INSTITUTE OF MODERN LANGUAGES RESEARCH
UNIVERSITY OF LONDON

BITHELL SERIES OF DISSERTATIONS
VOLUME 46

The Emergence of Post-Hybrid Identities: A Comparative Analysis of National Identity Formations in Germany's Hip-Hop Culture

INSTITUTE OF MODERN LANGUAGES RESEARCH

BITHELL SERIES OF DISSERTATIONS

Launched in 1978 by the then Institute of Germanic Studies, the Bithell Series of Dissertations is designed to help young scholars publish recent work of high quality which has been accepted for the award of a research degree by a University in the United Kingdom or the Republic of Ireland. Volumes 14 to 41 were published in conjunction with the Modern Humanities Research Association. From 2015 onwards, publication has been resumed by the Institute of Modern Languages Research (IMLR). For a list of previous volumes in the series, see http://modernlanguages.sas.ac.uk/publications/bithell-series-dissertations/.

Theses for possible inclusion in the series are considered by the Bithell Editorial Board twice annually, in May and November. Recommendations for theses to be considered should be made by the supervisor and/or examiner(s), should be accompanied by a copy of the Examiners' Report and Abstract, and sent to Dr Godela Weiss-Sussex at the Institute of Modern Languages Research, University of London, Senate House, Malet Street, London WC1E 7HU (email: godela.weiss-sussex@sas.ac.uk).

The Emergence of Post-Hybrid Identities:
A Comparative Analysis of National Identity Formations in Germany's Hip-Hop Culture

by

Marissa Kristina Munderloh

Institute of Modern Languages Research
2017

Published by the

Institute of Modern Languages Research
School of Advanced Study, University of London
Senate House, Malet Street, London WC1E 7HU
http://modernlanguages.sas.ac.uk

Cover image: Reproduced with kind permission of Tasek

First published 2017

ISBN 978 0 85457 255 7
ISSN 0266-7932

CONTENTS

LIST OF FIGURES

ACKNOWLEDGEMENTS

First I thank Prof Michael Gratzke, who has provided constant guidance throughout the process of thinking, researching and writing. At the same time I am extremely indebted to my parents, for without their support this project would not have been possible. I would also like to express my gratitude towards all members of the School of Modern Languages at the University of St Andrews who have shared their expertise with me along the way. I especially thank Dr Colette Lawson, Dr Michael White and Dr Emily Finer. Thank you also to Dr Tom Cheesman and Dr James Hodkinson for their detailed feedback on my research, as well as to Prof Jannis Androutsopoulos for enabling me to work with the Graduate School for Media and Communication (GMaC) at the University of Hamburg. Furthermore, I would like to thank Prof Andreas Stuhlmann for his support throughout my entire stay at the GMaC. I would further like to express great appreciation to Henry Dallek and DJ Dope for providing me with a starting point for my ethnographic research in the respective hip-hop communities of Oldenburg and of Hamburg. I especially thank Axel Zielke, Tim Beam and Oswald Achampong for introducing me to artists and for providing me with access to events in Hamburg. I am, of course, greatly indebted to all of my fifty-four interview partners, for without their knowledge and experiences this book would not have been possible. Finally, I thank Morven, Sarah and Jutta, with whom I was able to share the pain and pleasures of research; Melody and all the Blue Angels; the Tavern at Strathkinness; and Jorina, Frank, Ole, Ronny, Daniel and Thilko, who always offered good moments of distraction when needed. Lastly, I want to thank Sascha, whose ongoing support has been indispensable throughout this research project.

NOTE ON REFERENCING

The following abbreviations are used in the text:

Book Titles

THSP	Edward W. Soja, *Thirdspace: Journeys to Los Angeles and Other Real-and-Imagined Places* (Cambridge, MA: Blackwell, 1996)
LOC	Homi K. Bhabha, *The Location of Culture* (London: Routledge, 1994)
STGM	Erving Goffman, *Stigma: Notes on the Management of Spoiled Identity* (New York: Simon Schuster, 1963)
PSEL	Erving Goffman, *The Presentation of Self in Everyday Life* (New York: Anchor Books, 1959)

Abbreviations

AAVE	African-American Vernacular English
CDU	Christlich-Demokratische Union Deutschlands (Christian Democratic Union of Germany)
CSU	Christlich-Soziale Union (Christian Social Union of Germany)
DDR	Deutsche Demokratische Republik (German Democratic Republic = GDR)
PEGIDA	Patriotische Europäer gegen die Islamisierung des Abendlandes (Patriotic Europeans against the Islamization of the West)
SPD	Sozialdemokratische Partei Deutschlands (Social Democratic Party of Germany)

INTRODUCTION

> Wir als Union treten für die deutsche Leitkultur und gegen Multikulti ein – Multikulti ist tot.[1]
>
> [We as a union stand for a German dominant culture and against multi-culti – multi-culti is dead.]

> Mann, diese Politiker haben nicht gerafft, dass ich das Lied nicht als Ausländer, sondern als Deutscher geschrieben habe![2]
>
> [Man, these politicians haven't understood that I wrote this song not as a foreigner but as a German!]

This research project began in 2010, coinciding with the time when the Chairman of the CSU Horst Seehofer and the African-American German rapper Harris made the statements cited above. The German Chancellor Angela Merkel further added to Seehofer's stance that 'der Ansatz für Multikulti [...] gescheitert [ist], absolut gescheitert' [the approach towards multi-culti has failed, utterly failed].[3] However, this monograph offers a perspective on Germany's contemporary cultural state that echoes Harris's identity dilemma. By looking at contemporary German hip-hop culture, this study aims to show how this artistic movement in Germany already comprises multiculturalism. It therefore re-considers the romantic notion of 'Germany's predominant or guiding culture',[4] which, according to Hartwig Pautz, has been 'forged on the

1 Horst Seehofer, in 'Integrationsdebatte: Von Der Leyen versus Seehofer: "Eintrittsschwellen Senken"', *Frankfurt Allgemeine Zeitung für Deutschland – Inland*, 16 October 2010, Video, http://www.faz.net/aktuell/politik/inland/integrationsdebatte-von-der-leyen-versus-seehofer-eintrittsschwellen-senken-11056459.html [accessed 27 February 2014]. All translations are the author's own.

2 Harris, quoted in Khuê Pham, 'Deutscher Patriot: Der Rap-Musiker Harris ist dunkelhäutig – und stolz auf sein Land. In seinen Texten beschimpft er Integrationsverweigerer', *Die Zeit – Politik*, 47, 18 November 2010, p. 17. (No details of the interview are given.) Harris refers to his song 'Nur ein Augenblick' (2010), which was used as the soundtrack by the German Federal Government during a political campaign for integration.

3 Angela Merkel, in 'Integration: Merkel erklärt Multikulti für Gescheitert', *SPIEGEL ONLINE*, 16 October 2010, http://www.spiegel.de/politik/deutschland/integration-merkel-erklaert-multikulti-fuer-gescheitert-a-723532.html [accessed 25 February 2014].

4 Hartwig Pautz, 'The Politics of Identity in Germany: the *Leitkultur* Debate', *Race & Class*, 46 (2005), 39–52 (40).

belief that different, sequestered cultures should remain separate in order to retain their identities and avoid otherwise inevitable cultural conflicts'.[5]

To capture aspects of the multiculturality of contemporary Germany via hip-hop may seem a paradox at first. At the time of the eruption of the German *Leitkultur* debate in 2010, hip-hop in Germany was still being primarily represented through the commercial circulation of German gangsta rap, which was based on disseminating provocative messages that promoted physical aggression, misogyny and socio-cultural segregation from a racial-minority perspective as well as from an extreme German nationalist point of view.[6] Hence, commercially speaking, it seemed as though German hip-hop's image reflected Seehofer's and Merkel's political statements on Germany's culturally divided status. However, this research project has little to do with that particular subgenre of German rap, whose domination overshadowed the knowledge and richness of the overall movement that comprises hip-hop.

According to hip-hop founding father DJ Kool Herc, hip-hop culture's entirety is captured by 'the four hip-hop elements: DJing, B-Boying, MCing, and Graffiti'.[7] This study draws upon DJ Kool Herc's outline of hip-hop's main art forms and examines the ways in which each of them has become meaningful and authentic in a German cultural context.[8] Indeed, German graffiti artist Tasek claims: 'Wenn du deine eigene relevante Sprache daraus [aus Hip-Hop] entwickelst, dann gewinnst du langsam an Authentizität, aber das ist eben halt echt genau dieses Spannungsfeld, was im Hip-Hop auch, glaube ich, *echt* interessant ist' [If you develop your own relevant language from hip-hop, that is when you slowly become authentic, but that is also this area of tension which is, I think, *really* interesting in hip-hop].[9] In order to

5 Pautz, 'The Politics of Identity in Germany', 40.

6 Cf. Andreas Hartmann, 'Hip-Hop in Deutschland', *Musik*, September 2007, http://www.goethe.de/kue/mus/pop/de2621937.htm [accessed 15 January 2014]; cf. Andre Peschke, 'Breite Aufmerksamkeit seit Aggro Berlin und Gangster Rap', in *Hip-Hop in Deutschland – Analyse einer Jugendkultur aus pädagogischer Perspektive* (Hamburg: Diplomica, 2010), pp. 113–21.

7 Kool Herc, quoted in Jeff Chang, *Can't Stop, Won't Stop: A History of the Hip-hop Generation* (New York: Picador, 2005), p. xi. MCing is a synonym for rapping, derived from the rapper's initial role of being the 'Master of Ceremonies'.

8 While the art of beat boxing is often also considered one of hip-hop's main elements, it was not pursued as a communal practice during the time of my fieldwork and therefore does not feature in this study.

9 Tasek, interviewed by author, 20 August 2012. The concept of 'authenticity' in this quotation and throughout this study will appear with reference to the production of hip-hop art. 'Realness' is also employed as a synonym for authenticity by the hip-hop community and both terms describe the norm of creating art in line with the original practices, functions and aims of hip-hop: to be an honest reflection of the performer's personality and lifestyle, to aim at channelling creativity in a positive way and to be practised in an urban space. For

trace hip-hop's development into a relevant form of expression for artists in Germany, the national focus of this study has been narrowed down to the two local German hip-hop communities of Hamburg and Oldenburg.

Hamburg, with over 1,700,000 inhabitants, is considered a metropolitan area that is able to offer a '"big city" life, replete with the requisite opportunities and problems that come with living in an urban environment, giving what practitioners believe is an air of authenticity to the city's hip-hop practices'.[10] Moreover, Hamburg is home to 'the highest proportion of residents without an ethnic German background, at 27.5%'.[11] This multicultural composition is also reflected in its hip-hop community, which comprises many different ethnic heritages. Lastly, hip-hop in Hamburg is widely pursued as a profession, thus providing insights into the commercial realm of German hip-hop culture.

Oldenburg, on the other hand, with just under 170,000 residents,[12] provides an interesting contrast to Hamburg. Local graffiti artist Asek states: 'National gesehen ist Oldenburg, glaube ich, da echt so ein Provinzstädtchen!' [Seen in national terms, I think that Oldenburg really is a provincial town!].[13] Within its small, cosy urban space, Oldenburg's hip-hop community engages in this art form as an underground movement and as a communal leisure activity motivated by forces beyond monetary gains. Furthermore, the local hip-hop community almost exclusively comprises ethnic Germans. Hence, the two cities capture two divergent social and cultural compositions of German hip-hop while being geographically connected through a shared northern German region.

By comparing hip-hop's manifestation in Hamburg and in Oldenburg as a relevant German cultural practice, this study presents the first integrative study that evaluates German hip-hop culture in its full and complex artistic foundation, namely as a 'mehrdimensionale kulturelle Praxis, deren Bestandteile mit mehreren semiotischen Codes operieren: Bild, Sound, Typografie, Körperbewegung, Sprache' [multi-dimensional cultural practice

---

more information on hip-hop's constructed authenticity, especially in a gangster-rap context, see Kembrwe McLeoud 'Authenticity within Hip-Hop and Other Cultures Threatened with Assimilation', in *That's the Joint! The Hip-Hop Studies Reader*, ed. by Mark Anthony Neal and Murray Forman, 2nd edn (New York: Routledge, 2012), pp. 165–78.

10 Inez H. Templeton, 'What's so German about It? Cultural Identity in the Berlin Hip Hop Scene' (unpublished doctoral thesis, University of Stirling, 2005), p. 207, https://dspace.stir.ac.uk/bitstream/1893/75/1/Inez%20Templeton%20-%20Thesis%20PDF%20Version.pdf.

11 Anonymous, 'Census Reveals German Population Lower than Thought', *BBC News Europe*, 31 May 2013, http://www.bbc.co.uk/news/world-europe-22727898 [accessed 31 May 2013].

12 Stadt Oldenburg, 'Statistik', *Entwicklung der Einwohnerzahl 1978–2012* (Fachdienst Stadtinformation und Geodaten, 2012), http://www.oldenburg.de/fileadmin/oldenburg/Benutzer/PDF/40/402/0202-2012-Z-Internetx.pdf [accessed 20 March 2012].

13 Asek, interviewed by author, 21 March 2012.

in which the components operate with many semiotic codes: pictures, sounds, typography, body movement, language].[14] Moreover, this study also aims at deconstructing the common (mis)understanding of German hip-hop as merely consisting of gangsta rap. As German hip-hop scholar Ayla Güler Saied observes: 'Schaut man sich die öffentlich medial bekannten Künstler an, so scheint das Zusammenspiel zwischen Ghetto-Bezug aus der Unterschicht und Rap-Karriere unumgänglich. Dazu gehört auch eine Knastkarriere, um die Credibility und Authentizität zu unterstreichen' [If you look at the artists known to the public through the media, then it seems the interplay between a relationship to the ghetto due to lower-class origins and a rap career is inevitable. This includes a career in jail in order to underline credibility and authenticity].[15] In contrast to the socially harmful lyrical messages and images promoted by gangsta rap, this study will show how hip-hop artists also attempt to contribute to social and cultural integration through their art forms.

In order to understand how hip-hop can achieve these socio-cultural aims, this study briefly outlines the circumstances in which hip-hop emerged as an artistic movement in New York City. It then looks at the ways in which hip-hop's art forms were introduced into West Germany and imitated by German practitioners before being eventually adapted as a self-stereotypical German movement. This study will also show how artists incorporated other cultural influences into hip-hop's art forms, which has resulted in a mixture or hybridization of German hip-hop. This hybridization has, at some points, even revealed itself as an expression of Germanness that consists of multiculturality. It is these expressions of identity that this work highlights, naming them formations of post-hybrid identities. In order to highlight these developments as a relevant factor in understanding the cultural complexity and the multicultural struggle within contemporary Germany, the following section will provide a brief overview of the on-going debates concerning the German *Leitkultur*, the supposed problems of multiculturalism in Germany, as well as the challenges of the cultural hybrid, or even the post-hybrid, in a German national context.

A Multicultural Germany?

The previously mentioned political notion of Germany as a separated cultural landscape and one in which new cultural lifestyles (brought by immigrants)

14 Jannis Androutsopoulos, 'Einleitung', in *HipHop – Globale Kultur, Soziale Praktiken*, ed. by Jannis Androutsopoulos (Bielefeld: transcript, 2003), pp. 9–23 (p. 15).

15 Ayla Güler Saied, *Rap in Deutschland – Musik als Interaktionsmedium zwischen Partykultur und urbanen Anerkennungskämpfen* (Bielefeld: transcript, 2012), p. 160.

should conform to the values and norms of a supposed German dominant culture is not a recent development. In 1998 Brandenburg's Minister of the Interior, Jörg Schönbohm, introduced the term *Leitkultur* into Germany's national political debate about its immigration issues.[16] Two years later the concept became more prominent when it was appropriated by Friedrich Merz, the parliamentary party leader of the CDU. He stated:

> Das Aufnahmeland muss tolerant und offen sein. Zuwanderer, die auf Zeit oder auf Dauer bei uns leben wollen, müssen ihrerseits bereit sein, die Regeln des Zusammenlebens in Deutschland zu respektieren. Ich habe diese Regeln als die 'freiheitliche deutsche Leitkultur' bezeichnet. Die Formulierung hat reflexartig Empörung ebenso ausgelöst wie breite Zustimmung.[17]
>
> [The country receiving the immigrants has to be open and tolerant. Immigrants who want to live with us temporarily or for good have to be prepared to respect the rules of coexistence in Germany. I have termed these rules the 'liberal German leading culture'. This formulation has triggered outrage as well as vast approval.]

While the last sentence highlights the divided opinions towards needing, having and respecting a supposedly dominant German culture, Merz also admits that in Germany and for Germans there does not actually exist a definition of 'was wir unter unserer Kultur verstehen' [what we understand under the definition of our culture].[18] It is seemingly only understood as a counter-model to a multicultural German society.

As noted above, this understanding has been shared by CDU colleagues Merkel and Seehofer and has gained further public prominence through the opinions of the banker and SPD-member Thilo Sarrazin. In 2010 the former Berlin Senator for Finance published the book *Deutschland schafft sich ab: Wie wir unser Land aufs Spiel setzen*, which elaborated on his previous provocative comments regarding Germany's cultural and social state. In 2009, for instance, Sarrazin had claimed that '[d]ie Türken [...] Deutschland genauso [erobern], wie die Kosovaren das Kosovo erobert haben: durch eine höhere Geburtenrate. [...] Ich muss niemanden anerkennen, der [...] ständig neue kleine Kopftuchmädchen produziert' [[t]he Turks are conquering Germany just as the Kosovars conquered Kosovo: through a higher birth rate. [...] I do

16 Tilman Turpin, 'Die Leitkultur-Debatte: Fragen nach Identität und Integration in Deutschland', in *Die Zukunft der Demokratie: L'avenir de la démocratie*, ed. by Thomas Bedorf, Felix Heidenreich and Marcus Obrecht (Berlin: LIT, 2009) p. 105.

17 Friedrich Merz, 'Einwanderung und Identität', *Die Welt*, 25 October 2000, http://www.welt.de/print-welt/article540438/Einwanderung-und-Identitaet.html [accessed 10 January 2015].

18 Merz, 'Einwanderung und Identität'.

not have to acknowledge anyone who […] constantly produces new little headscarf girls].[19] According to Saied, such statements clearly and dangerously parallel racist and nationalistic discourses: 'Was diese Diskurse vereint, ist die Fokussierung auf die völkische Nation und der demografische Wandel, demnach die "Deutschen" auszusterben drohen' [What unites these discourses is the focus on the ethnic nation and the demographic change which threatens to make the "Germans" extinct].[20] Such nationalistic interpretations of the German migration debate will be touched upon in more detail later in this section.

In connection with the demographic change due to Turkish (and Muslim) immigrants, politicians and researchers have also warned about the development of a 'parallel society' (*Parallelgesellschaft*) in Germany. The term was coined by the German sociologist Wilhelm Heitmeyer, who, in an interview with *Die Zeit* in 1996, stated that immigrants in Germany were living in their own exclusive and isolated society and hence parallel to the German one.[21] While migration scholar Andrea Schmelz criticizes Heitmeyer's statement for its lack of empirical proof, she explains that the term has nevertheless manifested itself in public debate, conjuring an:

> image of an ethnically homogenous population group which separates itself spatially, socially and culturally from the mainstream society. At the same time, the term implies massive criticism of the immigrants' way of life and signals a demand for cultural assimilation.[22]

However, with no exact definition of German leading culture to which immigrants can assimilate, the actual problem, according to migration researcher Klaus J. Bade, is 'dass wir in Deutschland inzwischen eine multikulturelle Gesellschaft haben, ob wir das so wollten oder nicht – Punkt. Die Frage ist, wie man damit umgeht' [that we, in Germany, already have a multicultural society, whether we want it or not – full stop. The question is how to deal with it].[23] In an interview with *Spiegel Online*, Bade reverses the issue

19 Thilo Sarrazin, in 'Sarrazin droht Ausschluss aus der SPD', *taz.de*, 5 October 2009, http://www.taz.de/1/archiv/digitaz/artikel/?ressort=ba&dig=2009/10/05/a0116&cHash=500e526491 [accessed 10 January 2015].

20 Saied, *Rap in Deutschland*, p. 142.

21 Andrea Schmelz, 'Immigration and Integration Policies and Practices in Germany', in *Immigration Worldwide: Policies, Practices, and Trends*, ed. by Uma A. Segal, Doreen Elliot and Nazneen S. Mayadas (New York: Oxford University Press, 2010), pp. 63–78 (p. 75).

22 Schmelz, 'Immigration and Integration', p. 57.

23 Klaus J. Bade, '"Leitkultur"-Debatte: "Zuwanderung wird als Bedrohung empfunden"', *SPIEGELONLINE*, 24 November 2004, http://www.spiegel.de/kultur/gesellschaft/leitkultur-debatte-zuwanderung-wird-als-bedrohung-empfunden-a-329285.html [accessed 10 January 2015].

of the *Parallelgesellschaft* and the *Leitkultur* debate by explaining that 'es nicht um eine leitende Kultur als solche gehen kann, sondern eben um den Umgang mit kulturellen Unterschieden' [it cannot only be about a dominant culture as such but about dealing with cultural differences].[24] Bade thus concludes: 'Die Parallelgesellschaften gibt es in den Köpfen derer, die Angst davor haben: Ich habe Angst, und glaube, dass der andere daran Schuld ist' [The parallel societies exist in the minds of those who fear them: I am afraid and believe the other is to blame].[25]

The issue regarding migration in Germany's socio-political landscape is therefore the development of a cultural anxiety, since '[i]n Deutschland [...] der Begriff negativ [ist]: Migration als Bedrohung' [in Germany, the term is negative: migration as threat].[26] This notion can be linked to the public influence of Heitmeyer, who, together with Reimund Anhut, published a book on Germany's supposedly disintegrating socio-cultural state called *Bedrohte Gesellschaft. Soziale Desintegrationprozesse in ethnisch-kulturellen Konfliktkonstellationen*. As with Sarrazin's publication – indeed, both books appeared in 2010 – Saied claims that merely reading the title already suggests 'einen automatischen Zusammenhang von ethnischer Zugehörigkeit, Desintegration und Konfliktpotenzial und [...] sich somit in den hegemonialen Diskurs ein[reiht], der ethnische Zugehörigkeit mit negativen Konnotationen belegt' [an automatic connection between belonging, disintegration and the potential for conflict and [...] therefore aligns itself with the hegemonial discourse which loads ethnic belonging with negative connotations].[27]

This negative connotation of ethnic difference has been strengthened with the PEGIDA movement in Germany. The acronym stands for *Patriotische Europäer Gegen die Islamisierung des Abendlandes* and was founded in Dresden in late 2014. As the BBC reports, the PEGIDA supporters who take part in weekly demonstrations 'want Germany to curb immigration, accusing the authorities of failing to enforce existing laws. It challenges what it sees as liberal political correctness and multiculturalism in Germany'.[28] While the demonstrations have attracted extreme right-wing groups, such as neo-Nazis and hooligans, its supporters also include middle-class citizens, including Sarrazin, who claims that '[e]in wachsender Teil der muslimischen Mitbürger in Europa [...] die westliche Werteordnung nicht [teilt], [...] sich kulturell

24 Bade, '"Leitkultur"-Debatte'.
25 Bade, '"Leitkultur"-Debatte'.
26 Bade, '"Leitkultur"-Debatte'.
27 Saied, *Rap in Deutschland*, p. 129.
28 Anonymous, 'Who goes to German Pegida "anti-Islamisation" rallies?', *BBC News Europe*, 13 January 2015, http://www.bbc.com/news/world-europe-30776182 [accessed 13 January 2015].

nicht integrieren [will] und [...] sich in Parallelgesellschaften ab[schottet]' [a growing proportion of Muslim fellow citizens in Europe do not share Western values, do not want to be culturally integrated and isolate themselves in parallel societies].[29] Sarrazin's criticism thus highlights anxiety about a culturally divided and hence unstable status of Germany where religion is, again, used as an all-encompassing category that equals migration-related foreignness. Indeed, the re-use of Islam as an umbrella term for any form of 'otherness' is not uncommon. Ethnologist Gerd Baumann explains that 'because religion sounds so absolute, it can be used as a translation for other, more relative, forms of conflict. In complex situations of social strife, one can often find ethnic, national, or migratory boundaries transformed into religious ones'.[30] Nonetheless, just as the *Leitkultur* debate has divided opinion, thousands of Germans, including high-profile celebrities and politicians, have condemned the PEGIDA movement and have participated in counter-demonstrations to prove their support for Germany's multiculturalism.

The question that nevertheless remains is the following: why does anxiety about multiculturalism exist? According to the sociologist and migration scholar Nira Yuval-Davis, in a national context 'there are two kinds of social and cultural differences: those which threaten and those which do not. Multiculturalism is aimed at nourishing and perpetuating the kind of differences which do not'.[31] Yuval-Davis further elaborates that:

> there is a continuous debate about the limits of multiculturalism between those who want a continued construction of the national collectivity as homogenous and assimilatory, and those who have been calling for the institutionalisation of ethnic pluralism and the preservation of the ethnic minorities' cultures of origin as legitimate parts of the national project.[32]

The anxiety is, therefore, spurred first by the construct of the nation itself, where members of 'one or several ethnic groups [...] think, or are thought in some way, to "own" a state, that is, to carry a special responsibility for it'.[33] Nevertheless, in this national context Baumann notes that modern nation-states have also actively 'included some ethnic groups and excluded others,

29 Thilo Sarrazin, in 'Merkels Aussage vernebelt das Problem', *Die Welt*, 20 January 2015, http://www.welt.de/politik/deutschland/article136566652/Merkels-Aussage-zum-Islam-vernebelt-das-Problem.html [accessed 21 January 2015].

30 Gerd Baumann, *The Multicultural Riddle – Rethinking National, Ethnic, and Religious Identities* (New York and London: Routledge, 1999), p. 23.

31 Nira Yuval-Davis, 'Ethnicity, Gender Relations and Multiculturalism', in *Debating Cultural Hybridity*, ed. by Pnina Werbner and Tariq Modood (London and New Jersey: Zed Books, 1997), pp. 193–208 (p. 197).

32 Yuval-Davis, 'Ethnicity, Gender Relations and Multiculturalism', p. 197.

33 Baumann, *The Multicultural Riddle*, p. 30.

or privileged some and marginalized others. It is precisely this exclusion that turns numbers of people into "minorities" and thereby creates the key problem between nation-state and the multicultural project'.[34]

In Germany, the exclusion of ethnic groups has been most notably achieved through West Germany's guest-worker treaties of the 1960s and 1970s.[35] The term 'guest' in 'guest worker' [*Gastarbeiter*] not only reveals the idea of the invited worker returning home, it also implies that the workers who choose to settle in Germany remain guests – guests who are, however, not welcome anymore. Thanks to the continued referral to these new German citizens as such, the problem in contemporary Germany, according to Saied, is that:

> Die Bundesrepublik Deutschland hat sich im internationalen Vergleich erst relativ spät dazu bekannt, ein Einwanderungsland zu sein. Obwohl Migrationsbewegungen historisch gesehen seit jeher vorhanden gewesen sind und maßgeblich zum Wachstum und Entstehen von Großstädten beigetragen haben, wird Migration in vielerlei Hinsicht problematisiert, skandalisiert und durch Migrationsregime versucht zu regulieren.[36]
>
> [By comparison with other nations the Federal Republic of Germany has admitted very late that it is a country of immigration. Even though migratory movements have, historically, always existed and have made a decisive contribution to the growth and creation of cities, migration is often problematized, made into a scandal and subject to attempts to regulate it through systems of migration control.]

Within this problematization of migration, Saied adds that 'ethnische Kategorien [...] hierbei ein Instrument [sind], um Unterschiede immer wieder neu zu konstruieren und den Diskurs damit immer wieder zu aktivieren' [ethnic categories are an instrument used to re-construct differences anew and continously to re-active the discourse].[37] Ethnicity is, therefore, not only used as a political tool to locate a problem but is also treated as a self-contained category with no room for re-adjustment, despite Baumann's explaining that 'ethnicity is not an identity given by nature, but an identification created through social action'.[38] In this social, and hence subjective, context, ethnic

34 Baumann, *The Multicultural Riddle*, pp. 31–32.

35 For more information on the different nations and treaties linked to guest workers in West Germany see Carolin Butterwege, 'Von der "Gastarbeiter-Anwerbung" zum Zuwanderungsgesetz, Migrationsgeschehen und Zuwanderungspolitik in der Bundesrepublik', *Grundlagendossier Migration* (Bundeszentrale für politische Bildung, 15 March 2005), http://www.bpb.de/gesellschaft/migration/dossier-migration/56377/migrationspolitik-in-der-brd?p=all [accessed 20 January 2015].

36 Saied, *Rap in Deutschland*, p. 122.

37 Saied, *Rap in Deutschland*, p. 124.

38 Baumann, *The Multicultural Riddle*, p. 21.

identities are something fluid and negotiable and can therefore 'be stressed or unstressed, enjoyed or resented, imposed or even denied, all depending on situation and context'.[39] Often, however, Baumann states that the common perception or the 'idea of ethnicity appeals, first and foremost, to blood from the past. It invokes biological ancestry and then claims that present-day identities follow from this ancestry'.[40]

This idea is especially relevant in the German national context, for its citizenship law of *ius sanguini* has been the defining factor for becoming a German citizen from 1871 onwards. It was changed in 2000, adding a rule which allows German citizenship when born on German territory.[41] However, due to the long-standing tradition of citizenship through bloodline, German journalist Frida Thum reports in her article 'Und woher kommst du wirklich?' [And where are you really from?], published in *Die Zeit* in 2014, that 'die alte tief verwurzelte Vorstellung, dass nur deutsch ist, wer auch deutsche Vorfahren hat, in Schulen, am Arbeitsplatz und auch sonst im Alltag present [ist]' [the old, deeply rooted idea that only by having German ancestors can one be truly German is still present in schools, at work and even in everyday life].[42] Saied specifically blames ongoing political categorization for this exclusively ethnic understanding of Germanness. She adds that '[d]ie Kategorie "Personen mit Migrationshintergrund" [...] vom Statistischen Bundesamt in den Mikrozensus 2005 eingeführt [wurde] und [...] so gesehen die rechtlich verankerte Form der Stigmatisierung [ist]. [...] hierbei [gilt] selbst die dritte Generation noch als Person mit Migrationshintergrund' [the category of "people with a migrational background" was introduced into the micro-census by the Federal Office of Statistics in 2005 and is therefore the legally anchored form of stigmatization. [...] [H]ere even a member of the third generation is still regarded as a person with migrational background].[43]

In an everyday context, the simplest and often commonest categorization of having a 'Migrationshintergrund' [migrational background] is determined by visible traces of 'otherness', such as the headscarf mentioned by Sarrazin

39 Baumann, *The Multicultural Riddle*, p. 64.

40 Baumann, *The Multicultural Riddle*, pp. 19–20.

41 For detailed information on the conditions regarding German citizenship through place of birth, see Beauftragte für Migration, Flüchtlinge und Integration, 'Staatsangehörigkeit: Das Geburtstortprinzip' (Presse- und Informationsamt der Bundesregierung, 2015), http://bundesregierung.de/Webs/Breg/DE/Bundesregierung/BeauftragtefuerIntegration/Staatsangehoerigkeit/geburtsortprinzip/_node.html [accessed 20 January 2015].

42 Frida Thurm, 'Und woher kommst du wirklich?', *Zeit Online*, 16 September 2014, http://www.zeit.de/gesellschaft/zeitgeschehen/2014-08/deutsch-identitaet-migranten-sarrazin [accessed 10 January 2015].

43 Thurm, 'Und woher kommst du wirklich?'.

as a threatening difference to Germany's culture.[44] Aside from different dress codes, visible 'otherness' can also be interpreted in skin colour, especially when contrasted to 'whiteness', for as Alastair Bonnet observes, in western Europe '[n]on-white identities, by contrast [to white identities], have been denied the privileges of normativity, and are marked within the West as marginal and inferior'.[45] Relating this situation to Germany, Saied similarly claims: 'Während heute beispielsweise Weiße [*sic*] französische, schwedische oder nordamerikanische MigrantInnen, die in der Bundesrepublik leben, fast nie zum Ausgangspunkt politischer und öffentlicher Debatten werden, werden Türken, Araber oder pauschal die Moslems immer wieder fokussiert' [Whereas today, for example, White French, Swedish or North American migrants who live in the Federal Republic almost never become the starting point for political or public debate, attention is repeatedly focused on Turks, Arabs or generally on "the" Muslims].[46]

The problem of multiculturalism lies, therefore, in the fact that not all ethnicities in the 'multi'-prefix are included in the debate, while those ethnic minorities that want to become part of the homogeneous majority should ideally achieve this without losing their uniqueness in order to create an enriching national ethnic pluralism, as mentioned by Yuval-Davis. It comes as no surprise, then, that Baumann concludes: 'A multicultural nation-state is, in some ways, a contradiction in terms'.[47] However, just as assimilation to a German *Leitkultur* seems ironic when German politicians do not even know what it actually entails, a definition of it would always need to change over time anyway. As Baumann explains, culture is:

> two things at once, that is, a dual discursive construction. It is the conservative 're'-construction of a reified essence at one moment, and the pathfinding new construction of a processual agency at the next moment. It vacillates between two poles, and therein lies [*sic*] the sophistication and dialectical beauty of the concept.[48]

44 Cf. Thilo Sarrazin, 'Zuwandering und Integration', in *Deutschland schafft sich ab: Wie wir unser Land aufs Spiel setzen* (Stuttgart: Deutsche Verlags-Anstalt, 2010), pp. 255–330.

45 Alastair Bonnett, 'Constructions of Whiteness in European and American Anti-Racism', in *Debating Cultural Hybridity*, ed. by Werbner and Modood, pp. 173–92 (p. 188).

46 Saied, *Rap in Deutschland*, p. 138.

47 Saied, *Rap in Deutschland*, p. 32.

48 Saied, *Rap in Deutschland*, p. 95. The term 'culture' is used throughout this study to describe two things. On the one hand, it serves as an umbrella term for national traditions and ideologies that unite an imagined community as German. On the other hand, the term appears in the context of 'hip-hop culture'. The latter serves to describe a lifestyle which adheres to the aesthetic norms, artistic practices and communal beliefs that shape hip-hop.

Thus, the constant development of a culture is linked to constant change and vacillation. In particular, the 'conservative "re"-construction of a reified essence at one moment, and the pathfinding new construction of a processual agency' mentioned by Baumann can refer to processes of cultural hybridization, where the blending of an old cultural element with a new one creates and re-creates cultural traditions. This notion of culture that exists through cultural mixing thus challenges the wishful ideal of having a homogeneous national culture linked to a conserved past and remaining identifiable through its supposedly 'natural' and hence unchangeable state. As German cultural scholar Tom Cheesman summarizes it: 'The challenge that hybrid cultural innovations present to traditional, homogeneous and monolithic concepts of national identity is a focus of much debate'.[49]

Indeed, within the German *Leitkultur* debate, cultural hybridity can be understood as a threat since Baumann, for example, explains: 'In dealing with strangers, it helps one to stereotype them with the greatest of ease and to make common sense predictions of how these others might think and what they might do next'.[50] Nevertheless, since processes of cultural hybridization can alter the fixed image of the stereotype, Baumann poses the question: 'How do I predict the opinions of anyone with a crosscutting or multidimensional identity?'.[51] It is this lack of being able to stereotype in order to help to make sense of the 'other' that seems to be overwhelming for some Germans, despite multidimensional or crosscutting identities having become a normal feature in their society. With multiculturalism being a living part of contemporary Germany, some politicians and citizens need rather to re-frame the term 'multi-kulti' as 'a proactive awareness of these crosscutting cultural cleavages and a culture concept to deal with them'.[52]

Such a culture concept as Baumann proposes can be detected by the fifteen-year-old Germans Dzeko and Kamyar who feature in Thurm's aforementioned article. Thurm writes that the two boys are faced with the common situation in which 'selbst die angepasstesten und integrationswilligsten Kinder ein Problem haben, solange an ihren Namen oder ihrem Aussehen zu erkennen ist, dass ihre Familie nicht seit zehn Generationen in Deutschland lebt' [even the most assimilated children who are keenest to be integrated have a problem as long as their name or their appearance suggests that their family have not been living in Germany for the last ten generations].[53] However, she

49 Tom Cheesman, 'Polyglot Pop Politics – Hip Hop in Germany', *Debatte*, 6 (1998), 191–214 (p. 193).

50 Baumann, *The Multicultural Riddle*, p. 84.

51 Baumann, *The Multicultural Riddle*, p. 84.

52 Baumann, *The Multicultural Riddle*, p. 85.

53 Thurm, 'Und woher kommst du wirklich?'.

also reports that through recording a rap track called 'Generation Sarrazin (Deutsch so wie Du)' [Generation Sarrazin (As German as You)] the two boys can assert that they are:

> Deutsche und begreifen sich als solche und haben doch das Gefühl, dass andere das immer wieder hinterfragen. Es beginnt bei der Frage nach der 'wirklichen' Herkunft und hört bei Sarrazins Thesen auf. [...] Doch sie schaffen sich auch eine neue, ganz eigene Identität,[54] indem sie die deutschen Alltagscodes, die sie von klein auf kennen, mit dem kombinieren, was ihnen aus dem Heimatland und der Religion ihrer Eltern übermittelt wird. Die Zugehörigkeit zu diesen beiden Kulturen muss für sie kein 'Dazwischen' sein, sondern kann ein 'Zusammen' werden, aus dem sie ein neues Selbstbewusstsein schöpfen.[55]
>
> [German and understand themselves to be German – and still have the feeling that others repeatedly question this. It begins with the question of their 'real' ancestry and ends with Sarrazin's propositions. [...] However, they also manage to create their new, very own identity by combining German everyday codes, which they have known from an early age, with what is conveyed to them from their home country and their parents' religion. For them, belonging to these two cultures does not have to mean being 'in between' but can become a form of 'togetherness' out of which they create new self confidence.]

However, by rapping about their new, combined and hence hybrid identities, these and other German rappers take the risk that their lyrical presentations might not resonate as a new form of Germanness with the common listener. This dilemma has already been hinted at in Harris's introductory statement to this study. Even Thurm refers to the foreign 'Heimatland' of Szeko and Kamyar's parents, despite the fact that they could have been born in Germany as well. This problematic of the perception of the German hybrid has also been highlighted by Todd Herzog, who, in particular, investigates German writers of Jewish and hence 'other' ethnic heritage.

Herzog begins his analysis by re-stating that in previous German national discourse the culturally hybrid human being had a specific name, namely the *Mischling* [mongrel], and was viewed 'as a pathological character and held the floor in German racial science from the late 1800s until 1945'.[56] Hybridity was, therefore, initially treated as a racial category. Herzog elaborates that the *Mischling* was also seen as 'a particularly dangerous figure in German racial

54 Cf. Naika Fouroutan, in '"Junge Muslime möchten das Land mit gestalten" – Naika Foroutan im Gespräch', *Goethe Institut: Migration und Integration*, June 2012, http://www.goethe.de/lhr/ prj/daz/mag/igd/de9494836.htm [accessed 22 January 2015].

55 Thurm, 'Und woher kommst du wirklich?'.

56 Todd Herzog, 'Hybrids and Mischlinge: Translating Anglo-American Cultural Theory into German', *The German Quarterly*, 70 (1997), 1–17 (p. 2).

science, alternately a psychologically unbalanced hysteric lacking a stable identity and a dangerous monster whose "repressed" identity returns in an even more concentrated form'.[57] Relating this social threat to contemporary Germany, Saied claims that this concept of human race continues to live on as a translation of 'culture': 'Nachdem der Rassebegriff in Europa durch den Nationalsozialismus negativ belegt ist, wird in diesem Zusammenhang der Kulturbegriff als Markierung von Differenz herangezogen' [After the concept of race became negatively tainted by National Socialism the concept of culture is often used as a marker of difference in this context].[58] From this perspective, the issue of the multicultural within German political discourse could also be understood as the problematic of the multiracial or the multi-ethnic.

Herzog's studies on contemporary Jewish-German authors, who write for fellow German citizens and therefore market themselves in their homeland, reveal an issue of the multicultural which indeed translates to a problematic of the multi-ethnic: the impossibility of the hybrid identity being accepted as German. By comparing four authors, Herzog observes that as soon as German-Jewish writers reveal even a slight identification with Judaism, they are understood and essentialized as Jewish, hence non-German and 'other', despite expressing themselves in the shared German language. In Herzog's words, 'the German Jewish hybrid is read at all levels as the Jew in hiding whose ethnicity suddenly becomes visible'.[59] He concludes that:

> not only does contemporary cultural theory not provide a way to escape this model, a path by which to get beyond the body as a marker of identity, it, in fact, seems to repeat this fascination with the difference – even the monstrosity – of the hybrid.[60]

Thus, the success of cultural hybridization as a strategy towards the normalization of cultural or ethnic pluralism within the nation-state is dependent on the hybrid individual's reception by the consumer. While Herzog's study reveals the difficulty for mixed identities to be accepted as fully German, other analyses on similar topics concerning literary or lyrical expressions in Germany have also shown other outcomes. Returning to rap, Cheesman, for instance, observes that 'the integration of ethnic minority youth has been achieved de facto in pop, as nowhere else in German culture'.[61] He even suggests that:

57 Herzog, 'Hybrids and Mischlinge', 2–3.
58 Saied, *Rap in Deutschland*, p. 155.
59 Herzog, 'Hybrids and Mischlinge', 8.
60 Herzog, 'Hybrids and Mischlinge', 15. The contemporary cultural theory mentioned by Herzog will be discussed in 'Theoretical Overview'.
61 Cheesman, 'Polyglot Pop Politics', 194.

> the encounter between hip hop subculture and the state and market institutions may yet be in some sense cultural models for much-needed broader initiatives in social policy. Certainly, this seems to be the only sector in the German public sphere in which both ethnic plurality and bi- and multilingualism are taken entirely for granted.[62]

In line with Cheesman's outlook, this work will further investigate this supposedly normalized state of pluralism in German hip-hop, despite the differing and often problematic perspectives of multiculturalism in contemporary German political debate. The insights will therefore contribute to a better understanding of the current cultural dynamics that are shaping Germany's urban society. In order to highlight the scholarly relevance and the positioning of this research project within the academic field, the next section will provide a review of current scholarship on hip-hop culture.

Literature Review

Hip-hop culture has been a subject of German academic research since its establishment in Germany during the 1980s. The majority of early hip-hop scholars focused on the ways in which this artistic movement was adapted by Germany's minority youth, who re-translated hip-hop into their own strategy of cultural resistance. These observations were often embedded in a Turkish-German discourse, with the engagement in hip-hop positioned as an expression against mainstream German culture.[63] However, Cheesman also writes in 1998 that 'German-Turkish working class youth, in particular, have adopted and adapted rap in this manner – although Germany's hip-hop subculture is extremely diverse, and in fact white rappers have hitherto achieved most chart success.'[64] While, therefore, already revealing the participation of ethnic German rappers, Cheesman observes that, in general, 'rappers in Europe are

62 Cheesman, 'Polyglot Pop Politics', 199.

63 Cf. Ayhan Kaya, *Constructing Diasporas: Turkish Hip-Hop Youth in Berlin* (Warwick: University of Warwick, 1997) and '"Scribo Ergo Sum": Islamic Force und Berlin-Türken', in *HipHop: Globale Kultur – Lokale Praktiken*, ed. by Jannis Androutsopoulos (Bielefeld: transcript, 2003), pp. 246–72; Dietmar Elflein, 'From Krauts with Attitudes to Turks with Attitudes: Some Aspects of Hip-Hop History in Germany', *Popular Music*, 17 (1998), 255–65; Stefanie Menrath, *Represent what... Performativität und Identitäten im HipHop* (Hamburg: Argument, 2001); Levent Soysal, 'Rap, Hiphop, Kreuzberg: Scripts of/for Migrant Youth Culture in the WorldCity Berlin', in *Multicultural Germany: Arts, Media, and Performance*, ed. by Deniz Göktürk and Barbara Wolbert (= *New German Critique*, 92 (2004)), pp. 62–81; Murat Güngör and Hannes Loh, *Fear of a Kanak Planet: HipHop zwischen Weltkultur und Nazi-Rap* (Höfen: Hannibal, 2002).

64 Cheesman, 'Polyglot Pop Politics', 192.

seen and heard as "voices from the ethnic ghetto", speaking out on behalf of new generations of post-migrant "communities"'.[65]

This perception coincides with Arlene Tickner's observation that 'the ways it [hip-hop] is appropriated in different settings are intimately linked to how specific social actors, primarily marginal youth, experience the world and the places they occupy in it'.[66] However, more recent studies on rap in Germany reveal other trends regarding hip-hop culture's purpose and positioning in German society.[67] In her comprehensive analysis of contemporary rap in Germany, Saied, for example, criticizes the fact that '[d]ie Medien [...] einen Mythos [schaffen], der lautet "Durch die Musik raus aus dem Ghetto und raus aus der Kriminalität"' [the media create a myth which proclaims 'escape the ghetto and criminality through music'].[68] Stefan Burkard's study *Hip-Hop am Pranger – Wie die Medien eine Kultur verteufeln* even affirms that German media aim at representing German rap as a negative and even harmful socio-cultural movement, despite promoting it as an escape from crime.[69] Saied attempts to deconstruct this mediated image of rap by explaining that the dissemination of lyrical messages concerning social deviance or racial marginality 'somit weder im Rap noch im Alltag von Jugendlichen mit sogenannter Migrationsgeschichte selbst aus[geht], sondern [...] immer als interaktionistische Reaktion auf hegemoniale Zuschreibungs- und Stigmatisierungs-Praktiken bezogen [ist]' [does not originate from rap or from the everyday life of youth with a so-called migrational history but is always an interactionist reaction to hegemonial practices of ascription and stigmatization].[70] In other words, the assumed relationship between engaging in rap and belonging to a harmful and disrespectful ethnic and social minority in Germany is not cultivated within the art form as such, but maintained by the media as a provocative marketing strategy.

Saied therefore concludes that the 'Bezug auf ethnische Kategorien [...] in diesem [Rap] Kontext vielmehr dazu [dient], die Zugehörigkeit zu der deutschen Gesellschaft zum Ausdruck zu bringen und [...] somit eine politische Forderung nach Anerkennung und Zugehörigkeit und Gleichberechtigung [ist]' [reference to ethnic categories in this [rap] context

65 Cheesman, 'Polyglot Pop Politics', 191.

66 Arlene B. Tickner, 'Aquí en el Ghetto: Hip-Hop in Colombia, Cuba and Mexico', *Latin American Politics and Society*, 50 (2008), 121–46 (p. 122).

67 Cf. Templeton, 'What's so German about It?'; Saied, *Rap in Deutschland*; Maria Stehle, *Ghetto Voices in Contemporary German Culture* (New York: Camden House, 2012).

68 Saied, *Rap in Deutschland*, p. 160.

69 Cf. Stefan Burkard, *HipHop am Pranger – Wie die Medien eine Kultur verteufeln* (Hamburg: Diplomica, 2013).

70 Saied, *Rap in Deutschland*, p. 284.

serves to express belonging to German society and [...] is therefore a political claim to acknowledgement and belonging and equality].[71] This perspective on German rap's intentions is also shared by Maria Stehle, who researched the 'ghetto voices' expressed in contemporary German literary texts, films and rap music. She emphasizes the existing pluralism of rappers' different expressions of Germanness:

> [N]on-white Germans use the idea of 'nation' to claim citizenship and challenge and change notions of national belonging. Some artists [...] shift this demand for citizenship to a reassertion of white Germanness. Some artists use rap and hip-hop soundscapes to claim essentialized notions of the other, non-German national belonging, [...]; others reject Germanness and consciously place themselves outside of any national discourses; yet others consciously frame their perceived otherness as a positive – and new – kind of German identification.[72]

This study especially builds on Stehle's last observation pertaining to the positive German identification expressed through rap. In so doing, it also includes 'white' German hip-hop artists, engaging in Inez H. Templeton's claim about the importance of looking at all skin colours that participate in German rap. During her research on non-Germans, Afro-Germans and Germans who rap in Berlin, Templeton writes that the:

> intersection of hip-hop music and youth identities in Germany is not just an issue for non-whites. Unpacking complicated notions of German identity and looking at different negotiations with both Germanness and hip hop culture sheds much light on contemporary German society and culture.[73]

While rap music has provided a platform from which to present new and different national identity formations, these recent studies also highlight an important link between hip-hop culture and wider discourses on national identity, despite a common trend in the 'burgeoning literature on globalization [which] has often argued that established national allegiances and forms of organization are becoming increasingly irrelevant in a world of intensifying flows of people, products, ideas and images'.[74] This study supports the notion that national identity continues to be relevant for contemporary culture and society and therefore aims at examining the ways in which hip-hop culture can help to understand the different formations and expressions of identity within two hip-hop communities in Germany.

71 Saied, *Rap in Deutschland*, p. 284.

72 Stehle, *Ghetto Voices in Contemporary German Culture*, p. 151.

73 Templeton, 'What's so German about It?', p. 212.

74 Michael Skey, 'Why Do Nations Matter? The Struggle for Belonging and Security in an Uncertain World', *British Journal of Sociology*, 64 (2013), 81–98 (p. 81).

By narrowing the national focus to the two cities of Hamburg and Oldenburg, this monograph not only expands hip-hop scholarship on national identity constructions, it also adds to the existing scholarship of ethnographic studies conducted on local German hip-hop communities, since Hamburg and Oldenburg have remained unexamined by previous ethnographic Hip-hop studies. The cities which have featured most commonly in these studies include Berlin,[75] Frankfurt am Main[76] and Mannheim.[77] Bennett's observations on hip-hop practised in Frankfurt am Main especially highlight that 'im Rahmen der zeitgenössischen Gesellschaft das "Lokale" nicht nur ein hoch komplexer, sondern auch ein hoch bestrittener Raum geworden ist, der unter dem Aufschwung miteinander ringender und oft gegensätzlicher Ideale leidet' [in the context of contemporary society, the "local" has become not only a highly complex but also a highly contested space which suffers from the upsurge of many struggling and often opposing ideals].[78] In this sense, Hamburg and Oldenburg are not treated as two holistic entities but rather serve as urban arenas in which to assess the complexity and heterogeneity of Germany's hip-hop communities.

Furthermore, this study can be seen as a contribution to and continuation of Murray Forman's insights on race, space and place in rap practices. In his book *The 'hood Comes First: Race, Space, and Place in Rap and Hip-Hop* Forman writes that '[t]he "city" (or, more appropriately, cities) is central to the discussion of race, space, place, and hip-hop'.[79] Previous studies which have focused on hip-hop's socio-urban manifestation in Germany have not considered its complex urban entirety but have mostly examined a certain spatial condition or attribute, such as 'the street' or 'the ghetto'.[80] Thus,

75 Kaya, *Constructing Diasporas*, '"Scribo Ergo Sum"' and 'German-Turkish Transnational Space: A Separate Space of Their Own', *German Studies Review*, 30 (2007), 483–502; Soysal, 'Rap, Hiphop, Kreuzberg'; Templeton, 'What's so German about It?'; Güngör and Loh, *Fear of a Kanak Planet*, pp. 179–216.

76 Andy Bennett, 'Hip-Hop am Main: Die Lokalisierung von Rap-Musik und HipHop-Kultur', in *HipHop: Globale Kultur – Lokale Praktiken*, ed. by Androutsopoulos, pp. 26–42; Güngör and Loh, *Fear of a Kanak Planet*, pp. 230–33.

77 Menrath, *Represent what...*; Gabriele Birken-Silverman, '"Isch bin New School und West Coast … du bisch doch ebe bei de Southside Rockern": Identität und Sprechstil in einer Breakdance-Gruppe von Mannheimer Italienern', in *HipHop: Globale Kultur – Lokale Praktiken*, ed. by Androutsopoulos, pp. 273–96.

78 Bennett, 'Hip-Hop am Main', p. 29.

79 Murray Forman, *The 'hood Comes First: Race, Space, and Place in Rap and Hip-Hop* (Middletown, CT: Wesleyan University Press, 2002), p. 35.

80 Gabriele Klein and Malte Friedrich, 'Populäre Stadtansichten. Bildinszenierungen des Urbanen im HipHop', in *HipHop: Globale Kultur – Lokale Praktiken*, ed. by Androutsopoulos, pp. 85–101; Sebastian Schröer, 'Raum und Inszenierung', in *HipHop Meets Academia: Globale Spuren eines lokalen Kulturphänomens*, ed. by Karin Bock, Stefan Meier and Gunter

Friedrich and Klein, for instance, conclude that the emphasis on 'the street' in rap becomes 'vor allem ein Ausstattungsmerkmal, ein theatralisches Mittel, um lokale Identität herzustellen und den Glauben an Authentizität zu befördern' [above all a feature of its general equipment, a theatrical device used to create a local identity and to promote authencity].[81] This relationship between particularly deviant urban spaces and hip-hop authenticity is related to a dominant trend established in American commercial rap, whereby according to Forman:

> the conflation of the ghetto as a privileged sociospatial site and an idealized image of black authenticity within hip-hop discourse has continually threatened to override other possible images of lived cultural space among the hip-hop generation, regardless of one's racial identity.[82]

Since this theatrical framing of the urban ghetto has featured most prominently in commercial German gangsta rap, this work aims to deconstruct the ghettoesque spatial discourse that has influenced the common image of German rap. In order to do so, this analysis treats the city, or a particular urban attribute, beyond its function as a theatrical device in which 'the symbolic meanings of spaces and places both reflect and affect the ways in which race, class, gender, generational identities, and so on are constructed and understood'.[83] Rather, it will look at the variety and diversity of spaces, both material and metaphorical, within a city and their appropriation within hip-hop's different artistic practices, meanings and messages.

This wider focus on urban space goes hand in hand with the inclusion of hip-hop's four main art forms. Since urban spatial analyses of hip-hop culture have often centred on rap music, this study aims at unveiling whether urban space and identity discourses are treated differently by hip-hop's other elements, such as 'through the sonic appropriation of aural space, the appropriation of street corners (where, at an earlier stage in hip-hop's development, rap improvisation and breakdancing were common), or appropriation of the city's architecture through the ubiquitous display of spray-painted graffiti'.[84] A significant amount of scholarship has been devoted to studies on hip-hop's

---

Süss (Bielefeld: transcript, 2007), pp. 247–62; Malte Friedrich, *Urbane Klänge. Popmusik und Imagination der Stadt* (Bielefeld: transcript, 2010), pp. 137–49; Stehle, *Ghetto Voices in Contemporary German Culture*, pp. 129–75.

81 Klein and Friedrich, 'Populäre Stadtansichten. Bildinszenierungen des Urbanen im HipHop', p. 87.

82 Forman, *The 'hood Comes First*, p. 61.

83 Forman, *The 'hood Comes First*, p. 59.

84 Forman, *The 'hood Comes First*, p. 42.

other main art forms.[85] However, few have compared the different art forms' strategies of national identity construction to their available material and imagined spaces within one urban locale.

Hence, this monograph will present the first study that considers the ways hip-hop artists occupy, understand and experience their urban space, deeming it relevant towards understanding their ways of constructing a German identity for themselves. In order to grasp the interconnectedness between space, culture and German identity throughout this study, the comparative analyses will be guided by a three-dimensional theoretical framework, which will be introduced in the following section.

Theoretical Overview

Spatiality – The Material and Metaphorical Cityspaces of Hip-Hop

> Which spatial modes are of most significance to the cultural processes and social practices that underlie the hip-hop culture, and through what spatial apparatuses is the relative significance expressed and articulated?[86]

85 On graffiti see: Craig Castleman, *Getting Up: Subway Graffiti in New York* (Cambridge, MA: The MIT Press, 1982); Nancy MacDonald, *The Graffiti Subculture: Youth, Masculinity, and Identity* (London and New York: Palgrave Macmillan, 2001); Berhard Van Treeck, 'Styles – Typographie als Mittel zur Identitätsbildung', in *HipHop: Globale Kultur – Lokale Praktiken*, ed. by Androutsopoulos, pp. 102–10; Stefan Meier, 'Stylelife: Graffiti als "typographisches" Ausdrucksmittel sozialen Stils', in *Express yourself! Europas kulturelle Kreativität zwischen Markt und Underground*, ed. by Eva Kimminich and others (Bielefeld: transcript, 2007), pp. 193–208; Ayhan Kaya, 'German-Turkish Transnational Space: A Separate Space of Their Own', *German Studies Review*, 30 (2007), 483–502. On hip-hop dance see: Sally Banes, *Writing Dancing in the Age of Postmodernism* (Hanover, NH: University Press of New England, 1994); Arnd-Michael Nohl, 'Interkulturelle Bildungsprozesse im Breakdance', in *HipHop: Globale Kultur – Lokale Praktiken*, ed. by Androutsopoulos, pp. 297–320; Thomas F. DeFrantz, 'The Black Beat Made Visible: Body Power in Hip Hop Dance', in *Of the Presence of the Body: Essays on Dance and Performance Theory*, ed. by Andre Lepecki (Middletown, CT: Wesleyan University Press, 2004), pp. 64–81; Dorit Rode, *Breaking. Popping. Locking. Tanzformen der HipHop-Kultur* (Marburg: Tectum, 2006); Heidi Salaverría, 'Tanz um Anerkennung. Ästhetik und Alterität – von Breaking bis Krumping', in *Express Yourself!*, ed. by Eva Kimminich and others, pp. 209–38; Carla Stalling Huntington, *Hip Hop Dance: Meanings and Messages* (Jefferson, NC: McFarland, 2007); Joseph Schloss, *Foundation: B-boys, B-girls, and Hip-hop Culture in New York* (Oxford: Oxford University Press, 2009). On DJing and music production see: Adam Krims, *Rap Music and the Poetics of Identity* (Cambridge: Cambridge University Press, 2000); Joseph Schloss, *Making Beats – The Art of Sample-based Hip-hop* (Middletown, CT: Wesleyan UP, 2004); Steffen Lepa and Malte Pelleter, '"Sampling" als kulturelle Praxis des HipHop', in *HipHop Meets Academia*, ed. by Bock, Meier and Süss, pp. 199–213; Mark Katz, *Groove Music – The Art and Culture of the Hip-Hop DJ* (New York: Oxford University Press, 2012).

86 Forman, *The 'hood Comes First*, p. 9.

In order to answer these questions posed by Forman, first of all it must be clarified what kind of 'space' is addressed throughout this analysis. As the research project is concerned with understanding a socio-cultural phenomenon which is tied to an urban environment, it is most useful to engage in ideas of space that have been subject to the wider *spatial turn* in Humanities. According to urban geographer Edward W. Soja, this space constitutes:

> *gesellschaftlich produzierter Raum.* Das Wort Verräumlichung wird manchmal verwendet um sicherzustellen, dass nicht nur der physikalische Raum gemeint ist. Wir meinen weder den Raum der Physik noch den Raum der Natur, wenn wir von neuem Raumdenken reden. Wir meinen gesellschaftlich erschaffenen Raum im Sinne eines dynamischen Prozesses.[87]
>
> [*socially produced space.* The word spatialization is sometimes used to make perfectly certain that not only physical space is meant. We do not mean space as understood by physics or space as we find it in nature when we talk about new ways of thinking about space. We mean socially produced space in the sense of a dynamic process.]

While Soja has been a prominent contributor to the *spatial turn* since the late 1980s, the initial 'turn' dates back to the 1960s. Its beginning has most notably been attributed to the French scholars Henri Lefebvre and Michel Foucault who began to address the importance of socially produced space in everyday contexts.[88] Ultimately, the aim was to equate spatial thinking to historical thinking when analysing social and cultural structures. According to Soja, this means:

> dass das, was wir im Hinblick auf die Geschichte annehmen, auch für Raum gilt: Alles, was existiert, jemals existiert hat, je existieren wird, hat eine wichtige räumliche Dimension, und eine kritische räumliche Perspektive auf alles, was als existent denkbar ist, kann uns eine wesentliche Hilfe sein, die Welt zu verstehen.[89]
>
> [that what we assume in terms of history is also valid for space: everything that exists, that has ever existed, that will ever exist, has an important spatial dimension; and a critical spatial perspective on everything which can be imagined as existing can be an essential support in understanding the world.]

87 Edward W. Soja, 'Vom "Zeitgeist" zum "Raumgeist". New Twists on the Spatial Turn', in *Spatial Turn: Das Raumparadigma in den Kultur- und Sozialwissenschaften*, ed. by Jörg Döring and Tristan Thielmann (Bielefeld: transcript, 2008), pp. 241–62 (pp. 252–53). This German translation by Thomas La Presti and Jörg Döring provides the only written and published transcript of the original talk by Soja.

88 Soja, 'Vom "Zeitgeist" zum "Raumgeist"', pp. 241–62.

89 Soja, 'Vom "Zeitgeist" zum "Raumgeist"', p. 252.

Thus, the *spatial turn* was mobilized as a response to a previous historical dominance, which privileged historical accounts over spatial ones in order to make sense of social and cultural dynamics. It is this unbalanced perspective which Soja aims to counteract in his book *Thirdspace: Journeys to Los Angeles and Other Real-and-imagined Places*, in which he looks at spatial, historical as well as social contexts *simultaneously*, since these perspectives 'contain each other; they cannot successfully be understood in isolation or epistemologically privileged separately'.[90] Soja calls this triad of spatiality, historicality and sociality the ontological 'trialectics of being' (*THSP*, p. 71).

It is this trialectics that will also frame this research project, for the art forms of hip-hop are deeply linked to the 'postindustrial city, which provided the context for creative development among hip hop's earliest innovators, [and] shaped their cultural terrain, access to space, materials, and education' within a desolate social environment.[91] By taking hip-hop's trialectics of being into consideration, the idea is that the combined insights will provide a more detailed understanding of the way hip-hop has evolved into becoming a German cultural movement and how, in so doing, it reflects upon Germany's urban, cultural and social landscapes.

Beginning the theoretical overview with Soja's spatial component of the trialectics, this study will appropriate Soja's terminology in order to identify physical and imagined urban spaces that appear meaningful for the hip-hop communities of Oldenburg and Hamburg. Hence, the adaptation of Soja's spaces relates to 'cityspace', which 'refers to the city as a historical-social-spatial phenomenon, but *with its intrinsic spatiality highlighted* for interpretive and explanatory purposes'.[92] Soja distinguishes this intrinsic spatiality by dividing it into 'firstspaces', 'secondspaces' and 'thirdspaces' (*THSP*, p. 74).

The 'firstspace' serves to define the 'human occupance of the surface of the earth, the relations between society and nature, the architectonics and resultant geographies of the human "built environment"' (*THSP*, p. 75). 'Firstspaces' are therefore acknowledged by their objective, material and factual characteristics. In the 'secondspace', on the other hand, 'spatial knowledge is primarily produced through discursively devised representations of space, through the spatial workings of the mind' (*THSP*, p. 75). Thus, 'secondspaces' are imagined and subjective spaces in contrast to 'firstspaces' and are 'entirely ideational, made up of projections into the empirical world from conceived

90 Edward W. Soja, *Thirdspace: Journeys to Los Angeles and Other Real-and-imagined Places* (Cambridge, MA: Blackwell, 1996), p. 72 (In the following quoted as *THSP*).

91 Tricia Rose, *Black Noise – Rap Music and Black Culture in Contemporary America* (Middleton, CT: Wesleyan University Press, 1994), p. 34.

92 Edward W. Soja, *Postmetropolis: Critical Studies of Cities and Regions* (Malden, MA: Blackwell, 2000), p. 8.

or imagined geographies' (*THSP*, p. 75). However, Soja emphasizes that this 'does not mean that there is no material reality, no Firstspace, but rather that the knowledge of this material reality is comprehended essentially through thought, as *res cogito*, literally "thought things"' (*THSP*, p 75).

The relevance of distinguishing between these spatialities is, according to Soja, due to the fact that:

> many in the so-called spatial disciplines (Geography, Architecture, Urban and Regional Studies, and City Planning, with capital letters used to signify the formally constituted discipline) as well as scholars in other disciplined fields tended to concentrate almost entirely on only one of these modes of thinking, that is either on Firstspace or Secondspace perspectives (*THSP*, p. 10).

In an attempt to bridge the divided notions of and investigations into space, Soja introduces the 'thirdspace'. This space proposes a new academic awareness of spatiality by fusing the 'first-' and 'secondspaces' into a third perspective. Soja describes this 'thirdspace' as a 'product of "thirding" of the spatial imagination, the creation of another mode of thinking about space that draws upon material and mental spaces of the traditional dualism but extends well beyond them in scope, substance, and meaning' (*THSP*, p. 11). In other words, the 'thirdspace' is a subjective space in which physical and imagined worlds come together to create the living reality. It captures the way in which human subjects culturally and socially perceive the 'firstspace' when situated within it. This all-encompassing space ultimately opens up:

> an-Other [*sic*] way of understanding and acting to change the spatiality of human life, a distinct mode of critical spatial awareness that is appropriate to the new scope and significance being brought about in the rebalanced trialectics of spatiality – historicality – sociality (*THSP*, p. 10).

This differentiation of spaces in Soja's terms is particularly useful for an analysis of hip-hop culture. The artistic performance and lyrical messages of rap, for instance, comprise:

> the physical city and its material features, including architectural edifices, the above- and belowground crossroads, and the public and private spaces within delineated geographic boundary, as well as the symbolic city, which is to say the representational city, encompassing images, verbal articulations, or other artistic expressions of urban cultures, experiences, and identities.[93]

While Forman's brief observations therefore reveal an inherent distinction between 'first-', 'second-' and potentially even 'thirdspaces' in rap production,

93 Forman, *The 'hood Comes First*, p. 35.

they also raise the question of whether hip-hop's other art forms employ these spaces in the same way. This assumption is based on Forman's identification of communicative forms within all of hip-hop's elements, since the:

> call and response in rap, whether referring to what are termed 'shout outs' (in the positive) or 'disses' (in the negative), the use of sampled musical passages, or recordings that comment on or appropriate the work of other artists does in fact offer a cultural connection across time and space. So, too, do the physical confrontations of break-dance competitions or the cross-spatial circulation of names and identities through graffiti art and tagging (the unsanctioned writing of names or crew logos on walls and other public surfaces).[94]

Dancers who perform on 'firstspaces' at live 'thirdspace' events will almost always communicate their art form directly to their opponent or audience. Music producers will, however, only disseminate their sampled musical messages to an audience in a mediated form in which the spatial component becomes referenced and spatial communication is therefore created in an imagined 'secondspace'. Graffiti artists, on the other hand, need to communicate their art form by writing on 'firstspaces' such as walls or other public surfaces for their art form to be understood as graffiti art. Lastly, rap has been successfully implemented in all spatial spheres, since it can communicate *about* a 'secondspace' through lyrics, as well as *in* a 'firstspace' through the rapper's presence at a concert in front of a live audience.

Having thus explored the different theoretical approaches to cityspaces it should also be mentioned that 'space' in critical theory can also signify a non-physical location. German urban geographer Julia Lossau, for instance, writes that the 'symbolische Semantik [des Raums] [...] sich insbesondere in poststrukturalistischen, differenz- und machttheoretischen orientierten Strömen [findet]. "Raum" fungiert als Chiffre für die Anerkennung unterschiedlicher Stellen, Orte oder Standpunkte, von denen aus Bedeutung in kontextspezifischer Art und Weise produziert wird' [symbolic semantics [of space] is especially found in post-structuralist movements and those theoretically oriented towards difference and power. 'Space' functions as a code for the acknowledgement of various positions, places or standpoints from which meaning is produced in a manner specific to a given context].[95] Such symbolic 'spaces' resonate, for example, with post-colonialist Homi K. Bhabha's use of the 'third space', which refers to a moment in time in which the process of cultural

94 Forman, *The 'hood Comes First*, p. 66. To 'diss' means to disrespect, which is primarily achieved by verbally insulting a real or imagined opponent in rhyme form.

95 Julia Lossau, 'Spatial Turn', in *Handbuch Stadtsoziologie*, ed. by Frank Eckhard (Wiesbaden: VS Verlag für Sozialwissenschaften, 2012), pp. 185–98 (p. 187).

mixing or hybridity appears. This approach will serve to capture the historicality of hip-hop's trialectics as presented in the following section.

Historicality – Hip-Hop as a Culturally Hybrid Art Movement

According to Soja, Bhabha's theory of the 'third space' 'is occasionally teasingly on the edge of being a spatially ungrounded literary trope, a floating metaphor for a critical historical consciousness that inadvertently masks a continued privileging of temporality over spatiality' (*THSP*, pp. 141–42). In other words, Bhabha's 'third space' is embedded in a historical narrative which points to a crucial diversion from Soja's conception of 'thirdspace', both orthographically and epistemologically. While Soja's 'thirdspace', spelled as one word, derives from a physical spatiality, Bhabha's 'third space', written separately, is rooted in a cultural-*historical* discourse, as the 'non-synchronous temporality of global and national cultures'.[96] This understanding serves to frame the temporal development of hip-hop culture in Germany and its process of cultural hybridization, with Alan O'Connor noting that:

> the notion of cultural hybridity seems particularly attractive to studies of popular music. After all, nothing seems to travel so easily as a musical riff, drum rhythm and subcultural style and in the process to mutate into a musical hybrid.[97]

However, as previously touched upon by Herzog,[98] the concept of hybridity rather implied a negative status before describing the 'attractive' movement and composition of music and style, especially regarding the biological mixing of human races. In German Nazi history the demand for a racially pure German *Volk* was based on the idea that racial or ethnic crossbreeding would reduce the chance of survival. Racial or ethnic 'hybrids' were therefore strategically eliminated from Germany's social landscape in the early twentieth century.[99] While Papastergiadis continues to assert that in the 'antagonistic framework of institutional politics, hybridity is usually confined to a negative position',[100] the tainted concept of hybridity eventually became re-appropriated within

96 Homi K. Bhabha, *The Location of Culture* (London: Routledge, 1994), p. 312 (In the following quoted as *LOC*).

97 Alan O'Connor, 'Local Scenes and Dangerous Crossroads: Punk and Theories of Cultural Hybridity', *Popular Music*, 2 (2002), 225–36 (p. 225).

98 Cf. Herzog, 'Hybrids and Mischlinge', 2.

99 Nikos Papastergiadis, *The Turbulence of Migration: Globalization, Deterriolization and Hybridity* (Cambridge: Polity, 2000), p. 173.

100 Nikos Papastergiadis, 'Hybridity and Ambivalence: Places and Flows in Contemporary Art and Culture', *Theory, Culture and Society*, 22 (2005), 39–64 (p. 58).

critical theory as a metaphorical and cultural extension of its original use. In the process the adoption of the term 'cultural hybridity' shifted to refer to 'a person who represents the blending of traits from diverse cultures or traditions, or even more broadly it can be a culture, or element of culture, derived from unlike sources; that is, something heterogeneous in origin or composition.'[101]

In *The Location of Culture* Bhabha positions the concept of 'cultural hybridity' in a post-colonial context, explaining that hybrid or 'postcolonial temporalities force us to rethink the sign of history *within* those languages, political or literary, which designate the people "as one"' (*LOC*, p. 220). He furthermore emphasizes cultural hybridity's ability to weaken and ultimately to deconstruct previously uncontested concepts of cultural authority or political supremacy, especially in contrast to the hegemonic and holistic notion of the nation state or of Western colonial empires. Thus, Bhabha explains that:

> [a]t the point at which the precept attempts to objectify itself as a generalised knowledge or a normalising, hegemonic practice, the hybrid strategy or discourse opens up a space of negotiation where power is *unequal* but its articulation may be *equivocal*. Such negotiation is neither assimilation nor collaboration. It makes possible the emergence of an 'interstitial' agency that refuses the binary representation of social antagonism.[102]

The refusal of the binary specifically presents itself in what Bhabha terms the 'intervention of the Third Space of enunciation which makes the structure of meaning and reference an ambivalent process' (*LOC*, p. 54). He elaborates that '[s]uch an intervention quite properly challenges our sense of the historical identity of culture as a homogenizing, unifying force, authenticated by the originary Past [*sic*], kept alive in the tradition of the People' (*LOC*, p. 54). The 'third space' can therefore be seen as a rupture of the temporal sequencing of a chronological national narrative which has been constructed and maintained in order to make sense of one's belonging.

At this point it will also be noted that not every culturally hybrid process, product or person results in a cultural space of thirdness. Cultural hybridity does not need to exist in a new state, which the concept of the 'third space' suggests, in order to challenge existing norms, values and realities. Rather, the sheer process of mixing without creating something new is equally an act of re-organizing previously opposed and separated phenomena. The historical perspective of this analysis therefore enables one to trace the processes through

101 Brian Stross, 'The Hybrid Metaphor: From Biology to Culture', *The Journal of American Folklore*, 112 (1999), 254–67 (p. 254).

102 Homi K. Bhabha, 'Culture's in Between', *Artforum International*, 32 (1993), 167–70 (p. 168).

which a foreign cultural art form, such as hip-hop, can become representative of something familiar through cultural 'hybridization, that is, an appropriation via negotiation on the incoming pop culture products based on the specific structure, traditions, and needs or interests of the indigenous culture(s)'.[103] Hip-hop's art forms in particular seem to be an interesting cultural movement through which to observe this hybridization. Not only has Tasek mentioned hip-hop's development into an authentic and relevant German language but in the case of popping dancer Azad hip-hop has also been treated as a cultural 'Mixer, der Sachen zusammennimmt und daraus was Neues macht oder auf einer ganz anderen, neuen Ebene präsentiert, weil es rebelliert gegen Sachen die da vorher da waren' [mixer that unites things and that creates something new or presents something at a completely different level because it revolts against things that were there before].[104]

Furthermore, a comparison between ethnically German and culturally hybrid hip-hop practitioners in this study will offer additional insights into determining how hip-hop culture has been able to resonate meaningfully amongst these supposedly disparate cultural sensibilities. By creating a German cultural product through cultural exchange, the hip-hop artists of Oldenburg and Hamburg ultimately:

> question the dominant assumption on the relationship between traditional authenticity and contemporary culture and test the limits of artistic agency and institutional structures. From these new cultural practices in contemporary art there is a possibility to explore more broadly the impact of hybridity on the social and political landscape of modernity.[105]

These cultural practices further highlight the fact that Soja's cityspace and Bhabha's 'third space' cultivate a mutual relationship for 'the context or environment in which a hybrid is produced is so important to interpreting the meaning of the hybrid, as well as for shaping the form and destiny of the cultural hybrid, that it cannot be ignored'.[106] While Stross therefore highlights the influence of the 'first-', 'second-' and 'thirdspace' experiences on the hybrid artist and the art form, one may also consider the hybridization of Soja's spaces. This occurs when the 'secondspace' identity of a place does not relate to its actual 'firstspace' materiality. Such a hybrid spatiality still creates a 'thirdspace' experience but one which exists as a culturally hybrid construct. In this case the 'thirdspace' can be treated as a 'third space' as well. It is

103 Peter Auer, 'A Post-Script: Code-switch and Social Identity,' *Journal of Pragmatics*, 37 (2005), 403–10 (p. 406).

104 Azad, interviewed by author, 24 May 2012.

105 Papastergiadis, 'Hybridity and Ambivalence', 40.

106 Stross, 'The Hybrid Metaphor', 266.

important to emphasize this rather complex overlapping of the terminology of spatiality as it becomes relevant to determining the hybridity of Germanness when considering the location of hip-hop performances. In order to bridge the connection between cultural hybridity, its spatial manifestation and, as mentioned by Papastergiadis, its impact on the socio-political landscape of modernity, the following section will provide the final theoretical component of hip-hop's trialectics of being, namely 'sociality'.

Sociality – The Presentation and Management of the National Self

This third and final section of the theoretical overview presents two micro-sociological theories derived from the sociologist Erving Goffman. The first stems from Goffman's book *Stigma: Notes on the Management of Spoiled Identity*. The concept of stigmatized identity relates to the racial concept of cultural hybridity when one considers that the 'origin of hybridity has been drenched in the shame-soaked ideology of miscegenation and cut through with stigmatic associations'.[107]

According to Goffman, Anglo-American and hence Western society 'is organized on the principle that any individual who possesses certain social characteristics has a moral right to expect that others will value and treat him in an appropriate way'.[108] In other words, one's actions and appearances are always tied to preconceived norms, values and practices, which are interpreted by an other:

> [W]hen a stranger comes into our presence, then, first appearances are likely to enable us to anticipate his category and attributes, his 'social identity' [...]. We lean on these anticipations that we have, transforming them into normative expectations, into righteously presented demands.[109]

Goffman delves deeper into this everyday social process by observing the ways in which 'evidence can arise of his [the stranger's] possessing an attribute that makes him different from the others in the category of persons available for him to be, and of less desirable kind' (*STGM*, pp. 3–4). Goffman calls this attribute that affects the ways individuals are perceived and judged by others a 'stigma' and lists three categories of 'stigmata'.

The first refers to physical disabilities, which Goffman describes as the 'abominations of the body' (*STGM*, p. 4). If physically-related features are not

107 Papastergiadis, 'Hybridity and Ambivalence', 60.

108 Erving Goffman, *The Presentation of Self in Everyday Life* (New York: Anchor, 1959), p. 13 (in the following quoted as *PSEL*).

109 Erving Goffman, *Stigma: Notes on the Management of Spoiled Identity* (New York: Simon Schuster, 1963), p. 2 (in the following quoted as *STGM*).

the source of a social 'stigma', Goffman reverts to the second category that comprises 'blemishes of individual character' (*STGM*, p. 4). More specifically, this stigma can be a reflection of a 'weak will, domineering or unnatural passions, treacherous and rigid beliefs, and dishonesty' (*STGM*, p. 4). The third 'stigma' type that Goffman mentions is 'the tribal stigma of race, nation, and religion' (*STGM*, p. 4). The 'tribe' thus defines the cultural characteristics of a person that can, for example, comprise language, skin colour or the participation in particular culturally related rituals.

The importance of addressing and theorizing social 'stigmata' lies in the fact that they have the power to make an other be 'reduced in our minds from a whole and usual person to a tainted, discounted one' (*STGM*, p. 3). In this ideological sense, 'stigmata' are always a social construct and as such never constitute a fixed reality. Their creation is, rather, motivated by their disruption of a common, cultivated notion of a 'stereotype of what a given type of individual should be' (*STGM*, p. 3). Therefore, 'stigmata' are deeply connected to personal bias or to subjectively constructed identity norms. Indeed, while Goffman chooses to call the stigmatized characteristic of a person his or her 'attribute', he makes clear that an 'attribute that stigmatizes one type of possessor can confirm the usualness of another, and therefore is neither creditable nor discreditable as a thing in itself' (*STGM*, p. 3).

In order for a 'stigma' to be accepted in society, Goffman proposes the strategy of easing tension during social contact, such as by converting the 'stigma' into a social asset. Furthermore, he suggests the strategy of 'passing' when the 'stigma' remains invisible, describing it as 'the management of undisclosed discrediting information about self' (*STGM*, p. 42). In a hip-hop context commercial African-American rappers may therefore manage their 'attribute' of black skin by purposely emphasizing it as an asset in order to support their credibility as pertaining to the social and racial minority of American society.[110] In graffiti art, however, the same 'attribute' is deemed irrelevant, for the artist's physical body and hence skin colour are removed from the presentation of the artwork itself. Contrary to rap, then, graffiti art 'manages stigmata like class, "race" and physical appearance by paralysing their influence'.[111] Hence, a comparison between the ways in which 'stigmata' are managed within hip-hop's individual art forms may reveal differing outcomes depending on each element's norms and practices.

By considering this relationship between 'stigma'-management and hip-hop's artistic practices, further differences may even appear in terms of the

110 Cf. Raquel Z. Rivera, *New York Ricans from the Hip Hop Zone* (New York: Palgrave Macmillan, 2003), pp. 97–100.

111 MacDonald, *The Graffiti Subculture*, p. 192.

'management of Germanness'. Keeping in mind that '[s]tigma management is an offshoot of something basic in society, the stereotyping or "profiling" of our normative expectations regarding conduct and character' (*STGM*, p. 51), the consideration of 'stigmata' in this analysis will provide a useful guideline in determining what constitues the German stereotype or German cultural norms. In so doing, this study will reveal the ways in which different cultural heritages, ethnic backgrounds and skin colours are 'managed' in order to become part of the German national narrative.

The second social theory applied in this work stems from *The Presentation of Self in Everyday Life*. In this study, Goffman observes the ways in which people interact in everyday life under the influence of their 'firstspatial' environment. In order to theorize this socio-spatial aspect, Goffman applies theatre terminology to differentiate spaces and the behavioural norms attached to these. At the same time, the sociologist emphasizes that his report:

> is not concerned with aspects of theatre that creep into everyday life. It is concerned with the structure of social encounters – the structure of those entities in social life that come into being whenever persons enter one another's immediate physical presence (*PSEL*, p. 254).

Goffman distinguishes between structures that are created by direct verbal expression, by 'giving' or by other communicative forms which Goffman terms 'giving off'. This latter form of expression presents the core of his study, relating to the 'more theatrical and contextual kind, the non-verbal, presumably unintentional kind, whether this communication be purposely engineered or not' (*PSEL*, p. 4). Thus, Goffman's social theory simultaneously builds on spatiality as he shifts his focus to the 'kind of social life that is organized within the physical confines of a building' (*PSEL*, p. xi), indicating a continued interrelatedness between the three components of Soja's 'trialectics of being'.

The social encounter with and presentation of the self to an other are what Goffman defines as a social 'performance'. This comprises 'all the activity of a given participant on a given occasion which serves to influence in a way any other of the participants' (*PSEL*, p. 15). At this point it needs to be clarified that aside from Goffman's understanding of performance as a social act, this study is also concerned with another understanding of performance in terms of entertaining, artistic events. Goffman's definition suits the analysis of both types of performance. This is because hip-hop norms emphasize a 'keeping it real' state of mind whilst performing on stage.[112] This suggests that staged hip-

112 For an in-depth account of hip-hop culture's attitude of 'keeping it real' see Gabriele Klein and Malte Friedrich, *Is this real? Die Kultur des HipHop* (Frankfurt am Main: Suhrkamp, 2003); and Menrath, *Represent what…*, pp. 92–102.

hop performances at concerts or competitions are not supposed to diverge from the artists' everyday presentation of self but should reflect their common social behaviour and identity.

Moreover, a performer may also be part of a larger performance 'team' 'who co-operate in staging a single routine' (*PSEL*, p. 79). The staging occurs on a 'front' whose physical confines are marked by its 'setting', i.e., the 'furniture, décor, physical layout, and other background items which supply the scenery and stage props for the space of human action played out before, within, or upon it' (*PSEL*, p. 22). In this 'front' space, the performer also has his or her 'personal front' constructed by 'clothing; sex, age and racial characteristics; size and looks; posture; speech patterns; facial expressions; bodily gestures; and the like' (*PSEL*, p. 24).

From the identifying of a 'front' region on which a performance is staged, it can be deduced that there exists a 'back' region as well. Indeed, in contrast to the norms established in the 'front' Goffman describes the 'back' region, which is often spatially adjacent to the 'front', as the place 'where the suppressed facts make an appearance' (*PSEL*, p. 112). These are most likely to be 'relative to a given performance, where the impression fostered by the performance is knowingly contradicted as a matter of course' (*PSEL*, p. 112). The remaining places situated beyond the 'front' and 'back' regional discourse are described as the 'outside' (*PSEL*, pp. 134–35). Lastly, it remains to be said that the individuals' roles are defined by these spaces in that 'performers appear in the front and back regions; the audience appears in the front region; and the outsiders are excluded from both regions' (*PSEL*, p. 145).

The relevance of Goffman's socio-spatial divisions for analysing hip-hop culture becomes evident in a micro-sociological study conducted at a German hip-hop festival. By applying Goffman's social theory, German sociologist Sebastian Schröer is able to capture the interrelatedness between spaces and social class, i.e., the perks enjoyed by 'very important people' who move freely within the public *and* the backstage area of the festival versus the restricted access of the audience who remain solely in the 'front'.[113] Indeed, in order to keep the divided roles of the individuals intact, the 'front' and hence the audience are usually kept separated from the 'back' (*PSEL*, p. 113). Having access to both sides, Schröer is able to compare the 'thirdspace' experiences of the 'front' contrasted to the 'back' by observing that:

> [w]ährend in der *Public area* häufig (jedoch nicht immer) eine Orientierung an den gängigen szenetypischen Klischees z.B. in Bezug auf Kleidung, Verhalten und Interaktion (performatives Handeln in Form von lässigen Posen, auffallende Verwendung szenespezifischer Begriffe und Sprachcodes[)] sowie

113 Cf. Schröer, 'Raum und Inszenierung', p. 259.

> 'perfektionierte' Kulissen bei der Inszenierung auffallen, wird im V.I.P.-Bereich ein eher spielerischer Umgang damit gepflegt.[114]
>
> [[w]hile in the public *area* there is often (but not always) a striking orientation towards the current clichés typical of the scene, e.g. with reference to clothes, behaviour and interaction (performative action in the form of cool posing, the striking use of scene-specific terms and language codes[)], as well as 'perfectioned' scenery in the actual presentation [of the show], these elements are dealt with somewhat more playfully in the V.I.P. area.]

In terms of hip-hop culture, an examination of the social spaces which comprise a performative hip-hop setting may therefore provide interesting insights into the concept and norm of 'keeping it real', especially when examining performances in non-commercial 'settings'. This comparison will be achieved by looking at the Oldenburg hip-hop artists who engage in this art form as a leisure activity in contrast to the professional pursuit of hip-hop in Hamburg. However, not only does Schröer's micro-social theorization of hip-hop's performative spaces reveal the importance of taking spaces into consideration for social analyses, it also shows that in order to do so the researcher is required to be physically present in the spaces himself. This aspect will be elaborated on in the following section, shifting from theory to methodology and towards an explanation of the construction of the corpus of this study.

Methodology

Constructing a Corpus

The corpus of this monograph is formed by qualitative data gathered during a period of fieldwork between January 2012 and September 2012. The qualitative approach to this research project aims at better understanding the nuances of cultural formation by taking subjective accounts into consideration and by *de*constructing the ways in which 'people construct the world around them, what they are doing or what is happening to them in terms that are meaningful and that offer rich insight'.[115]

Many studies on hip-hop continue to be conducted without ethnographic insights and hence without subjective accounts.[116] This especially refers to

114 Schröer, 'Raum und Inszenierung', p. 259.

115 Michael Angrosino, *Doing Ethnographic and Observational Research* (London: Sage, 2007), p. xii.

116 Templeton, 'What's so German about It?', p. 40.

rap-music studies in which the convenience of analysing lyrics and music-video clips available from the Internet and therefore from the computer screen provides the simplest way of pursuing a hip-hop study. However, improvised rap, graffiti art, dance and DJ performances are not necessarily mediated and hence visible in the same way as the written dissemination of lyrics. These hip-hop elements still often remain undocumented, which makes ethnographic research an indispensable method of gaining insight into and knowledge of the art forms and the artists' identity formation. This becomes even more relevant when identity is understood as 'something one performs, rather than something one is'.[117] In this sense identity is something 'contingent and relational, reacting to context and situation'[118] that needs to be captured whilst happening in conversation or in certain spaces such as studios, practice rooms and backstage areas. Hence, an ethnographic study on national identity in hip-hop culture allows the researcher to witness these situations and gain a more detailed and deeper comprehension of hip-hop's performative processes and negotiations of identity.

At the same time, the challenge in such a qualitative ethnographic study is its tendency to become too subjective. Michael Angrosino warns that inevitably 'ethnographers, who bring their own baggage with them so to speak, will produce different images of what they have observed'.[119] In order to mitigate this situation I have attempted to enter the ethnographic field with the least baggage possible. Without having had a personal interest in or knowledge of hip-hop's aesthetics aside from the passive consumption of hip-hop dance performances, I was certain that my lack of previous personal engagement in hip-hop culture would secure an objectivity that was not distorted by pre-formed opinions, tastes or biases.

In order to gain a balanced insight into Oldenburg's and Hamburg's lived hip-hop scenes, the time spent in the field was divided between, first, three and a half months in Oldenburg and, subsequently, five and a half months in Hamburg. The reason for this time frame is related to Oldenburg's small cityspace and the fact that its current hip-hop movement only comprises two elements: rap and graffiti art. In Hamburg, however, hip-hop's presence is grounded in rap, graffiti art, dance and live DJing and music production, thus providing a wider range of material to cover and more time required to do so. Hence, the corpus of this monograph consists of six case studies framed by the four main elements of hip-hop practised in Hamburg and the two which remain actively pursued in Oldenburg.

117 Noel Castree, Rob Kitchin and Alisdair Rogers, 'Identity', in *A Dictionary of Human Geography* (Oxford: Oxford University Press, 2013), pp. 231–32 (p. 232).
118 Castree, Kitchin and Rogers, 'Identity', p. 232.
119 Angrosino, *Doing Ethnographic and Observational Research*, p. 11.

By conducting a comparative hip-hop analysis which looks at the same cultural formation at different sites, this corpus is, moreover, shaped by a multi-sited ethnographic study. According to cultural anthropologist Marcus George, such an approach:

> claims that any ethnography of a cultural formation in the world system is also an ethnography of the system, and therefore cannot be understood only in terms of the conventional single-site mise-en-scene of ethnographic research, assuming indeed it is the cultural formation, produced in several different locales, rather than the conditions of a particular set of subjects that is the object of study.[120]

While this work does not seek to explore the depths of multi-sited ethnography, a side effect of employing such an approach did indeed reveal two very different fieldwork experiences, which consisted of participant observation and semi-structured interviews, despite examining the same cultural movement using the same ethnographic methods. The following sections will elaborate on these methodological approaches, while the individually tailored method of close readings of hip-hop's art forms will be explained in the respective chapters.

Participant Observation

According to the editors of *Participant Observation: A Guide for Fieldworkers*, participant observation is an ethnographic method designed 'to collect data in naturalistic settings by ethnographers who observe and/or take part in the common and uncommon activities of the people being studied'.[121] It is therefore a precondition that the researcher is in the field, on site, where he or she can observe, participate and conduct first-hand empirical investigation. Angrosino further differentiates between levels of intensity within this method. One level of participant observation, for example, is what Angrosino terms the 'participant-as-observer', in which the researcher is immersed in the scene or community while at the same time being known as the ethnographer and permitted to conduct research within the community.[122] However, as soon as the ethnographer is more detached from the community, he or she, according to Angrosino, becomes the 'observer-as-participant'. At this level, the ethnographer will generally only interact with research participants

120 George E. Marcus, 'Ethnography in/of the World System: The Emergence of Multi-Sited Ethnography', *Annual Review Anthropology*, 24 (1995), 95–117 (p. 96).

121 Kathleen Musante DeWalt and Billie R. DeWalt, *Participant Observation: A Guide for Fieldworkers* (Lanham, MD: Rowman & Littlefield, 2011), p. 2.

122 Angrosino, *Doing Ethnographic and Observational Research*, p. 6.

through interviews and by observing them at selected events.[123] It is these two levels of participant observation which shaped this research project as well.

In Oldenburg, an immersion into the hip-hop community led me into becoming a 'participant-as-observer', since hip-hop was primarily practised as a personal activity and was therefore a private matter. This privacy was reflected in the rappers' domestic spatial occupancies, for rap was generally performed and recorded in living rooms, basements or bedrooms. Hence, in order to experience rap culture in Oldenburg it was necessary for me to share these domestic, indoor and underground 'firstspaces' with a male-dominated group of hip-hop artists. In this setting, my presence as a 'participant-as-observer' further became a sign of personal confidentiality, for local hip-hop artists began sharing private issues and asking for advice from a female perspective. This dynamic can be related to Joan Neff Gurney's observations on gender's auxiliary potential during fieldwork. She explains that a female ethnographer who enters a male-dominated setting may have an advantage in gaining further insight into the field by utilizing her gender as an asset since it presents less of a threat to the masculinity of her subjects.[124] While this observation resonates with my fieldwork experience, my access to the almost exclusively male hip-hop events and spaces was, however, seen as a threat by the artists' female partners. At one point, for example, I was denied access to a recording session as the studio was located in the producer's flat, which was also inhabited by his partner.

However, beyond moving in these domestic 'firstspaces' further participant observation in Oldenburg entailed the attendance of rap concerts (both by local rappers as well as by others who performed in Oldenburg at that time) with access to the 'front' as well as to 'back' regions. Other events included local hip-hop jams, video-clip shoots, graffiti-art sessions and visiting local 'halls of fame', meaning legal graffiti walls dispersed throughout Oldenburg. These observations also revealed a tight relationship between the local rap community and the graffiti artists who, on the whole, tended to support each other's art form: CD covers for local rap albums were often designed by local graffiti artists, while the graffiti-art studio was used as a background for rap video-clips or as a venue to host hip-hop jams and informal rap sessions.

Following this fieldwork experience in Oldenburg, I shifted into becoming an 'observer-as-participant' in Hamburg. Here, my role as a female academic and participant observer became immediately accepted by local hip-hop

123 Angrosino, *Doing Ethnographic and Observational Research*, p. 6.

124 Cf. Joan Neff Gurney, 'Female Researchers in Male Settings', in *Experiencing Fieldwork: An Inside View of Qualitative Research*, ed. by William B. Shaffir and Robert A. Stebbins (Los Angeles: Sage, 1991), pp. 53–61 (p. 56).

artists and their partners. This difference was due to the fact that the research participants in Hamburg engaged in hip-hop as a profession. Hence, when entering the local hip-hop field I found myself in offices, recording studios, rehearsal rooms, art galleries, backstage at high-profile hip-hop events as well as in youth centres. I therefore initially doubted my success as a fieldworker in Hamburg as I was lacking access into the hip-hop practitioners' private spheres to which I was accustomed in Oldenburg. However, I soon realized that such insight was not required in order to conduct an equally successful study on the local artists' relationship to hip-hop. In Hamburg, hip-hop culture simply functioned through a different system and on a different level, as each art form was, for the most part, practised as a professional occupation in separately designated spaces. Aside from attending various DJ concerts, dance battles, rap concerts and festivals, halls of fame and graffiti-art exhibitions, I also had the opportunity to participate in breakdance training sessions, employing my experience and knowledge as a dancer and gymnast to gain further insight into this particular art form. In the end, the two different observational experiences provided more detailed knowledge and awareness about the two local hip-hop communities than anticipated. This was further supported by information gathered through personal interviews, which will be addressed in the next section.

Interviews

The interviews conducted for this research project followed a semi-structured format which 'combine[s] the flexibility of the unstructured, open-ended interview with the directionality and agenda of the survey instrument to produce focused, qualitative, textual data'.[125] This means that certain questions relating to the topic of investigation were pre-formulated and can be read in the appendix.[126] The lengths of the interviews varied between twenty minutes and four hours, depending on the time available and the number of participants involved. In total, this provided an estimated seventy hours of interview material that was digitally recorded and subsequently transcribed.[127]

In Oldenburg, twenty-three interview participants engaged in this study, while in Hamburg interviews were conducted with twenty-nine research subjects. Due to instances in which meeting times were incompatible or

125 Stephen L. Schensul, Jean J. Schensul and Margaret Diane LeCompte, *Essential Ethnographic Methods: Observations, Interviews, and Questionnaires* (Walnut Creek, CA: AltaMira, 1999), p. 149.

126 Cf. Schensul, Schensul and LeCompte, *Essential Ethnographic Methods*, p. 149.

127 The transcriptions incorporated into this study have been amended from their spoken original for the sake of grammatical clarity and readability.

interview opportunities occurred unplanned, one interview was conducted via email while four are held on record through written notes. All interviews were conducted in German apart from one, which was held in English. While not all interviewees are cited, their stories and insights have shaped the overall perspective of German hip-hop culture reflected in this work. The interviewees were over eighteen years of age and comprised hip-hop artists from diverse ethnic backgrounds. Some were first- or second-generation immigrants whose mother and father had other nationalities, while others had one or both parents of German heritage. The interviewees were carefully chosen through previous knowledge or personal suggestions by artists during my time in the field; these also advised me to talk to rap-label managers, hip-hop journalists or hip-hop activists who were familiar with the local communities. This ensured a heterogeneous sample of perspectives and personal narratives, whereby interviewees were not always born and raised in the respective cities but rather contributed actively towards the hip-hop art form in their community during the time of investigation.

In both local hip-hop communities there remained, however, the same challenge in, and ultimately impossibility of, attaining contact with graffiti artists who pursued solely illegal graffiti art. Thus the graffiti artists who shared their insights in this study have, for the most part, left their illegal activity behind and now pursue graffiti art commercially or teach it as a legitimate art form. Nevertheless, graffiti art's illegal form of expression does appear in the form of close readings of visual documentation.

Chapter Overview

Each chapter is dedicated to one of hip-hop's main art forms, beginning with music, followed by dance, rap and graffiti art. All four chapters adhere to the same structure: a spatial, historical and social overview of each art form's emergence in the United States is followed by an outline of the chosen method for the close reading of the specific hip-hop element in the respective German case study. This is succeeded by a brief introduction on the ways in which hip-hop was initially practised in West Germany.[128] This will serve as a basis from which to understand the contemporary social, historical and spatial discourses that frame the contemporary local manifestations of hip-hop. While the first two chapters on music and dance only comprise analyses pertaining to Hamburg, the last two chapters on

128 Both Hamburg and Oldenburg lie in what used to be West Germany. The history of hip-hop in the GDR can therefore be omitted in an analysis of the respective local hip-hop communities.

rap and graffiti art comprise a comparative study of their manifestations in Hamburg *and* in Oldenburg.

The conclusion to this multi-sited hip-hop analysis will summarize the main findings and trends concerning contemporary identity formations in German hip-hop culture. Projected outcomes include a better understanding of what it means to be German in the twenty-first century for those who engage in hip-hop culture, of how hip-hop's four main art forms help to negotiate, manage and communicate local belonging and how, through this, hip-hop can be understood as a German cultural practice. These results present a perspective on German identity in which some ethnicities, mentalities and skin colours become part of contemporary Germanness, while others do not. The former state is captured in the concept of 'post-hybridity' – a term that is introduced into this monograph to describe multicultural and at the same time German identity formations which are particularly mobilized in hip-hop culture.

CHAPTER 1

Hip-Hop Music

The Backbone of Hip-Hop Culture: The DJ

> Hip hop began explicitly as dance music to be appreciated through movement, not merely listening. It was originally designed for live performance, where one could admire the dexterity of the DJ.[1]

These live performances, as outlined by Richard Shusterman, specifically unfolded in the New York City borough of the Bronx. Indeed, the Bronx has been most commonly cited as the birthplace of hip-hop music and hence of hip-hop culture in the year 1973.[2] At the time, the Bronx's 'thirdspace' experience was defined by financial instability, ethnic segregation and social marginality,[3] with Forman emphasizing that 'nowhere was the human damage and social devastation of late 1970s and early 1980s America more evident than in the city's uptown boroughs where the hip-hop phenomenon originated'.[4]

This social devastation also reflected on the Bronx's urban 'firstspaces', which comprised 'rumbling highways and crumbling schools, towering apartment buildings and teeming playgrounds'.[5] However, Mark Katz also emphasizes that within these 'firstspaces' there existed, due to the cultural and ethnic amalgamation of African-American, Caribbean and Latino heritages, 'funk godfathers, soul queens, and disco DJs; street corner *salseros* and Jamaican sound system makers'.[6] In other words, despite the bleak urban circumstances of the Bronx it was also an arena for experiencing culturally rich and positive energies in the form of music and dance. Katz asserts that by encountering the Bronx from this perspective many of 'the early hip-hop DJs felt genuine affection for their city, taking deep pride in being a Bronxite rather than

1 Richard Shusterman, *Performing Live – Aesthetic Alternatives for the Ends of Art* (New York: Cornell University Press, 2000), p. 63.
2 Cf. Rose, *Black Noise*, p. 30; Katz, *Groove Music*, p. 17.
3 Cf. *Scratch*, Afrika Bambaataa, Mos Def and Fab 5 Freddy, dir. by Doug Pray (Palm Pictures, 2001) [on DVD].
4 Forman, *The 'hood Comes First*, p. 87.
5 Katz, *Groove Music*, p. 42.
6 Katz, *Groove Music*, p. 42.

protesting its harsh conditions'.[7] In fostering this pride, DJs began to engage in this local 'thirdspace' experience by employing their musical knowledge of the Jamaican sound systems in order to create live urban musical performances.[8]

The first DJs to do so were African-American DJs Grandmaster Flash and DJ Afrika 'Bam' Bambaataa, as well as Jamaican DJ Kool Herc. Known as 'the "holy trinity" of hip-hop culture, as the three pioneers who laid hip-hop's foundation',[9] the three DJs started hosting local open-air events. These became known as 'block parties', firmly linking this party movement to its 'firstspace', i.e., to the architectonics of the neighbourhood block. In so doing, DJs engaged in spatial discourses by, on the one hand, converting an urban space into a Goffmanian 'front' and, on the other hand, by demarcating *their* territory within the wider cityspace. Thus, local DJ Grandmaster Flash remembers that:

> Kool Herc had the West Side, Bam had Bronx River. DJ Breakout had way uptown past Gun Hill. Myself, my area was like 138th Street, Cypress Avenue, up to Gun Hill, so that we all had our territories and we all had to respect each other.[10]

This respect was primarily negotiated through 'spatial praxis, the transformation of (spatial) knowledge into (spatial) action in a field of unevenly developed (spatial) power' (*THSP*, p. 31). The spatial power came in the form of the sonic volume released by the DJ's sound system, for '[p]artygoers and passersby who heard – and felt – a sound system from afar were not just hearing music, they were witnessing a raw demonstration of the DJ's might and receiving a clear message: *you are entering my territory*'.[11] However, not only does Katz interpret the DJ's aural demarcations as important signals for his social 'audience' as well as for 'outsiders', he further infers that 'the output of such extravagant volume can also be interpreted symbolically: both as a display of power and as a defence mechanism'.[12]

More specifically, this aural shield defended against the constant traffic noise of engines and motors conjured up by the American Expressway – a highway complex built straight through the Bronx.[13] The sheer material factor of the highway cutting through the New York borough consequentially created

7 Katz, *Groove Music*, p. 40.

8 Katz explains that these sound systems were 'often homemade assemblages of turntables, amplifiers, speakers, and miles of cable. And they were enormous – some systems had as many as fifty speakers' (Katz, *Groove Music*, p. 26).

9 Katz, *Groove Music*, p. 51.

10 DJ Grandmaster Flash, quoted in Murray Forman, '"Represent": Race, Space and Place in Rap Music', *Popular Music*, 19 (2000), 65–90 (p. 66).

11 Katz, *Groove Music*, p. 36.

12 Katz, *Groove Music*, p. 39.

13 Katz, *Groove Music*, p. 38; Rose, *Black Noise*, pp. 31–33.

a 'thirdspace' filled with constant sonic turbulence. Hence, for the 'pioneering hip-hop DJs, merely to exist in the Bronx was to experience near-constant noise'.[14] With this in mind, it is hardly surprising that the first hip-hop DJs not only absorbed the noise but worked against it and simultaneously 'created it, and through their massive sound systems, they indelibly shaped the Bronx soundscape'.[15]

The musical sound in conjunction with the material conditions of the cityspace also influenced the establishment of a distinct musical aesthetic beyond the volume that was being played. Through the advent of specific technical inventions with which to play vinyl records, the DJ's focus shifted from negotiating respect via sonic and hence spatial power towards negotiating it through technical dexterity.[16] The most prominent of such technical inventions came in the form of the 'scratch' technique. Commonly acknowledged as having been accidentally invented by Bronx DJ Grandwizzard Theodore who manually moved a vinyl record back and forth, the scratch has become the most recognized aesthetic element of hip-hop music.[17]

Whilst it was primarily employed to scratch an additional rhythm pattern into a recorded sound, Katz connects this invention to the urban experience, namely 'as a celebration of the notoriously noisy city of the Bronx, for it transformed what could be considered sonic blight into music'.[18] In other words, even the emerging aesthetics and techniques that created hip-hop music were mobilized through the local 'thirdspace' experience, again highlighting the influence and relevance of spatiality on hip-hop music's development. In this context other aesthetic practices were invented by the 'trinity of hip-hop' at the neighbourhood block parties as well:

> Herc set the cornerstone, a powerful, bass-heavy break beat; Bam, the Master of Records, supplied the bricks through his vast and eclectic selection of songs and sounds; and Flash [...] provided the mortar – the means of joining hip-hop's diverse sonic materials into a solid, unbroken structure.[19]

The break beat, or simply the 'break', refers to a short percussion solo generally heard in funk music, although a break 'may show up anywhere in a song,

14 Katz, *Groove Music*, p. 39.

15 Katz, *Groove Music*, p. 39.

16 Katz, *Groove Music*, p. 49.

17 *Scratch*, dir. by Pray; and Katz, *Groove Music*, pp. 49–51. According to Grandwizzard Theodore, '[t]he scratch is something the Hip Hop world cannot live without' (Grandwizzard Theodore, quoted in *Born in the Bronx – A Visual Record of the Early Days of Hip Hop*, ed. by Johann Kugelberg (New York: Rizzoli International, 2007), p. 202.

18 Katz, *Groove Music*, p. 66.

19 Katz, *Groove Music*, p. 49.

and really, anywhere in music'.[20] Typically, there is an underlying 'funkiness' uniting these breaks, such as a syncopated rhythm pattern played by a small selection of instruments. This provides the break beat with a somewhat naked feeling in contrast to the full sonic force of the overall musical track.

In particular, break beats owe their cornerstone status to local dancers who performed 'their showiest moves during these percussive breaks'.[21] While originally composed as a short musical divergence within the main theme of the song, the newly formed purpose of these breaks required an artificial musical extension in order to make the dancing last longer. This extension was created by Grandmaster Flash who 'developed more sophisticated ways of repeating breaks, using two copies of a record on two turntables and employing a mixer to switch quickly and seamlessly between the two discs'.[22] So-called 'looping' was born, which meant playing the same segment of a break over and over again – like a loop. From this invention onwards, Joe Schloss explains that the:

> breakbeat focus of the Bronx deejays set in motion a number of social trends that would give birth to a music known as hip-hop. These included the development of a substantial body of knowledge about the nature and location of breakbeats, an oral tradition and culture to preserve this knowledge, a worldview that valorized the effort necessary to find breaks, and an aesthetic that took all of these concerns into account.[23]

This hip-hop music aesthetic eventually spread to other parts of the country as well. New turntable techniques were most notably being invented by DJs in Philadelphia and on the West Coast of the United States.[24] However, these advances also disconnected the practice of DJing from being a lived dance experience in a public urban space. By the 1990s, hip-hop DJing branched into 'turntableism', which became a 'separate movement, independent from dancers and MCs. The music of these DJs was meant for listening, not dancing, for head-nodding, not rump-shaking'.[25] On the other hand, within this new movement the turntable finally gained an identity of its own. It became considered an autonomous musical instrument, indeed, a hybrid musical instrument with the possibility of creating new music by simultaneously *re*-producing previously recorded sounds.[26] The requirement of 'real-time manipulation' through specific turntable techniques such as 'backspinning,

20 Katz, *Groove Music*, p. 49.
21 Katz, *Groove Music*, p. 15.
22 Katz, *Groove Music*, p. 16.
23 Schloss, *Making Beats*, pp. 32–33.
24 *Scratch*, dir. by Pray; Katz, *Groove Music*, pp. 101–08.
25 Katz, *Groove Music*, p. 127.
26 Katz, *Groove Music*, p. 62.

slip-cueing, punch phrasing, and, of course, scratching'[27] further legitimized the turntable's status as a musical instrument beyond its initial purpose to create dance music in the blocks of the Bronx.

A similar shift in terms of performative priorities took place when DJs re-located from the outdoor public space into an indoor music studio.[28] This new branch of DJing completely stopped engaging with the live 'audience' which had previously framed the DJs' 'thirdspace' experience as performers. Rather, DJs who started working in studios started calling themselves music producers and employed their musical skills for 'the creation of the instrumental tracks over which MCs rhyme'.[29] The contrast between making music in a performative 'front' versus in a private 'back' region is highlighted by German DJ Stylewarz, who explains that:

> beim Auflegen kriegst du halt relativ schnell ein Feedback. Viele Leute denken 'Ja du legst halt auf und die Leute tanzen'. Aber [...] das [ist] so ein Geben und Nehmen. Und im Studio bist du in deiner kleinen eigenen Welt. Und fährst deinen Film. Bist am Basteln. Und dann schaust du halt irgendwie was du damit machst und ob eventuell andere Leute deinen Film nachvollziehen können.[30]
>
> [while you're deejaying you get feedback quite quickly. Many people think, 'Yeah, you deejay and then people dance'. But [...] it's giving and taking. And in the studio you are in your own little world. Doing your own thing. And are crafting. And then you just look and see what you are going to do with it and whether other people might understand your world.]

DJ Stylewarz's act of 'basteln' refers to the creation of musical 'beats', which can be understood as 'musical collages composed of brief segments of recorded sound'.[31] These segments can include a 'fraction of a waveform, a single note from an instrument or voice, a rhythm, a melody, a harmony, or an entire work or album'[32] and are individually referred to as 'samples'. The selected samples employed in music production are frequently 'the same ones that DJs had been spinning for years'.[33] This aesthetic practice of composing musical collages from past sounds therefore still provides a historical bond and a sense

27 Katz, *Groove Music*, p. 62.
28 Forman, *The 'hood Comes First*, p. 79.
29 Katz, *Groove Music*, p. 62.
30 DJ Stylewarz, interviewed by author, 12 June 2012.
31 Katz, *Groove Music*, p. 2.
32 Justin A. Williams, 'Musical Borrowing in Hip-hop Music: Theoretical Frameworks and Case Studies' (unpublished doctoral dissertation, University of Nottingham, 2009), p. 14, http://eprints.nottingham.ac.uk/11081/1/JustinWilliams_PhDfinal.pdf [accessed 19 July 2016].
33 Katz, *Groove Music*, p. 122.

of continuity to the original practice of DJing. It is here that hip-hop music's historicality becomes most apparent since the aesthetic of sampling creates musical texts that fuse past sounds into a contemporary sonic mixture.

Hip-hop scholar Tricia Rose, in particular, relates this aesthetic of hip-hop music to an African-American cultural and historical discourse, whereby recognizing samples 'affirms black musical history and locates these "past" sounds in the "present"'.[34] Moreover, Rose writes that the 'distinctive, systematic use of rhythm and sound, especially the use of repetition and musical breaks, are part of a rich history of New World black tradition and practices'.[35] The turntable technique of looping break beats, i.e., of repeating a segment of a song, is what Rose understands as being inherently African – especially in contrast to classical European musical traditions. Basing her findings on James A. Snare's studies on African music, Rose explains that 'European culture "secrets" repetition, categorizing it as a progression or regression, assigning accumulation and growth or stagnation to motion, whereas black cultures highlight the observance of repetition, perceiving it as circulation, equilibrium'.[36] The practice of looping is thus, according to Rose, 'repositioned as repetition, as equilibrium inside the rupture' – the rupture being the cutting of the break beat out of its entire song.[37] Hence, Rose's conclusion is that the hip-hop DJs' technical invention 'uses repetition and rupture in new and complex ways, building on long-standing black cultural forces'.[38]

Schloss further supports this cultural-historical perspective of hip-hop music production practices by linking the aesthetic of sampling to the vernacular African-American tradition of 'signifying'.[39] Originally cultivated by black slaves in the United States, this tradition engages in the potential ambiguity of words and sentence structures in order to re-contextualize language by extracting the supposed clearness and directness from utterances made by the 'white' authority.[40] The act of signifying thus turns language into a playful and clever 'semantic inversion and indirection, feigned simplicity, and covert parody'.[41] In terms of the appearance and manifestation of signifying in hip-hop music productions, Schloss explains that by 'turning samples of single notes and linear musical phrases into cycles and using virtually all material in an ambiguous or double-voiced

34 Rose, *Black Noise*, p. 89.
35 Rose, *Black Noise*, p. 64.
36 Rose, *Black Noise*, p. 69.
37 Rose, *Black Noise*, p. 70.
38 Rose, *Black Noise*, p. 70.
39 Schloss, *Making Beats*, pp. 196–97.
40 Ulf Poschardt, *DJ Culture* (Hamburg: Rogner und Bernhard, 1995), p. 191.
41 Shusterman, *Performing Live*, p. 62.

way, hip-hop can simultaneously "Africanize" material from any source and hide its African sensibility'.[42]

However, it remains problematic to ground all of hip-hop's musical structures and hence hybridization processes in an African or African-American context, for 'only one group other than African Americans was involved from the very beginning – Latinos, particularly those of Puerto Rican heritage'.[43] According to Katz, this Latino influence appeared 'through the work of individual DJs and, more broadly, though the impact of Latin music'.[44] Katz elaborates on this aspect, stating that the 'Latin contribution is not just in the tinge – it's at the core' of hip-hop music.[45] This cultural contribution can be traced back to the 'thirdspace' perspective of the Bronx since hip-hop music's break beat tradition 'owes a great deal to the salsified soundscape of the Bronx'.[46]

It can, of course, also be argued that salsa was influenced by African instruments and traditions before it was 'exported' to the Bronx by the cultural heritages of its inhabitants. However, if this were the case a clear distinction between African-American and Latino cultural heritages would not be made by hip-hop scholars or by its practitioners. Rather, Jeffrey O. G. Ogbar concludes that the 'centrality of Puerto Ricans is ignored for the sake of the "black aesthetic"'[47] which has manifested itself as a key racial discourse in hip-hop culture.[48] Aside from describing its musical aesthetic, the 'attribute' of blackness became an identity norm for the first hip-hop DJs in the Bronx which simultaneously stigmatized other skin colours and ethnicities that did not reflect Africanness. Latino DJ Charlie Chase from the Bronx, for instance, claims that he 'encountered scepticism and prejudice'[49] at hip-hop parties due to his Latino heritage: 'Dancers at his first gigs were sometimes shocked to see that the DJ who emerged from the shadows was Puerto Rican, not black, and early on he was frequently harassed at parties by security who assumed he didn't belong'.[50] Similarly, local Puerto Rican DJ Disco Wiz was confronted by fellow Latinos asking: 'You're trying to be black, you hanging out with black people? [...] Stick to your kind, you disgrace'.[51] These statements thus

42 Schloss, *Making Beats*, pp. 196–97.
43 Katz, *Groove Music*, p. 27.
44 Katz, *Groove Music*, p. 27.
45 Katz, *Groove Music*, p. 32.
46 Katz, *Groove Music*, p. 32.
47 Jeffrey O. G. Ogbar, *Hip-Hop Revolution – The Culture and Politics of Rap* (Lawrence, KA: University Press of Kansas, 2007), p. 44.
48 Rivera, *New York Ricans from the Hip Hop Zone*, pp. 79–97.
49 Katz, *Groove Music*, p. 28.
50 Katz, *Groove Music*, p. 28.
51 Katz, *Groove Music*, p. 28.

touch upon the cultural expectation of the 'stigmatized' individual to remain loyal to his 'tribe'. The Latino and African-American inhabitants therefore saw themselves as individual cultural entities:

> who have a common history and culture (and often a common national origin), who transmit their membership along lineage lines, who are in a position to demand signs of loyalty from some of the members, and who are in a relatively disadvantaged position in society (*STGM*, p. 145).

This loyalty was evidently negotiated through skin colour, where 'blackness' signified an inherent segregation within the Bronx's racial-minority community despite sharing the same cityspace. However, since 'attributes' are always subject to social constructions of reality, it needs to be said that the signifier of black skin remains an arbitrary cultural sign of Africanness. This is best highlighted by black New York DJ Rob Swift, who states: 'I'm Spanish. My parents are from Colombia'.[52]

From these discordant socio-racial discourses taking place in the lived urban space of the Bronx, the development of DJing in other cityspaces not only contributed to the advancement of turntableism and studio production practices but also changed the need to have certain racial 'attributes' in order to be an authentic hip-hop DJ. The establishment of turntableism as an independent art form has, for example, been indebted to 'the rise of a Filipino American turntableist scene [and] must be recognized as one of the key developments in the history of the hip-hop DJ'.[53] Moreover, Canadian DJ A-Trak even emphasizes the established integration of races and ethnicities in hip-hop DJ culture, stating that today's 'DJs come from all backgrounds. It's not like the rap scene which is predominantly black, and where you constantly hear about white MCs having to prove themselves. It's really great, actually, how multicultural DJing is'.[54]

Thus, as an interim summary, this section has served to trace the aspects of spatiality, historicality and sociality that have formed and defined hip-hop's musical element. As the 'firstspace' of the Bronx in the 1970s comprised disintegrating buildings which were predominantly inhabited by African-American and Latino residents, the constant sound of traffic as well as the open-air lifestyle created a noisy yet lively 'thirdspace' experience. Engaging in this urban condition, hip-hop DJs re-appropriated their neighbourhood blocks as 'firstspatial fronts', namely as the material areas on which to perform their block parties. Whilst their status and respect as DJs was negotiated

52 DJ Rob Swift, in *Scratch*, dir. by Pray.

53 Katz, *Groove Music*, p. 137.

54 DJ A-Trak, quoted in Katz, *Groove Music*, p. 137. A-Trak's statement concerning the racial composition of hip-hop's lyrical element will be further explored in the chapter on rap.

according to territorial boundaries and sonic volume, their musical creations and performances also served to maintain a cultural bond and historical continuity with the cultural narratives of their urban community. This has been most notably achieved through the practice of sampling, namely by relying on previous cultural knowledge of musical pieces in order to create a musical experience in the present.

Lastly, it remains to be said that sampling is also able to hybridize musical texts as the '*referenced* version takes on *alternative lives and alternative meanings* in a fresh context'.[55] It is here where new histories may be composed, simultaneously creating new cultural meaning. Indeed, the cultural norms and performative practices of DJing have already expanded since leaving the original urban 'firstspace' of the Bronx. What was once deemed a post-industrial, urban enunciation of 'blackness' has become a musical expression for artists pertaining to other spatial, historical and social contexts. Therefore, even though studies suggest that hip-hop's musical aesthetic especially 'resonates with black cultural priorities in the age of digital reproduction',[56] other hip-hop scholars such as Tony Mitchell oppose this view by stating that contemporary hip-hop culture 'cannot be viewed simply as an expression of Afro-American culture; it has become a vehicle for global youth affiliations and a tool for reworking local identity all over the world'.[57] This local identity nevertheless remains expressed through hip-hop music's aesthetics and the practice of 'citation, of the relentless sampling of sonic and verbal archives'.[58] In order to capture this aesthetic, the following section will turn to intertextual theory with which to offer a close reading of hip-hop music's contemporary texts and to detect its hybrid musical meanings and messages in a German cultural context.

Reading the Intertextual Aesthetic of Hip-Hop Music

Originally, the method of close reading was applied to literary texts, in which words and sentences became critically read with 'depth, precision, acuity, and patience'.[59] While this study follows the same critical approach,

55 Rose, *Black Noise*, p. 90.

56 Rose, *Black Noise*, p. 75.

57 Tony Mitchell, 'Introduction: Another Root – Hip-Hop Outside the USA', in *Global Noise: Rap and Hip-Hop Outside the USA*, ed. by Tony Mitchell (Middletown, CT: Wesleyan University Press, 2001), pp. 1–38 (pp. 1–2).

58 Russel A. Potter, *Spectacular Vernaculars: Hip-hop and the Politics of Postmodernism* (Albany, NY: State University of New York, 1995), p. 53.

59 Andrew DuBois, 'Close Reading: An Introduction', in *Close Reading: The Reader*, ed. by Frank Lentricchia and Andrew DuBois (Durham: Duke University Press, 2003), pp. 1–40 (p. 4).

it also applies close readings to cultural texts which are created without the written word. These include musical, and later choreographed, lyrical and typographic texts.

Close readings of hip-hop music that has been created through DJing and music production are influenced by Serge Lacasse's approach to sampled musical texts.[60] In 'Intertextuality and Hypertextuality in Recorded Music' Lacasse adapts Gerard Genette's theory of *transtextuality* and applies it to popular musical texts that specifically make use of the sampling technique.[61] As explained in *Palimpsestes: la littérature au second degré*, Genette employs the all-encompassing term *transtextuality* when referring to 'all that sets the text in a relationship, whether obvious or concealed, with other texts'.[62] *Intertextuality* is therefore understood as a subcategory of *transtextuality* and used to 'identify a relation of copresence between two texts or among several texts; that is to say eidetically and typically as the actual presence of one text within another'.[63]

Genette refers to the most direct intertextual practice as the act of *quoting*,[64] yet also mentions *allusions* as a paradigm for *intertextuality*, defining these as 'an enunciation whose full meaning presupposes the perception of a relationship between it and another text, to which it necessarily refers by some inflections that would otherwise remain unintelligible'.[65] These acts of *intertextuality* are captured by Lacasse through the simultaneous reworking of Nelson Goodman's understanding of *allographic* and *autographic* art forms.[66] In so doing, Lacasse defines the two main intertextual categories found in sampled popular music as *autosonic* and *allosonic* quotations.[67]

The former quotation is 'characterised by the actual insertion of an excerpt from a given text within another'.[68] In musical terms, an *autosonic* quotation is therefore 'intimately linked with recording techniques'.[69] This quotation can be simply understood as the re-playing of a part of an already recorded track.

60 Serge Lacasse, 'Intertextuality and Hypertextuality in Recorded Music', in *The Musical Work: Reality or Invention?*, ed. by Michael Talbot (Liverpool: Liverpool University Press, 2000), pp. 35–58.
61 Lacasse, 'Intertextuality and Hypertextuality in Recorded Music', pp. 35–58.
62 *Palimpsests: Literature in the Second Degree*, trans. by Channa Newman and Claude Doubinsky (Lincoln and London: University of Nebraska Press, 1997), p. 1 (original: Gerard Genette, *Palimpsestes: la littérature au second degré* (Paris, Ed. du Seuil, 1982)).
63 Genette, *Palimpsests*, pp. 1–2.
64 Genette, *Palimpsests*, p. 2.
65 Genette, *Palimpsests*, p. 2.
66 Nelson Goodman, *Languages of Art: An Approach to a Theory of Symbols* (New York: Bobbs-Merrill, 1968), pp. 112–15.
67 Lacasse, 'Intertextuality and Hypertextuality in Recorded Music', p. 38.
68 Lacasse, 'Intertextuality and Hypertextuality in Recorded Music', p. 38.
69 Lacasse, 'Intertextuality and Hypertextuality in Recorded Music', p. 38.

Lacasse also mentions exceptions to this rule, such as *allosonic* quotations, which may want to sound *autosonic*. This happens when a producer attempts to mimic the original music as if it were directly taken from the live recording.[70] However, *autosonic* quotations are generally slightly re-adjusted through accelerations or diminuendos, or modified with a reverb, echo or looping, for example.[71] The *allosonic* quotation, on the other hand, refers to a quoted text passage that has been distinctly altered compared to its original. This can be achieved through a live improvisation of the citation or through being performed by another instrument or musician. Hence, in an *allosonic* quotation 'the shared bit between original text and intertext is abstract' and is 'not typical for recording techniques'.[72]

The purpose of employing *allosonic* and *autosonic* quotations in hip-hop music is, according to Rose, 'about paying homage, an invocation of another's voice to help you say what you want to say. It is also a means of archival research, a process of musical and cultural archeology'.[73] This archival research connects to Katz's aforementioned pursuit of previous musical pieces known as the act of 'digging in the crates', i.e., searching for unknown break beats and samples on vinyl records stashed in crates. Therefore, Rose further argues that musical samples function 'as a challenge to know these sounds, to make connections between the lyrical and musical texts'.[74] From this perspective, the dual distinction between *autosonic* and *allosonic* quotations within the sampled musical text also reveals the location and appearance of cultural hybridization. While Papastergiadis notes that the creation of cultural hybridity and identity 'involves the performance of two tasks simultaneously: it requires memory and experience',[75] the intertextual understanding of sampling does just that: it activates memory and creates an experience in the present which bridges differences between one's own cultural traditions and the ones introduced through African-derived musical aesthetics.

The challenge that lies in this particular method, however, is the risk of the recipient not sharing the cultural codes transmitted by the producer and hence not comprehending the intertextual references. As Lothar Mikos points out: 'Intertextualität ist daher ein Moment des Kommunikationsprozesses zwischen Autor/Produzent und Hörer/Rezipient' [Intertextuality is therefore a moment in the communication process between author/producer and

70 Lacasse, 'Intertextuality and Hypertextuality in Recorded Music', p. 40.
71 Lacasse, 'Intertextuality and Hypertextuality in Recorded Music', p. 39.
72 Lacasse, 'Intertextuality and Hypertextuality in Recorded Music', p. 38.
73 Rose, *Black Noise*, p. 79.
74 Rose, *Black Noise*, p. 89.
75 Papastergiadis, *The Turbulence of Migration*, p. 98.

listener/recipient].[76] Furthermore, intertextuality is 'auf der Rezeptionsseite bestimmt durch alle Texte, die die Hörer an einen HipHop-Track herantragen, sowohl ihr Wissen um HipHop-Tracks als auch ihre Erwartungen an HipHop-Tracks. Intertextualität kann also nur relativ bestimmt werden [determined, in its reception, by all the texts which the listeners bring to a hip-hop track, both their knowledge of hip-hop tracks and their expectation of hip-hop tracks. Intertextuality can, therefore, only be determined relatively].[77]

Moreover, as the practice of sampling not only employs musical segments but any type of media deriving from television, cartoons, films or computer games, as well as random sounds that may comprise the DJ's social space, it should also be mentioned that not all intertextual quotations need to be culturally meaningful. German producer Sleepwalker explains that 'alles was summt und brummt [...] Inspirationsquelle für einen Musiker [ist]' [anything that hums and buzzes is a source of inspiration for a musician].[78] Similarly, German DJ and producer Mirko Machine emphasizes the infinity of sounds that can serve as samples, explaining:

> Ich sample einfach auch alles. So ... Aber es gibt genug! Das ist ja auch einfach das Gute im Hip-Hop. Man kann ja einfach alles samplen! So, ne? Wenn das Glas jetzt runterfällt, ich habe das cool aufgenommen gerade mit einem Mikrofon irgendwie [*laughs*] und finde das klingt cool und ich schneide das noch mal und setz das neu und dann kann ich auch daraus einen Beat machen.[79]
>
> [I just sample everything. Like ... But there is enough! That is just simply the good thing about hip-hop. You can just sample everything. Like, you know? If the glass were just to fall down now, and I somehow just recorded it cool with a microphone [*laughs*] and I think it sounds cool and I cut it again and re-set it, then I can make a beat out of it.]

These statements therefore contradict Rose's aforementioned conclusion that relates sampling to a black cultural priority. They also problematize Steffen Lepa's and Malte Pelleter's findings, which state that hip-hop beats are 'nie "l'art pour l'art", sondern [...] immer auch ihre soziale und kulturelle Funktion

76 Lothar Mikos, 'Interpolation and Sampling: kulturelles Gedächtnis und Intertextualität im HipHop', in *HipHop: Globale Kultur – Lokale Praktiken*, ed. by Androutsopoulos, pp. 64–84 (p. 72).

77 Mikos, 'Interpolation and Sampling', p. 73. Intertextual references that appear in the following examples have been analysed with information that was gathered from interviewing the relevant DJs and producers. This also applies to the remaining three art forms and the close readings of their cultural texts and intertextuality.

78 Sleepwalker, interviewed by author, 5 June 2012.

79 Mirko Machine, interviewed by author, 10 May 2012.

im Sinne von Bedeutungsstrukturen und Fixpunkten der HipHop-Kultur erfüllen [müssen]' [never 'l'art pour l'art' but always have to fulfil their social and cultural function in terms of hip-hop culture's meaningful structures and benchmarks].[80] Rather, as Peter Manuel claims, the postmodern 'combination of elements from disparate discourses' such as hip-hop music's 'sampled passages [often] function as simulacra, as free-floating signifiers to be enjoyed for their very meaninglessness, their obvious artificiality, in a characteristically postmodern exhilaration of surfaces'.[81] Researching sampled music can therefore entail exploring a fine line between locating signification in a text and dismissing it as being intentionally irrelevant. With this in mind, the next section will turn to hip-hop music's practices and performances in Germany by providing a brief overview of hip-hop music's establishment as a musical movement in West Germany followed by an analysis of its manifestation in Hamburg.

The Establishment of Hip-Hop Music in West Germany

> Der einzige Unterschied ist: er wohnt in New York, ist schwarz, und ich wohne in Deutschland und bin weiß. Das ist der *einzige* Unterschied. Und wenn wir auf *Knowledge* kommen mach ich ihn nass, weil er nämlich *nix* weiß, außer, dass er da wohnt![82]
>
> [The only difference is: he lives in New York, is black, and I live in Germany and am white. That is the *only* difference. And when we get to knowledge then I'll thrash him because he doesn't know a single thing except that he lives there!]

Mirko Machine's dismissal of the supposed racial and spatial superiority of a black DJ from New York City already captures the altered dynamics of hip-hop's musical element since its adaptation to other social, historical and spatial contexts. While the identity norm of the 'black aesthetic' has been invalidated, the cityspace of New York has equally lost its 'secondspatial' relevance of being the 'birthplace of hip-hop'.[83] Instead, Mirko Machine's statement implies that contemporary authentic hip-hop productions are not subject to a fixed discourse on race and place anymore but now rely

80 Lepa and Pelleter, '"Sampling" als kulturelle Praxis des HipHop', p. 209.

81 Peter Manuel, 'Music as Symbol, Music as Simulacrum: Postmodern, Pre-modern, and Modern Aesthetics in Subcultural Popular Musics', *Popular Music*, 14 (1995), 227–39 (p. 233).

82 Mirko Machine, interviewed by author, 10 May 2012.

83 Katz, *Groove Music*, p. 38.

solely on the 'substantial body of knowledge'.[84]

This knowledge was transferred to West Germany a decade after hip-hop culture's emergence in the Bronx where hip-hop music became simultaneously introduced in the form of DJing and turntabling as well as in the form of studio production. Initially, hip-hop music reached parts of West Germany through the presence of American soldiers stationed in Bremerhaven, Bremen and southern Germany. Here, hip-hop music was either played in designated dance clubs located in close proximity to American army bases[85] or aired on the American Forces Network radio station (AFN) in its German broadcasting area.[86] However, more importantly, the main source through which hip-hop culture was introduced to the wider German audience consisted of American hip-hop films. These included Charlie Ahearn's *Wild Style* (1983), Tony Silver's and Henry Chalfant's *Style Wars* (1983), as well as Stan Lathan's *Beat Street* (1984).

Frankfurt rapper D-Flame in particular recalls the impact of *Wild Style*, explaining: 'Wir haben das so angeguckt und ich so: "Alter! Ich will alles sein in dem Film! Egal, ob Graffiti-Writer, Rapper, bla bla bla." Weißt du? [*Laughs*] Das war erst mal so weit entfernt, aber man hat die irgendwie so gefühlt!' [We were watching it and I was like: 'Man! I want to be everyone in this film! Whether graffiti artist, rapper, bla bla bla.' You know? [*Laughs*] It was so far away but you could somehow just feel it!].[87] While fascinated by hip-hop's aesthetics, D-Flame's memory also sheds light on the fact that thesocio-urban conditions of the Bronx, which nurtured this movement in the first place, became lost in the process of cinematic mediatization. Without further insight into the spatial, historical and social dynamics that shaped hip-hop music, DJ Stylewarz explains that in West Germany: 'Da hast du dir überhaupt gar keine Gedanken drüber gemacht *was* es ist, sondern wir waren einfach so sehr damit beschäftigt irgendwie *das* zu machen' [You did not really think at all about what it was you were doing, rather we were so totally busy just doing it].[88] This lack of contextual knowledge concerning hip-hop culture becomes even more apparent in D-Flame's reading of the 'tribal stigmata' on screen, whereby:

> die Puerto Ricaner haben mich an meine damaligen türkischen Freunde sehr erinnert und die Schwarzen waren halt ich! Und ich habe das auch mit Türken zusammen geguckt, mit zwei Türken zusammen, und wir haben dann uns so

84 Schloss, *Making Beats*, pp. 32–33.
85 DJ Ben Kenobi, interviewed by author, 2 July 2012.
86 DJ Stylewarz, interviewed by author, 10 June 2012.
87 D-Flame, interviewed by author, 26 July 2012.
88 DJ Stylewarz, interviewed by author, 10 June 2012.

> gegenseitig angeguckt: 'Krass! Die sehen ja sogar aus wie wir!' Weißt du so? [*Laughs*] 'Das sind wir!'.[89]
>
> [the Puerto Ricans reminded me of my Turkish friends back then and the Blacks were me! And I was also watching it together with Turks, together with two Turks, and we just looked at each other: 'Amazing! They even look like us!'. You know? [*Laughs*] 'That's us!'.]

While this statement by the German rapper, who is of Cherokee-Jamaican and Polish descent, reveals that the racial 'attributes' of the Bronx's hip-hop community resonated meaningfully as 'tribal stigmata' in Germany, it also reveals the ambivalence of these social signifiers when introduced into a different cultural context.

Furthermore, without realizing that hip-hop was about gaining a respected identity through creativity and innovation, early German DJs and producers rather engaged in hip-hop music as a mimetic cultural practice. Thus, their choice of samples echoed those played by American DJs.[90] In other words, early West-German hip-hop music productions did not turn to the sounds of past German music with which to create a contemporary German hip-hop sound. The reason for this cultural disengagement is provided by Hamburg rapper and producer Samy Deluxe, who explains that:

> das Ding in Deutschland ist ja, dass wir ja nicht so eine wirkliche eigene Musikkultur haben, auf die wir irgendwie stolz zurückblicken können, wie wenn du in Amerika aufwächst und einfach weißt so: 'Meine Eltern haben immer James Brown gehört und irgendwie das war unser Shit damals. Ich habe noch die *childhood memories*, wie die im Wohnzimmer dazu tanzen und dann sample ich das mal'. Dann hat es natürlich einen ganz anderen Bezug, als wenn ich jetzt sage: 'Oh, den kenne ich auch James Brown, seitdem ich ein Kind war, aber Samples...'. Und wir haben ja gar nicht das deutsche Pendant dazu. [...] In Frankreich ist [es] auch viel mehr, weißt du? Wenn du da lebst, dann hast du irgendwie direkt die Chansons mit denen du aufgewachsen bist. Die liebst *du*, die lieben deine Eltern, die lieben die weißen Leute, die lieben die schwarzen Leute.[91]
>
> [the thing in Germany is that we never really had our own music culture which we can look back at proudly, like, when you grow up in America and just know: 'My parents always listened to James Brown and that was somehow our shit back then. I still have the *childhood memories* of them dancing to his music in

89 D-Flame, interviewed by author, 26 July 2012.

90 Cf. Sleepwalker, interviewed by author, 5 June 2012.

91 Samy Deluxe, interviewed by author, 29 July 2012. For further information on the relationship between chansons and French rap culture, see Murat Güngör, 'Politisches Chanson und Rap', in Güngör and Loh, *Fear of a Kanak Planet*, pp. 43–46.

> the living room and that's why I'll sample it'. Then it has a completely different reference from me saying: 'Oh, I have also known James Brown since I was a child but samples …'. And we just don't have the German equivalent. […] In France it's also much more, you know? If you live there you have all these chansons with which you grew up. *You* love them, your parents love them, white people love them, black people love them.]

By explaining this cultural dilemma, Samy Deluxe engages in Rose's historical perspective of sampling, which functions as a memory discourse: only a personal memory of a particular song or artist is able to authenticate its use as a sample. Samy Deluxe specifically locates these memories within a 'thirdspace' experience, such as dancing to the song in the living room and hence consuming the music in a lived social space. This importance of 'living the sounds' is not only subject to the African-American inhabitants of the Bronx who listened to James Brown, it is also iterated in his example of France, insinuating that only by *living* in France can one experience and develop a full appreciation for French chansons. These even have a uniting effect across generations and different racial backgrounds. However, if, according to Samy Deluxe, German youth did not have any proud memory of experiencing music that was sung in the German language, there was little possibility of creating authentic German hip-hop music through the practice of sampling. Instead, the only German music that seemed most compelling for sampling at that time was found in the GDR with Samy Deluxe adding that his fellow rap colleague Dendemann 'mir damals mal so geile Funkmusikplatten aus dem Osten gezeigt [hat], also aus der DDR richtig' [back then showed me really awesome funk music records from the East, I mean really from the GDR].[92] The GDR was thus understood as being just as culturally foreign as funk music, with neither of them resonating with West German familiarity.

Indeed, it was not until the unification of Germany that the conscious transition from the production of music to the production of *meaning* through music happened.[93] In Hamburg, this transition occurred in the 1990s in a process peculiar to its urban spatial logics and cultural nuances. It is this cultural shift which will be explored in the following analysis, highlighting the ways and strategies with which Hamburg's contemporary DJs and music producers create hip-hop music as a meaningful German musical movement.

92 Samy Deluxe, interviewed by author, 29 July 2012. During this interview Torch, a member of hip-hop trio Advanced Chemistry from Heidelberg, also emphasized the plethora of useful music found in the GDR for sampling purposes.

93 DJ Stylewarz, interviewed by author, 10 June 2012.

Hamburg and the German Hip-Hop Sound

While hip-hop music was introduced through American films, Hamburg's early hip-hop music productions and turntabling practices were also highly influenced by the music's establishment as a 'hard core' genre in London known as 'Britcore'.[94] Hamburg music producer Sleepwalker even describes his early local hip-hop community as having been:

> ein Teil dieser Britcoreszene. Ich hatte erst so eine Band, die hieß erst 53,3 Extreme, so wegen Breitengrad Hamburgs. Und später hießen wir dann Readykill und [sind] dann auch mit Stylewarz zusammen ab '91 [...] auf Tour gewesen und so. Da hieß er No Remorze und wir hießen Readykill so, weißt du? Und wir haben ganz viel zusammen gemacht.[95]

> [part of this Britcore scene. I first had a band called 53.3 Extreme, you know, because of Hamburg's degree of latitude. And later we were called Readykill and then we were together with Stylewarz from '91 onwards [...] we went on tour and stuff. He was called No Remorze and we were called Readykill, like, you know? And we did a lot together.

Forming an extention of Britcore's outreach in Germany, Sleepwalker's hip-hop group symbolized their local allegiance to Hamburg by geographically mapping their northern German location as a 'secondspace'. Their choice of English names, on the other hand, alluded to the deviant and aggressive sound that defined Britcore, since 'der härteste Rap, den es eigentlich gab, [. . .] aus London [kam]' [the hardest rap in existence came from London].[96] DJ Ben Kenobi's location of 'hard' rap further highlights the ambivalence of cultural difference by disregarding the fact that hip-hop music's sound was supposedly a direct echo of the stigmatized experience of the American post-industrial city, which, according to Ogbar, 'gave hip-hop its force and character'.[97] Instead, Britcore was a reflection of an anarchistic political movement musically expressed through a fast tempo and a sound described by DJ Ben Kenobi as 'schon so angepunkt fast' [almost punky somehow].[98] Nevertheless,

94 Samy Deluxe, interviewed by author, 29 July 2012; cf. Gizmo, interviewed by author, 17 July 2012; DJ Ben Kenobi, interviewed by author, 3 July 2012; DJ Stylewarz, interviewed by author 10 June; Sleepwalker, interviewed by author, 5 June 2012; Tim Beam, interviewed by author, 8 August 2012.

95 Sleepwalker, interviewed by author, 5 June 2012. At this point DJ Stylewarz was still living in Bremerhaven, the only city other than Cologne to have shown interest in the Britcore genre. See Samy Deluxe, interviewed by author, 29 July 2012.

96 DJ Ben Kenobi, interviewed by author, 3 July 2012.

97 Ogbar, *Hip-Hop Revolution*, p. 41.

98 DJ Ben Kenobi, interviewed by author, 3 July 2012.

the technique with which the 'punky' sound was created continued to follow the aesthetic of sampling, for Sleepwalker explains: '[Die] Beats, die wir früher gemacht haben, die waren immer sehr Flow-lastig und die haben so gescheppert und das waren immer gesamplete Beatloops. Und die Engländer haben das auch gemacht, weißt du, und die Amis haben schon angefangen Beats zu programmieren' [[The] beats that we used to create were always very flowy and they always rattled and they were always sampled beat loops. And the English did the same thing, you know, and the Americans had already started programming beats].[99]

As Hamburg's hip-hop community was subject to this unique cultural influence from Britain, the fact that it even engaged in this European musical co-operation has been particularly related to Hamburg's geographical location. DJ Ben Kenobi elaborates on this aspect by quoting local rapper Jan Delay, who rapped:

> '[D]er Hafen ist die Bassline', sozusagen. Ja ich glaub schon, dass das [der Hafen] eine Rolle spielt und ich glaube jetzt im Nachhinein ist es schade oder ist es gut, dass hier keine Amis stationiert waren. Also ich glaube für die Musik war es auf jeden Fall ausschlaggebend auch. Oder es hat sich auf jeden Fall widergespiegelt in der Musik, dass es nicht so amerikanisiert war. [...] Natürlich haben wir Ami-Rap gehört, aber nicht nur. Wir waren da ein bisschen offener.[100]
>
> ['[T]he port is the bass line', so to speak. Yeah I do think that it [the port] plays a role and I think that now, with hindsight, it's unfortunate or it's good that no Americans were stationed here. I think it was certainly very decisive for the music as well. Or it was at least reflected in the music that it wasn't so Americanized. [...] Of course, we listened to American rap but not only that. We were a bit more open.]

In other words, the 'secondspace' of Hamburg's sea port, which in Jan Delay's full rapped verse is moreover 'das Herz, die Bassline' [the heart, the bassline][101] and the lack of American soldiers and their importation of American cultural products became the reason why local hip-hop musicians were more open towards foreign musical sounds. Hip-hop journalist Gizmo further supports

99 Sleepwalker, interviewed by author, 5 June 2012. The fact that American producers were programming beats rather than sampling was influenced by copyright infringement laws which made sampling an illegal practice in the USA (Tonya M. Evans, 'Sampling, Looping and Mashing ...Oh My!: How HipHop Music is Scratching more than the Surface of Copyright Law', *Fordham Intellectual Property, Media & Entertainment Law Journal*, 21 (2011), 843–904 (pp. 872–79).

100 DJ Ben Kenobi, interviewed by author, 3 July 2012.

101 Jan Delay, 'City Blues', on *Blast Action Heroes* (Buback/Motor, 2003) [LP/CD].

DJ Ben Kenobi's observation by adding that Hamburg is 'das Tor zur Welt' [the gateway to the world],[102] a remark which presents the German cityspace from a perspective that dates even beyond post-war Hamburg. Indeed, German historian Lars Ammenda explains:

> Hamburger entwickelten aufgrund der liberalen Traditionen und der geographischen Welt-Offenheit des Hafens eine besondere Bindung zur Stadt. Dies legt auch die erstaunliche Karriere des Schlagworts 'Tor zur Welt' nahe, das als Synonym und werbewirksames Etikett für Hamburg in den heutigen Zeiten der Globalisierung wieder sehr häufig verwendet wird. Das Bild vom Tor wurde bereits Ende des 19. Jahrhunderts gelegentlich gewählt, um die räumliche Lage von Hafenstädten und Küsten zu beschreiben.[103]
>
> [Hamburgers developed a special bond with their city due to the liberal traditions of the port and the fact that geographically it was open to the entire world. This is also suggested in the astonishing career of the catchphrase 'gateway to the world', which in this current age of globalization is still often used as a synonym and as an effective promotional label for Hamburg. The image of the gateway was already used occasionally at the end of the nineteenth century to describe the spatial location of ports and coasts.]

This particular 'secondspace' identity and identification with Hamburg as a culturally open-minded city even became influential beyond the Britcore movement since it was appropriated as a local sign for Hamburg's own hip-hop sound.

By 1998, Absolute Beginner, comprising rappers Jan Delay and Denyo as well as DJ Mad, released their album *Bambule*. The unique characteristic of this album is emphasized by D-Flame, who claims that 'die [Absoluten Beginner] [...] damals dann auch ganz woanders gesamplet [haben]' [they [the Absolute Beginners] also sampled from other sources].[104] Thus, the use of different musical and hence cultural sounds reflects the worldliness and open-mindedness of the city, which is influenced by its sea port. It is, therefore, no coincidence that *Bambule* begins its sonic narrative with a track called 'Das

102 Gizmo, interviewed by author, 17 July 2012.

103 Lars Amenda, '"Welthafen" Hamburg – Kultur- und Technikgeschichtliche Perspektiven', in *Hamburgs Geschichte Einmal Anders: Entwicklung der Naturwissenschaften, Medizin und Technik*, ed. by Gudrun Wolfschmidt, Nuncius Hamburgensis – Beiträge zur Geschichte der Naturwissenschaften, 7 (Norderstedt: on Demand, 2009), pp. 238–49 (p. 243).

104 D-Flame, interviewed by author, 26 July 2012; samples in *Bambule* include French composer Pierre Bachelet's 'O' Et L'Amour a Trois' (1992) in the track 'Hammerhart', while 'Nicht Allein' incorporates Cuban guitarist Silvio Rodriguez's song 'Debo Partirme en Dos' (1975). By remaining true to hip-hop's break-beat tradition in funk and soul songs, the track 'Füchse' samples from The Originals' hit 'You're my Only World' (1974), while Shuggie Otis's song 'Aht Uh Me Hed' (1974) appears in the track 'Liebes Lied'.

Boot', treating Hamburg as a 'mental or ideational field, conceptualized in imagery, reflexive thought, and symbolic representation'[105] since the naming of this sea vessel immediately places the listener in a maritime 'secondspace'. Incidentally, the title also signifies a German identity without necessarily requiring knowledge of the German language as it recalls the internationally successful German war film titled *Das Boot* (1981).[106] While the song's aural introduction does not begin in a German war submarine, it does, however, situate the audience in a local river ferry, by which means 'der spezifische Sound der verwendeten Samples lokale Bezüge [herstellt]' [the specific sound of the samples used create local connections].[107]

The track starts with samples of bustling and beeping, and an *autosonic* quotation of the ferry captain's announcement: 'Nächste Station: St. Pauli-Landungsbrücken. Und da gibt's dann … Bambule' [Next stop: St. Pauli-Landungsbrücken. And there you will find ... Bambule].[108] This sampled introduction connects the name of the hip-hop album to a socio-spatial discourse pertaining to Hamburg. While the term 'bambule' refers to an African-American prison protest tradition, it was also the name of a trailer park and hence of a local 'firstspace' which, at the time of the album's release, was situated in the *Karolinenviertel* of the St. Pauli district – a city district which borders on Hamburg's port and hence on the 'gateway to the world'.[109]

By aurally reflecting this maritime and at the same time global German 'secondspace', the hip-hop album not only employs samples from multiple cultural contexts but also makes use of German songs. D-Flame highlights this aspect by noting that 'das [...] damals noch keiner gemacht [hat], aber dann so deutsche Samples: "Dein Gesicht und mein Arsch könnten gute Freunde sein!" Weißt du? [*Laughs*] Das war einfach geil! Wir so: "Eeeeey fett, Alter!"' [Nobody was doing that back then, but then German samples like: 'Your face and my ass could be good friends!' You know? [*Laughs*] That was

105 Soja, *Postmetropolis*, p. 11.

106 The German feature-length film *Das Boot* had a further social impact on Germany and its image abroad as it re-formed the threatening perspective of German war submarines into humane items by providing insight into the feelings and fears of the young male crew operating the vessel (Michael L. Hadley, *Count Not the Dead: The Popular Image of the German Submarine* (Annapolis, MD: Naval Institute, 1995), pp. 4–5).

107 Lepa and Pelleter, '"Sampling" als kulturelle Praxis des HipHop', p. 207.

108 Absolute Beginner, 'Das Boot', *Bambule* (Buback/Universal Music, 1998) [CD].

109 Bambule was also the name of a German television film based on a script by later RAF terrorist Ulrike Meinhof which was aired in 1970. The film was briefly fashionable again in the 1990s with *Bambule* positively exploring the notion of solidarity as political action and hence as a precondition for the formation of an RAF collective identity (Sarah Colvin, *Ulrike Meinhof and West German Terrorism: Language, Violence, and Identity* (Rochester, NY: Camden House, 2009), p. 75).

just awesome! We were like: 'Eeeeey sick, man!'].[110] Aside from mentioning the innovative act of sampling from past German music, the equivocal act of cultural hybridity becomes evident as well, since D-Flame refers to the hip-hop track 'Nie Nett' by actually citing a verse from German singer and songwriter Udo Lindenberg which appears in 'Ich bin beim Bund' (1983):

> Der Spieß pöbelt rum, wie die letzte Sau.
> Der hat bestimmt Komplexe oder Trouble mit seiner Frau.
> Schreit hier rum, so 'n beknacktes Schwein.
> Ich sag': Dein Gesicht und mein Arsch könnten gute Freunde sein.[111]
>
> [The sergeant is cussing like the last sow.
> He probably has complexes or trouble with his wife.
> Screams around here like some crazy pig.
> I just say: Your face and my ass could be good friends.]

Lindenberg's last verse has been extracted from its original lyrical stanza and looped four times as an *autosonic* quotation at the end of 'Nie Nett'. Re-appearing in this new German hip-hop context, Lindenberg's dismissive statement, which expresses his discontent in needing to return to the military barracks whilst serving as a soldier in the German Bundeswehr, is re-directed as a boastful insult to other German rappers who are supposedly listening to the song. Hence, while the dialectical play of the two German songs engages in the same semantic relationship, the playful product of hybridity also creates a local bond beyond its hip-hop aesthetic. While Lindenberg is not originally from Hamburg, he and his voice have been closely associated with Hamburg's music scene since the 1970s. The act of sampling him in a Hamburg hip-hop track therefore creates a historical continuity and a musical narrative located in the same 'spatiality'.

However, the reason for choosing Lindenberg as a sample is, according to Jan Delay, the fact that Lindenberg is 'der größte lebende deutsche Poet. Er war der Grund, warum ich angefangen habe zu singen' [the greatest living German poet. He was the reason I started singing].[112] Hence, despite

110 D-Flame, interviewed by author, 26 July 2012. 'Wir' refers to the Frankfurt hip-hop community. The personal and national impact of this hip-hop album was also mentioned by Stee, interviewed by author, 26 July 2012; by DJ Ben Kenobi, interviewed by author 3 July 2012; and by Samy Deluxe, interviewed by author, 29 July 2012.

111 Udo Lindenberg und das Panikorchester 'Ich bin beim Bund', *Odyssee* (Polydor, 1983) [CD].

112 Oliver Fuchs and Hannes Ross, 'Udo Lindenberg und Jan Delay: "Wir haben den Nasensound"', *Stern*, 28 March 2008, http://www.stern.de/kultur/musik/udo-lindenberg-und-jan-delay-wir-haben-den-nasensound-615113.html [accessed 12 April 2013]. This article also touches upon the fact that Lindenberg and Jan Delay have even performed together on stage.

Samy Deluxe's previous account of Germany's youth supposedly lacking an emotional connection to past German music, this case highlights an exception which was relevant to the authentic practice of sampling as an act of re-living personal memories. Samy Deluxe acknowledges this case by explaining that 'Jan, zum Beispiel, immer solche Sachen, wie Udo Lindenberg [kannte]. Ist damit richtig aufgewachsen und deshalb macht es auch total Sinn [ihn zu samplen]' [Jan, for example, always knew such things as Udo Lindenberg. He really grew up with him and that is why it makes sense [to sample him]].[113]

From *Bambule* onwards, hip-hop music's techniques gradually enabled the wider discovery and revival of Germany's musical past by hip-hop artists. Even beyond Lindenberg, Jan Delay also sampled songs by *Neue deutsche Welle* artist Nena,[114] while DJ Mirko Machine mentions that in his contemporary hip-hop productions 'Hildegard Knef [...] gesamplet [ist]. Hier, Aphroe, 'Kleiner Mann' ist Susanne [*sic*] Haas. Ja, Udo Lindenberg. Drums habe ich schon gesamplet' [Hildegard Knef is sampled. Here, Aphroe 'Kleiner Mann' is Susanne [*sic*] Haas. Yes, Udo Lindenberg. I've sampled his drums].[115] In this way previous German popular music became consumable for these artists as it re-appeared in the guise of hip-hop, which created:

> 'newness' that is not part of the continuum of the past and present. It creates a sense of the new as an insurgent act of cultural translation. Such art does not merely recall the past as a social cause or aesthetic precedent: it renews the past, refiguring it as a contingent 'in-between' space, that innovates and interrupts the performance of the present (*LOC*, p. 10).

Nevertheless, this 'in-between space' remained firmly grounded in a German cultural context, for the newness of German hip-hop music became understood and accepted as a German cultural product. Samy Deluxe, for instance, highlights this seemingly self-contradictory development of German hip-hop music by stating: '[D]as erste, was ich auf Deutsch eben cool fand, waren eben die Jungs [Jan Delay and Torch] hier. So weißt du? Das war eben das erste, was für mich irgendwie Sinn gemacht hat' [[T]he first thing that I thought was cool in German were these boys [Jan Delay and Torch] here. You know? That was the first thing that made sense to me].[116] With German hip-hop representing the first viable form of consuming German popular music, Samy Deluxe's personal experience, and hence history, of German music thus begins with German hip-hop. It therefore comes as no surprise that in order for Samy Deluxe to engage in a historical discourse of German music, the

113 Samy Deluxe, interviewed by author, 29 July 2012.
114 Jan Delay, *Irgendwie, irgendwo, irgendwann* (EMI, 1999).
115 Mirko Machine, interviewed by author, 20 May 2012; the singer's name is Sandra Haas.
116 Samy Deluxe, interviewed by author, 29 July 2012.

timeline of his German samples only reaches back to the advent of German hip-hop music. While Jan Delay pays tribute to his role model Udo Lindenberg via the practice of sampling, Samy Deluxe engages in this aesthetic by paying tribute to his local idol Jan Delay. This becomes evident in Samy Deluxe's track 'Feuer, Verbrannt, Asche' (2012), in which the song title already alludes to Jan Delay's song 'Feuer' (2007).

While Samy Deluxe ironically re-appropriates the beat of 'Feuer' in order to boast about his rap skills, he repeatedly introduces the *autosonic* references of Jan Delay yelling 'Au ja'. Samy Deluxe strategically employs this utterance as an act of *hypertextuality* in which an identifiable segment of the earlier text, the *hypotext*, unites with the *hypertext*, i.e., Samy Deluxe's adaptation of it.[117] In this case, the *autosonic* quotation of Jan Delay's expression is aurally distorted as it is additionally chopped into many echoing breaks. Samy Deluxe moreover engages in a *metatextual* practice in which a text is united with another 'of which it speaks without necessarily citing it'.[118] At the end, Samy Deluxe verbally and hence *allosonically* quotes Jan Delay's original verse 'denn das wichtigste ist, dass das Feuer nicht aufhört zu brennen' when rapping:[119]

> Denn eines, was ich von meinem Mentor gelernt hab',
> Von dem ich mir den Beat hier geliehen hab',
> Ohne, dass ich vorher das Sample geklärt hab',
> Und ohne, dass ich grad ein Feature von ihm hab', ist,
> Dass das Feuer nicht aufhört zu brennen.[120]

> [One thing that I learned from my mentor,
> From whom I borrowed this beat here,
> Without having previously clarified the sample
> And without currently having a feature from him, is
> That the fire won't stop burning.]

While this example of sampling therefore serves to show how Samy Deluxe's understanding of German musical history *begins* with hip-hop, it also highlights the establishment of a local and historical musical continuity within Hamburg. From a social perspective, this sampled narrative also hints at a multicultural development of Hamburg's hip-hop music when one considers that Samy Deluxe is an Afro-German music producer who continues in the musical footsteps of the ethnic German hip-hop artist Jan Delay, influenced by ethnic German singer and songwriter Udo Lindenberg.

117 Cf. Genette, *Palimpsests*, p. 5.

118 Genette, *Palimpsests*, p. 4.

119 Jan Delay, in 'Feuer', *Mercedes Dance* (Buback/Universal Music Group, 2007) [CD].

120 Samy Deluxe, 'Feuer, Verbrannt, Asche' (2012), https://www.youtube.com/watch?v=Fe6IVrkGO1M [accessed 9 June 2016].

However, the question remains whether the multicultural approaches towards creating new local German narratives as exemplified by Absolute Beginner and by Samy Deluxe have sufficed for a musical innovation which not only Germanizes an already established foreign musical technique and aesthetic, but has also developed into a new hip-hop music-related genre. An answer to this question is provided during a conversation between Hamburg DJ Placeebo and D-Flame:

> D-Flame: Ich würde mir dann doch ein bisschen mehr wünschen, dass wir ein bisschen mehr wie Frankreich und England noch ein bisschen *mehr* da auch unseren eigenen Scheiß so rausziehen. Weißt du? Weil ich meine Franzosen fangen jetzt auch wieder an eher Ami-Beats zu machen. Du merkst dann immer wieder, wo man sich das herholt, aber man zieht es sich von da und macht noch sein eigenes Ding dazu.
>
> DJ Placeebo: Aber die sind mutiger!
>
> D-Flame: Aber die Franzosen, wie gesagt, sind ein bisschen mutiger. Wobei ich fahre eher natürlich auf England ab, weil England –'
>
> DJ Placeebo: Die Engländer sind auch mutiger! [...]
>
> D-Flame: Und seit Jahren machen die halt zum Beispiel Sachen, wie … weißt du, es gibt Reggae. Dann machen sie auf einmal Dub! Weißt du? Dann gibt's irgendwie Drum 'n' Bass, dann machen die Engländer [...] Two Step. Dann gibt es auf einmal Dub Step! Weißte? Die mixen immer. Alle zwei Jahre kommt ein neuartiger Musikstil, der *auch* die Wurzel aufgreift, aber trotzdem was Neues. [...] So was hörst du dann halt auch in Amerika nicht. Und das fehlt noch ein bisschen in Deutschland.[121]
>
> [D-Flame: 'I would wish for a bit more, that we create a bit more of our own shit, like France or England. You know? Because, I mean, the French are also starting to create rather American beats. You always notice where they take it from, but you take it from there and add your own thing.'
>
> DJ Placeebo: 'But they're more courageous.'
>
> D-Flame: 'But the French, as already said, are a bit more courageous. Whereby I really like England, because England –'.
>
> DJ Placeebo: 'The English are more courageous as well! […]'.
>
> D-Flame: 'And for years they are doing things, for example, like… You know, there's reggae. Then they all of a sudden do dub! You know? Then there somehow is drum'n'bass, then the English do […] two step. Then all of a sudden you have dub step! You know? They are always mixing. Every two years a new music style arrives, which *also* captures the root but it's still something new. […] That is what you also don't hear in America. And that is still missing a bit in Germany.]

121 D-Flame and DJ Placeebo, interviewed by author, 26 July 2012.

D-Flame's observation on the way DJs and producers in England have created new sounds is clearly identifiable as the act of creating 'third spaces' in which the mixing of musical styles and cultural influences enables new forms of music to emerge. While D-Flame and DJ Placeebo therefore conclude that the German producers are not bold enough in terms of innovation, DJ Stylewarz claims that the creation of new musical genres is also the result of 'thirdspace' experiences framed by social encounters and cultural exchange. Just as the inhabitants of the Bronx fused their cultural sensibilities with material knowledge to create hip-hop music, so have the different cultures comprising the British as well as the French hip-hop communities created new musical styles, which are nevertheless still identified as being 'British' or 'French'. In contrast to this situation abroad, DJ Stylewarz interprets German hip-hop's stagnant musical state as being due to the fact that:

> Deutschland relativ deutsch ist, so. Sieht in Frankreich schon wieder anders aus. Da hast du halt viele Afrikaner, noch mehr Araber und all das so. Das ist kulturell noch viel, viel größer. Und in Deutschland ist es nicht so. Oder in England zum Beispiel! Also was du da an Musik irgendwie hast. Du hast die ganzen Jamaikaner da. Und du kannst dem nicht entziehen! Also das wär eine Kunst das zu tun. Und das gibt es in Deutschland nicht. Das ist immer nur so Sparte mäßig. [...] Das heißt, es mischt sich überhaupt nicht. Das hast du in Frankreich, also in allen Ländern um Deutschland herum, hast du das halt nicht so.[122]
>
> [Germany is relatively German, like. It's different in France. There you have a lot of Africans, more Arabs and all that. It's culturally much, much bigger. And it's not like that in Germany. Or in England, for example! The amount of music you have there. You have all the Jamaicans there. And you can't escape it. To do so would be quite a skill. And that does not exist in Germany. Everyone keeps to their own little niche. [...] Which means there is no mixing. And you just don't have that in France, or in all the countries around Germany.]

In this case, DJ Stylewarz's critique echoes the contemporary German *Leitkultur* debate, in which the problem is not the existing multiculturalism in Germany but the lack of interaction and spatial connection between the cultures, since '[c]ultural exchange is the precondition of art'.[123] While DJ Stylewarz thus condemns Germany's supposed segregated cultural and musical state, claiming that the situation is different, indeed even better, in

122 DJ Stylewarz, interviewed by author, 10 June 2012. For further insights into France's adaptation of hip-hop music as a national form of artistic expression compared to Germany, see Murat Güngör, '"l'école du micro d'argent" – Ein Blick auf die französische Szene', in Güngör and Loh, *Fear of a Kanak Planet*, pp. 41–52.

123 Papastergiadis, *The Turbulence of Migration*, p. 125.

Britain and in France, a new hip-hop crew from Hamburg is attempting to create a local hip-hop sound.

'Rattos Locos Records', founded by its manager Blacky White in 2008, fuse different cultural sounds in order to create their own musical identity, which, in turn, is deeply connected to the aforementioned 'secondspace' perspective of Hamburg. While the port has already been described as 'the gateway to the world' as well as the 'bassline' of Hamburg, Rattos Locos appropriate this urban symbolism by further emphasizing the metaphorical multicultural-mindedness of Hamburg's past Hanseatic pirates. Rattos Locos member Nate57, for example, explains that his beats include:

> karibische Einflüsse und auch brasilianische Kuduro-Einflüsse. [...] Sogar Grime-Einflüsse gibt es auch. Und Piraten sind halt die Segler. Die gehen halt um die Welt. Wir sammeln die schönsten Sachen auf und kreieren neuen Sound! Jede Musikrichtung ist ja auch so entstanden aus anderen Musikrichtungen. Auch Reggae und so. Und wenn man es ja versucht eine eigene Identität zu machen, wird es halt doch ein anderer, eigener Sound. Wenn du dann dich daran setzt und sagst: 'Ich will jetzt einen *Dirty South* Beat machen', dann wird es halt auch ein *Dirty South* Beat, weil du dich daran auch hältst mit den High Hats und die Bass Drum so setzen. Und wir versuchen halt eine Mischung daraus zu machen und es klingt auch wirklich jetzt mittlerweile nach was ganz Neuem so. So U-Boot-Hamburg-mäßig.[124]
>
> [Caribbean influences and also Brazilian kuduro influences. [...] There are even grime influences as well. And pirates are real sailors. They go around the world. We collect the nicest things and create a new sound! Every music style originated that way from other music styles. Even reggae and so forth. And when you try to create your own identity, then it becomes a different, individual sound. If you sit down and say: 'I wanna create a *dirty south* beat', then it becomes a *dirty south* beat because you follow the norms, setting the high hats and the bass drum that way. And we really try to make a mixture from everything and it really does sound like something new now. Like submarine-Hamburg-wise.]

In his explanation, Nate57 captures the submarine imagery previously employed by Absolute Beginner in the title 'Das Boot'. In this case, the wartime cruises by the German submarines attacking the enemy become synonymous with the sea raids by the Hanseatic pirates. In this way the same social, spatial and historical discourse of the German maritime combat tradition becomes a metaphor for Hamburg's authoritative German hip-hop music. The most

124 Nate57, interviewed by author, 21 August 2012. Since the release of *Bambule* a submarine has been installed as a tourist attraction at the local *Fischmarkt* in St. Pauli, again underlying the connection between this sea vessel and the image of Hamburg.

intriguing aspect of this musical hybridization, however, is that the Afro-German or German-Pakistani artists who comprise Rattos Locos employ this strategy in order to represent their German identity. In other words, despite their innate hybridity, they mix cultural sounds in order to express their local German identity, in which, according to Papastergiadis, 'attention to its [the cultural exchange's] processes can not just register the transcendental signs of value or taste, but issue an inventory of the dynamics of change'.[125]

These dynamics of change reveal themselves in a state of post-hybridity in which the act of cultural mixing is supposed to affirm a local Germanness through cultural foreignness. Thus, Nate57, who is of Angolan origin – Angola being where the music genre of kuduro originated – does not employ kuduro as a cultural component and representation of his supposed 'tribal stigma'. Rather, through his employment of kuduro in its Latin American adaptation, the musical genre distances itself from its original affiliation with African culture and is used as a musical ingredient which represents Nate57's German affiliation to Hamburg's multicultural cityspace.

However, the success of Rattos Locos' new sound is dependent on other forces as well. These forces comprise the commercial realm and the cultural industries. Mirko Machine, for example, emphasizes German hip-hop music's marginalization on the German air waves by contrasting this situation to 'die Franzosen. [Die] sind da einfach nicht so behindert, wie wir hier. So. Da gibt es einfach französische Musik *immer* schon im Radio' [the French. They are just not as retarded as us. They have *always* played French music on the radio].[126] France's commercial protectionism and its rather exclusive attitude towards French music are therefore understood as a positive achievement by Mirko Machine, despite hip-hop music being celebrated for its necessary multicultural diversity of sounds. Gizmo even compares the musical output at dance clubs:

> [D]ieser Push die eigene Mucke auch im Club zu spielen, so weißt du? Die fehlt noch [in Deutschland]. Frankreich spielen immer ihren eigenen Kram. In Frankreich ist ja auch das Gesetz, dass 70% muss national sein. Klar, dass Hip-Hop dann auch permanent läuft.[127]
>
> [This push to play your own music in clubs, you know? That is still missing [in Germany]. France always play [*sic*] their own thing. In France it's also the law that 70% has to be national. Of course, hip-hop is played permanently there.]

125 Papastergiadis, *The Turbulence of Migration*, p. 125.

126 Mirko Machine, interviewed by author, 10 May 2012.

127 French air-play legislation requires 60% of the music played on the radio to be European-based, of which in turn 40% need to be French, i.e., sung in the French language. Gizmo, interviewed by author, 17 July 2012.

Indeed, DJ Ben Kenobi admits that 'im Club [...] ich eigentlich *nie* Deutschrap aufgelegt [hab']' [I really *never* played German rap in the club].[128] Initially, the reason for this selection was that early German hip-hop beats were simply not 'fett und Club-tauglich' [fat and suitable for the club].[129] Recalling listening to a track by local hip-hop crew Dynamite Deluxe in the 1990s, DJ Ben Kenobi describes their sound as having been 'ein bisschen mau. Da fehlte halt irgendwie die Fettness. Die war noch nicht da' [a bit meagre. It lacked the fatness somehow. It wasn't there yet].[130] It seems as though the fat, booming beats of American hip-hop music, which were created in direct connection to their 'firstspace', namely as a marker of urban territory and statement of sonic resistance against the noise of highway traffic, were not translatable into a German context where the cityspace did not provide a similar noise against which German DJs and producers had to react. The only instances in which DJ Ben Kenobi has played German hip-hop have been as homages towards local artists: 'Natürlich hab' ich mal einen Samy-Deluxe-Track gespielt und auch einen Schnabel-Track, aber das, ne? Wenn du hundert Lieder spielst und davon sind drei Deutschrap-Dinger, das ist eigentlich sehr mager' [Of course I used to play a track by Samy Deluxe and also a track by Schnabel, but that? If you play a hundred songs and three of them are German rap things, that is really a bit poor].[131] In other words, playing German tracks aimed not at disseminating German hip-hop music to a wider audience but at cultivating internal structures and hierarchies within the local hip-hop community.

However, in this club context, the question arises of whether the performative turntable element of DJing has become 'Germanized'. While this analysis has thus far explored German music productions, it needs to be considered whether the DJ tradition and turntable techniques have developed differently in Hamburg, despite the low number of German hip-hop music productions being played at dance events. This assumption is sparked by the supposed differences between American and European turntable approaches, with Mirko Machine defining the former as:

> so amerikanisch unsauber. Also bei den Amis war oft so ein Style, die haben die Nadel ungefähr da hingelegt, wo sie wissen wo sie hinmüssen und haben dann zwischendurch immer mal den Fader aufgemacht. Hier in Europa war man viel mehr darauf bedacht quasi das sauber zu machen und hat die Platten abgeklebt. So, dass du die Nadel *genau* an den Punkt setzen kannst, wo du

128 DJ Ben Kenobi, interviewed by author, 3 July 2012.

129 DJ Ben Kenobi, interviewed by author, 3 July 2012.

130 DJ Ben Kenobi, interviewed by author, 3 July 2012.

131 Mister Schnabel is a former rapper from Hamburg. DJ Ben Kenobi, interviewed by author, 3 July 2012.

> hinmusst. Und [du] konntest auch einfach *im* Takt, auf jeden Fall in zwei Takten, eine Scheibe wechseln, wenn ein neuer Beat kommt.[132]

> [so American-unclean. The Americans often had such a style, they always kind of put the needle roughly where they knew where they had to be and then opened the fader in between. Here in Europe you were much more careful to do it clean and you put tape on the records. So that you could put the needle *exactly* where you had to be. And [you] could also switch a record within a bar, definitely within two bars, when a new beat dropped.]

Without providing further reasons regarding these different approaches to turntabling DJ Ben Kenobi presents an insightful example of how European youth initially engaged in the 'foreign' art of turntableism. Prior to discovering the turntable as a musical instrument, the local hip-hop DJ was trained in classical percussion. The awareness of classical musical structures facilitated DJ Ben Kenobi's understanding of the drum-heavy hip-hop music, which, according to Rose, reflects 'critical priorities in many African and Afrodiasporic musical practices'.[133] DJ Ben Kenobi explains that the insights gained through his training in classical music were:

> für's DJing [...] natürlich top! [Eine] Art Taktgefühl und einen Auftakt und [beim] Sample die Länge zählen und deshalb ging das bei mir relativ schnell mit dem Mixen und dem Verständnis für den Beat. Und wann muss man wo wie rein.[134]

> [perfect for DJing! A feeling for the beat and [for] an upbeat and to count the length of a sample and that is why it went relatively fast for me with mixing and having an understanding for a beat. And when, where and how I have to enter].

DJ Ben Kenobi's last remark refers to 'beat matching', which is a technique of switching smoothly between two different songs and is a valued skill since DJs need to 'count where the first beat drops on a bar or a measure. They must be able to listen to music of one tempo in one ear and then adjust another song until it is the right tempo in the other ear.'[135] Thus, local DJ Vito concludes: 'Ich kenne keinen DJ, der besser beim Auflegen echte Remixe machen kann, dass manchmal Leute gedacht haben: "Oah, hast du das neue Lied gehört?" Der ist so *on point*! Ich kenne keinen, der das so gut kann wie er' [I don't know any DJ who is better at creating real remixes while deejaying, so that people

132 Mirko Machine, interviewed by author, 10 May 2012.

133 Rose, *Black Noise*, p. 66.

134 DJ Ben Kenobi, interviewed by author, 3 July 2012.

135 Hans Bakker and Theo Bakker, 'The Club DJ: A Semiotic and Interactionalist Analysis', *Symbolic Interaction*, 29 (2006), 71–82 (p. 72).

sometimes thought: 'Whoa, did you hear that new song?' He is so *on point*! I don't know anyone who is as good as him].[136]

DJ Ben Kenobi was able to perfect his turntable skills by combining knowledge of two disparate types of musical styles and cultural approaches. The fusion of classical music expertise and turntable technique has, moreover, resulted in a seemingly better ability to handle beats on a turntable and to create new musical 'texts', indeed a 'third space' of music, as Papastergiadis notes that '[b]y mixing things that were previously kept apart there is both a stimulus for the emergence of something new, and also a shift in position that can offer a perspective for seeing newness as it emerges'.[137] In line with this classical approach towards hip-hop music Samy Deluxe even proposes that 'man […] natürlich unglaublich viele geile Klassikkomponisten aus Deutschland samplen [könnte]!' [you could also sample many amazing classical composers from Germany!].[138]

Extending this idea of the 'classical' component within hip-hop DJing, Hamburg's DJ Orchester has blended classical and hip-hop performance traditions while engaging in the African-derived musical aesthetics of turntabling. Having split in 2013, the orchestra consisted of DJ Stylewarz 'der einfach alles zercuttet hat, was überhaupt nur geht. Mixwell, der so technisch vollkommen überlegen ist. Ein Mensch, der hat ein unglaubliches Taktgefühl. [...] und Mirko Machine' [who just cuts everything and anything possible into pieces. Mixwell, who is technically so utterly superior. A person who has an amazing feeling for the beat. [...] and Mirko Machine].[139] The distinct characteristics mentioned by DJ Vito highlight the individual styles and hence identities of the turntableists, something which confirms their skills and status as artists. Indeed, turntableist formations such as the DJ Orchester only made sense 'when the DJ could be accepted as self-sufficient, no longer understood primarily as a supplier of music to MCs or dancers. In other words, turntableism was a necessary precondition for the existence of turntable bands'.[140]

With a band name that fuses a juxtaposing duality, Mirko Machine recalls that 'die Leute [...] einfach mit diesem Namen "DJ Orchester" nichts anfangen

136 DJ Vito, interviewed by author, 21 June 2012.

137 Papastergiadis, 'Hybridity and Ambivalence', 57.

138 Samy Deluxe, interviewed by author, 29 July 2012. Indeed, Berlin-based rap and reggae artist Peter Fox sampled from Soviet composer Dmitri Shostakovich's Symphony No.7 in C Major (the 'Leningrad' Symphony) (1941) in his track 'Alles Neu' (2008). Consequently, London rapper Plan B entered at number 6 in the UK singles chart after having sampled Peter Fox's beat in his own song 'Ill Manors' (2012), *2012-04-07 Top 40 Official Singles Chart UK Archive* (The Official Charts Company, 7 April 2012), http://www.officialcharts.com/archive-chart/_/1/2012-04-07/ [accessed 21 February 2013].

139 DJ Vito, interviewed by author, 21 June 2012.

140 Katz, *Groove Music*, p. 147.

[konnten]. So. Konnte sich keiner was darunter vorstellen' [people really didn't get this name 'DJ Orchester'. So. Nobody could imagine what it was about].[141] Incidentally, the name was not coined by the DJs themselves but by the owner of a local dance club in Hamburg who aimed to hire all three DJs 'wie so ein DJ Orchester' [like some kind of DJ orchestra].[142] The local DJs thus engaged in this vision by blending the performance traditions of DJing with established stage practices at classical concerts. Mirko Machine, for instance, proposed that 'wenn wir so Orchester-mäßig uns so nennen, sollten wir uns auch einen Frack anziehen. Das wäre einfach fett!' [if we call ourselves something orchestra-like then we should also wear tails. That would be wicked!].[143] Hence, when performing as a DJ orchestra the three turntableists' 'personal front' comprised white shirts complete with bow ties and tails, while baggy jeans and trainers were, however, substituted for formal trousers and shoes.

Furthermore, by visualizing their name through the integration of symbolic codes on their 'personal fronts', the three DJs' '"[a]ppearance" may be taken to refer to those stimuli which function at the time to tell us of the performer's social statutes' (*PSEL*, p. 24). In this case, the DJs' social statement addresses class rather than race, as all three musicians are of 'white' German ethnicity, while DJ Stylewarz is half American as well. The DJ Orchester therefore employs the *classy* dress code in order to signify, albeit playfully, an adherence to a higher social class than that usually attributed to hip-hop artists, as they are often dismissed as self-sufficient, skilled musicians. This perception is triggered by their being paid less for their performance than DJs who play electronic music,[144] or by their being frequently confronted with a 'DJ-as-jukebox' attitude on the part of club audiences.[145] In order to accentuate this social recognition even further, the DJ Orchester re-framed the spatial characteristics of the dance club as well.

During the DJ Orchester's performances, the 'firstspace' of the club architecture was restructured according to a classical European performance 'setting'. A curtain devided the 'front' region between the 'audience' and the 'performer'. The DJ Orchester appropriated the tradition of curtain openings and closures in order to signal the beginning and end of their concert. Standing on an elevated stage facing the audience, the communal DJ Orchester's performance thus entailed 'a team of persons whose activity on stage in conjunction with available props will constitute the scene from which the

141 Mirko Machine, interviewed by author, 10 May 2012.
142 Mirko Machine, interviewed by author, 10 May 2012.
143 Mirko Machine, interviewed by author, 10 May 2012.
144 DJ Mixwell, interviewed by author, 19 June 2012.
145 DJ Stylewarz, interviewed by author, 10 June 2012.

performed character's self will emerge, and another team, the audience, whose interpretive activity will be necessary for this emergence' (*PSEL*, p. 253).

The available 'props' were, in this case, three turntables, while the interpretive activity of the audience, on the other hand, was influenced by the 'secondspace' identity of the location as a discothèque in which club norms were followed. Indeed, the DJs adapted these norms by beginning their concert 'um zwei [Uhr morgens] [...] und dann kommt ein Intro und dann geht der Vorhang auf und dann stehen wir da mit unserem *Stuff* und dann geht's los! Und dann rocken wir da auch reell so zusammen' [at two [o'clock in the morning] [...] and then an intro starts and then the curtain opens and then we are standing there with our *stuff* and then it begins! Then we really rock together].[146] The 'thirdspace' experience of their performance thus combined the expected danceable hip-hop sound with the classically-staged delivery as 'a simultaneously real-and-imagined, actual-and-virtual, locus of structured individual and collective experience and agency'.[147] In combining these two performance practices into a real-and-imagined experience, the DJ Orchester's hybrid approach to turntabling was further enforced by playing fixed and improvised musical sequences at their concerts:

> Wir haben eine Routine am Anfang. Machen noch irgendwas und gehen in Partymode über. Spielen dann zusammen wirklich Platten. Jeder guckt so, was geht mit den Leuten. So und wenn die Leute gut drauf sind, kommt wieder eine Routine. Und dann geht es wieder reihum und man spielt wieder ein bisschen Platten.[148]
>
> [We have a routine in the beginning. We do something and then switch into party mode. We really play records together. Everyone watches what is going on with the crowd. And if the people are in a good mood then we play a routine again. And then we switch again and everyone plays some records.]

On the one hand, the DJs engaged in the original musical practice which catered to the audience's and hence to the dancers' requirements. On the other hand, performing set routines gave the turntableists an air of artistic seriousness, as these routines were carefully planned and practised in advance. These preparations specifically unfolded in a designated 'back' region, namely at 'unser Orchester Probenplatz' [our orchestra rehearsal space],[149] a feature which again highlights the DJ Orchester's professional construction of their performed selves as they distinguished between the 'back region with its tools

146 Mirko Machine, interviewed by author, 10 May 2012.
147 Soja, *Postmetropolis*, p. 11.
148 Mirko Machine, interviewed by author, 10 May 2012.
149 Mirko Machine, interviewed by author, 10 May 2012.

for shaping the body, and a front region with its fixed props' (*PSEL*, p. 253). Their 'Probenplatz' [rehearsal space] is called the *Lab*, 'lab' having been a common term for referring to the hip-hop DJs' practice room. Katz writes that DJ Steve Dee 'calls the Harlem apartment bedroom where he developed [beat juggling] his *lab*'.[150] This 'secondspace' label of the 'firstspace' functioned to emphasize the experimental innovation and artistry of this musical tradition, comparing it to a field of science.[151]

The DJ Orchester's *Lab* is located in an industrial building situated in Hamburg's Schanzenviertel. It is furnished with 'tools' such as turntables, samplers, computers, vinyl records and other technical equipment required for practising turntable skills and for producing beats. Other material such as posters on the walls and books in shelves decoratively represent hip-hop culture as well. The outside architecture of the *Lab*'s 'firstspace' edifice does not, however, identify it as a place pertaining to hip-hop's musical art form. Rather, it is the 'secondspace' identity of the Hamburg neighbourhood which resonates with hip-hop since it is known for its alternative, multicultural and artsy scene. Nevertheless, the three DJs experience hip-hop as a private and secluded practice in contrast to its open-air manifestation in New York City. With their *Lab* distanced from housing areas, the local DJs are able to play in full sonic volume at any hour of the night without disturbing 'outsiders'. This backstage area thus fuses the practicality of its 'firstspace' with the symbolic 'secondspace' image of its neighbourhood in order to be a genuine 'thirdspace' for local hip-hop culture. Consequently this *Lab* also became the 'setting' for the DJ Orchester's promotional video teaser with which they once advertised their upcoming show. A close reading of the video's brief cinematic narrative will provide a more detailed insight into the ways in which the German DJs negotiate the three aspects of sociality, spatiality and historicality in their culturally hybrid turntable performance on screen.

Titled 'DJ Orchester – Mirko Machine, DJ Mixwell, DJ Stylewarz',[152] the video teaser begins with a sequence of close-up shots showing hands switching on a record player, releasing its needle onto a blue vinyl record and subsequently moving the record back and forth. The introductory images are accompanied by a female voice announcing: 'Sehr geehrte Damen und Herren, hören Sie nun das DJ Orchester' [Ladies and Gentleman, please now listen to the DJ Orchester] (0:04). This four-second German phrase is immediately followed by an accelerated *autosonic* quotation of the first two instrumental bars of the

150 Katz, *Groove Music*, p. 70.

151 Cf. Katz, *Groove Music*, p. 70.

152 'DJ Orchester – Mirko Machine, DJ Mixwell, DJ Stylewarz', *Guesi2007*, http://www.youtube.com/watch?v=Bxv2y5Izll4 [accessed 1 January 2012].

Figure 1: Hands on Vinyl

(Source: https://www.youtube.com/watch?v=Bxv2y5Izll4)

song 'Paranoid' (1970) by English rock band Black Sabbath. Rock music and hip-hop successfully collaborated in the 1980s[153] and Mikos explains that the appearance of rock-music samples in hip-hop creates a fusion in which 'die (echte oder vermeintliche) Authentizität des Hip-Hop mit der Authentizität des schmutzigen, ehrlichen Hardrock vereint [wird]' [the (real or alleged) authenticity of hip-hop is combined with the authenticity of dirty, honest hard rock].[154] During this instrumental introduction the face and hence the identity of the DJ continue to remain obscure. Rather, the musical sound and the visual captions of the turntable dexterity are at the centre of attention (see Figure 1).

Another sequence of close-up shots reveals more hands moving vinyl, pushing faders and turning buttons until fifteen seconds later a cut to a medium shot finally frames all three DJs standing between a shelf of vinyl records and a turntable played by DJ Mixwell. The DJs' appearance is defined by their performative selves and hence by their classy 'personal front'. Mirko Machine diverges slightly with his appearance as he has exchanged his white shirt for a T-shirt and his bow tie for a winter hat. The cut to the new cinematic frame is, moreover, accompanied by a new sonic layer over Black Sabbath's

153 In 1986, for example, African-American hip-hop duo Run-DMC had successfully sampled from Aerosmith's song 'Walk this Way' (1975), leading to a musical hit that the two bands eventually recorded and performed together.

154 Mikos, 'Interpolation and Sampling', p. 77; Forman also mentions that in terms of hip-hop music's commercial crossover to a wider American consumer public 'the images and aesthetic codes of urban black culture were carefully merged with the outlaw stances of white rockers' (Forman, *The 'hood Comes First*, p. 150).

guitar riff. A male voice is heard asking the audience in an American-English accent: 'Are you ready?' (0:15). This question is simultaneously lip-synced by Mirko Machine whilst pointing to the camera and is hence directed at the viewer. His ambiguous act of wordplay therefore characterizes him linguistically as American. Indeed, by engaging in such signifying practices through turntabling, DJs communicate through the manual manipulation of a pre-recorded voice rather than their own.[155]

The answer to Mirko Machine's question is, of course, not provided through live feedback by the intended audience but by DJ Stylewarz. A new cut shows him at the turntables, where he carries on looping the same *autosonic* quotation, yet enhances the guitar riff with a heavy drum base layer, thus musically underlining Mirko Machine's question (0:17). Following this communicative moment, DJ Stylewarz scratches 'twiddles', which were invented by London DJ Supreme during the Britcore movement. Having been part of the Britcore scene, this scratch style has established itself as a 'typische[n] Stylewarz Scratch auch. Das ist ein verspannter Unterarm und das geht halt derbe schnell' [typical Stylewarz scratch as well. It's a tense underarm and it just goes really fast].[156] DJ Stylewarz scratches a rhythm pattern into the female voice that was inserted at the beginning of the video teaser. Using the German word 'das' as an *allosonic* quotation and abstracting it through scratching, DJ Stylewarz eventually releases the vinyl record, allowing it to flow into the full resonation of 'das DJ Orchester' (0:20).

The remaining part of the teaser serves to introduce the individual members of the orchestra. In this way the DJs further engage in the turntable technique of word play. Mirko Machine, for instance, lip-syncs the announcement of his name, which is played by DJ Stylewarz (0:26). DJ Mixwell, on the other hand, plays his own autosonic introduction while merely directing his gaze into the camera (0:32). The full reference only unfolds when DJ Mixwell's colleagues point to him as the announcement appears. Last, DJ Stylewarz plays his name while also remaining muted behind the turntables. In this case, however, his identity remains ambiguous as he points to Mixwell and Mirko Machine behind him, with Mirko Machine lip syncing DJ Stylewarz's name instead (see Figure 2).

Within their unity as a German DJ orchestra, these individual acts of word play enable the DJs to take on different identities by playfully engaging in the African-American tradition of signifiying. Moreover, their performance depicts the way that 'the turntable is used in practice as a semiotic resource for making meaning. Together, the beat and the turntable are at the center

155 Katz, *Capturing Sound*, p. 133.
156 Mirko Machine, interviewed by author, 10 May 2012.

Figure 2: Stylewarz

(Source: https://www.youtube.com/watch?v=Bxv2y5Izll4)

of a structure of signs whose conventions and practice are under constant diachronic evolution'.[157] Closing the scene, the *autosonic* quotation of 'Das DJ Orchester' is played one last time, underlying the cinematic medium-shot that frames the three men for a final moment. The teaser subsequently ends with a change in the mise-en-scène in which the three DJs are seen affixing posters to walls in the Schanzenviertel (0:45). The music terminates with yet another *autosonic* citation saying 'Check it out ... Like this!' until the visual image fades to black with a superimposition of 'Uebel und Gefährlich' – the DJ Orchester's show location in Hamburg (0:49). In sum, this brief video clip presents the culturally hybrid manifestation of the DJ Orchester, who fuse two divergent performative and spatial practices into one. This is, first, achieved by providing a hybrid cinematographic setting in which a portion of the 'back' region of the *Lab* is re-mediated as the 'front'. This backstaged 'front' is, on the one hand, constructed though a mise-en-scène in which designated hip-hop 'tools' are re-functioned as staged 'props' and, on the other hand, through the DJs' 'personal front', which reflects their appearance on a live 'front' rather than their presentation of self in the 'back'.

In order to hybridize their music, the DJs 'Africanize' Black Sabbath's looped guitar riff by layering a drum beat on top of it. Moreover, in utilizing *intertextual* quotations from two different languages, German and English, and by engaging in word play with which the DJs alter their sense of place

157 Bakker and Bakker, 'The Club DJ', 72.

and identity, they blur the linguistic signifiers that commonly serve to identify a culture. Similarly, DJ Stylewarz's use of twiddles defines him musically as an English DJ rather than German-American: 'Stylewarz ist auf jeden Fall, das hört man am Scratch Stil so definitiv von den Engländern beeinflusst' [Stylewarz is definitely – you can hear it in the scratch style – influenced by the English].[158] The only direct reference to their German national identity is the aural introduction enunciated in German, which addresses a socially cultivated German audience comprising 'Damen' and 'Herren'.

Thus, the communal turntable performance of the DJ Orchester 'tracks the dynamism within displacement and emphasizes the agency within specific practices of ironic appropriation or critical incorporation. It stresses that cultural categories, when inserted into different contexts, tend to take on contrary meanings and values'.[159] In so doing, the DJ Orchester 'erases any essentialist claims for the inherent authenticity or purity of cultures' (*LOC*, pp. 83–84) as they do not specifically represent German culture, or the direct adaptation of an Afro-American one. Rather, the three DJs mix both cultural traditions in order to provide a unique performance located between European and African performative aesthetics.

Summary

After providing an overview of the spatial, historical and social conditions that have shaped hip-hop music, the second part of this chapter turned to its appropriation in West Germany and specifically looked at the ways in which DJing and music production were formed by Hamburg's urban dynamics. The case studies and interviews presented in this chapter have covered a broad range of important figures who have shaped and continue to shape the sound of hip-hop from Hamburg. They also revealed that the musical identity of the local hip-hop music community has relied heavily on Hamburg's 'secondspace' ideology, which promotes cultural open-mindedness and worldliness through the cultural flows and exchanges enabled by Hamburg's seaport. This open-mindedness also mobilized early hip-hop musicians to engage in the Britcore movement and hence in musical sounds and traditions beyond their American musical role models. This development stands in contrast to other ethnographic studies on hip-hop music, such as Andy Bennet's research on Frankfurt's hip-hop music in the early 1990s. Being part of the former American occupation zone, this city still had US-American army bases and hence a cultural flow

158 DJ Ben Kenobi, interviewed by author, 3 July 2012.
159 Papastergiadis, *The Turbulence of Migration*, p. 111.

of American cultural products and people, which, as Bennet observes, was relevant for the shaping of the local hip-hop scene and style.[160]

In Hamburg, however, without this American influence, the release of the album *Bambule* by Absolute Beginner in 1997 exemplified how local hip-hop artists used samples to represent their city. This included samples from Germany's own musical history. Since member Jan Delay listened to Udo Lindenberg during his childhood, his personal memories of this German singer became a symbol of authenticity in his sampling of Lindenberg in his own songs. Hence, by giving hip-hop a local German identity through the fusion of past sounds in present musical texts, which were identifiable by the German language, Absolute Beginner helped establish German hip-hop music in Hamburg.

This genre, in turn, became the first viable German music for other hip-hop artists such as Samy Deluxe. In continuing with the local historical narrative enabled by the aesthetic of sampling, Samy Deluxe has cited Jan Delay as a sign of his own cultural memories and past experiences of German music. While this example therefore emphasized local hip-hop music's cohesion in terms of spatial and historical continuity, it also served to highlight a social aspect whereby an Afro-German hip-hop artist becomes representative of the cultural continuity of Hamburg's musical history.

Nevertheless, the question remained as to whether hip-hop music has also cultivated a unique musical sound beyond recognition of the German language in particular samples. While D-Flame and DJ Placeebo refuted the existence of a German sound due to German hip-hop artists' lack of courage in taking the next step, DJ Stylewarz's reasoning addressed the supposed cultural stagnation in Germany which inhibits cultural exchange and hence the production of art and newness within art. These answers already suggest a divergence from and even contradiction of the supposedly unifying cultural force of hip-hop music, which allows different cultural and musical sounds to be combined into new arrangements. Hamburg's multicultural rap label 'Rattos Locos Records' has, however, shown that the aim exists of creating a local hip-hop 'U-boot sound'. In this way Rattos Locos engage in Hamburg's spatial-historical discourse that emphasizes its maritime connection and liberal attitude towards foreign cultures or, in this case, towards foreign styles of music. By representing Hamburg and their local affiliation through a multiculturally created hip-hop sound, the rappers also express a post-hybrid German identity, for their music represents their Afro-German or Pakistani-German bi-culturality as a part of their Hamburg locality.

160 Bennet, 'Hip-Hop am Main', 26–30.

While the analysis until this point engaged in music production, the following examples addressed the live, performative aspects of hip-hop music. These highlighted local artists' fusion of classical musical knowledge and performance practices with turntabling. DJ Ben Kenobi, for instance, learned how to DJ with previous knowledge of classical percussion, while the DJ Orchester blended cultural codes of classical musical performances and DJing into a hybrid turntabling spectacle. Nonetheless, despite their German ethnicity neither DJ Ben Kenobi nor the DJ Orchester aimed to express a local German identity through their music, unless one counts their clean approach towards turntabling and their use of the German language in their samples. Rather, the DJ Orchester engaged in a class discourse by attempting to elevate hip-hop music's social status as a professional art form through their incorporation of classical performance traditions. The DJs focus on their social struggles because their 'whiteness' is useless in making a statement on cultural or ethnic acceptance within German and even European society. Thus, DJ Stylewarz claims: 'Ich möchte nicht nur als der Hip-Hop DJ, sondern auch einfach als irgendwie Musiker wahrgenommen werden. Sei es beim Auflegen [oder] als Produzent' [I don't just want to be perceived only as the hip-hop DJ but also just as a musician. Whether this is while playing records or as a producer].[161]

Hip-hop music in Hamburg can therefore be seen as immersed in two identity discourses: one which emphasizes local belonging and one which aims towards a higher class-categorization. While the technique of sampling in music production has been employed to create a local identity in music, the use of specific turntable techniques played by local DJs expresses an affiliation to a European music community rather than to a local German one. Whether music is the only hip-hop art form that expresses such different social aspects and claims of identity and belonging will be explored in the next chapter, in which we turn to hip-hop dance in Hamburg.

161 DJ Stylewarz, interviewed by author, 3 July 2012.

CHAPTER 2

Hip-Hop Dance

Break Beats and Break Boys: The Emergence of Hip-Hop Dance

> See, the whole thing when hip-hop first started was the music was played in the parks and in the jams for the dancers, and those dancers were B-Boys.[1]

As this chapter turns to hip-hop's dance element, the statement by Bronx b-boy Crazy Legs serves to highlight the connection between the musical art form of hip-hop, initiated by the hip-hop DJs, and the emergence of b-boys and subsequently of hip-hop dance. This connection is already inherent in the term 'b-boy', which is believed to have derived from 'break boy', labelling the dancer who specifically danced during the break beats played by the DJ.[2] In his book *Foundation: B-boys, B-girls, and Hip-hop Culture in New York* Joseph Schloss, however, also explains that the abbreviation 'b-boy' may refer to a person who, 'in keeping with the slang of the time, temporarily loses his mind, or "breaks," and expresses that in the dance'.[3] In an interview with New York b-boy Trac 2, this dancer further suggests that the label derived from '"Bronx-boy" because that's where we come from. "Battle-boy," because that's what we were. Or a "beat-boy," because that's what moved us'.[4] Trac 2's account of the etymology of 'b-boy' also captures the spatiality, sociality and historicality of b-boying: the Bronx relates to the cityspace in which the art form emerged, the battle refers to the social context of the presentation of self, while the beats musically reflect the cultural histories of the Bronx's inhabitants.

Beginning with an overview of hip-hop dance from a spatial perspective, one needs first of all to return to the aforementioned 'thirdspace' experience of the Bronx, since the 'process of producing spatiality or "making geographies" begins with the body, with the construction and performance of the self, the

1 Crazy Legs, quoted in in S. H. Fernando Jr, *The New Beats: Exploring the Music, Culture, and Attitudes of Hip-Hop* (New York: Anchor/Doubleday, 1994), p. 17.

2 Kool Herc, quoted in Nelson George, 'Hip-Hop's Founding Fathers Speak the Truth', in *That's the Joint!*, ed. by Forman and Neal, pp. 43–55 (p. 46).

3 Schloss, *Foundation*, p. 59.

4 Trac 2, quoted in Schloss, *Foundation*, p. 59.

human subject, as a distinctively spatial entity involved in a complex relation with our surroundings'.[5] This particular urban geography of the Bronx was visibly defined by its 'street corner *salseros*',[6] who accompanied the rhythms and sounds of Puerto Rican and Cuban drummers in parks and other public venues. While living in this 'thirdspace' influenced the emergence of the DJs' neighbourhood block parties, it also legitimized dancing in urban spaces. As Schloss writes:

> Since early hip-hop jams took place in the same spaces as street drumming – sidewalks, parks, public beaches and schoolyards – the experience of dancing to an extended, Latin-style percussion break played by a deejay in a park would have been extremely similar to the experience of dancing to live drummers in that park.[7]

Not only does this comparison draw upon commonalities between hip-hop culture and the overall lifestyle of the Bronx during that particular time but Schloss also mentions the specific 'firstspaces' on which the dancing unfolded, namely on sidewalks, in parks and in school yards. The materiality of these asphalted surfaces was not only dirty but also harsh, especially when considering that the art of b-boying developed a high number of floor moves compared to salsa dancing. Even though a piece of cardboard or linoleum protected the dancers from direct contact with their dance floor, Schloss explains that '[c]oncrete happens to be more conducive to footwork'[8] and that 'the *idea* of concrete – and its association with urban environments (literally, "the streets") – has a certain rawness that reads as historical authenticity'.[9] While 'historical authenticity' can describe the local, albeit more abstract, continuation of the aforementioned street-corner salsa tradition and the cultivation of an outdoor urban lifestyle, it has also come to define the art of b-boying as being inextricably linked to this 'firstspace' condition. Hence, proving one's faithful engagement in this art form required a specific surface, 'leaving b-boys who unsuccessfully attempt air moves to nurse scrapes, sprains, and broken bones'.[10]

However, the rawness of the urban environment can also be understood beyond spatial terms, namely as a description of the social atmosphere of the Bronx. As b-boying gained its own autonomy as a dance form, it eventually transcended the initial party context and became a lesson about how 'one is

5 Soja, *Postmetropolis*, p. 6.
6 Katz, *Groove Music*, p. 42.
7 Schloss, *Foundation*, p. 20.
8 Schloss, *Foundation*, p.20.
9 Schloss, *Foundation*, p. 96.
10 Schloss, *Foundation*, p. 96.

to carry oneself in life, particularly with regard to the relationship between creativity and self-confidence'.[11] On the one hand, this presentation of self was influenced by the popularity of kung fu films in the 1970s.[12] The martial art's philosophical approach in particular nurtured b-boying's positive focus on creativity and individuality beyond its kinaesthetic expression.[13] On the other hand, self-assurance was fostered by a particular attitude that 'like the dance itself, requires a controlled aggressiveness [which] derives from the circumstances in which it arose: the New York streets of the '70s often required posture of barely restrained violence'.[14] While early b-boys inevitably represented 'the urban unrepentant poor [...] who are considered to be engaged in some kind of collective denial of the social order' (*STGM*, p. 144) due to living in a cityspace that was stigmatized by social marginality and financial despair, the local practice of b-boying became a strategy with which to gain a highly respected social status.

This strategy initially imitated the street gang culture and territorial wars within New York City's uptown neighbourhoods. In accordance with the social structures and hierarchies of these local street warriors, b-boys began forming dance crews following the same internal organization of these gangs.[15] In some cases they even substituted membership of a dance crew for their gang membership, which led to 'the general emphasis on defining one's identity through a superior dance style'.[16] Nevertheless, while gaining a social status through dance skills rather than through outright violence, b-boy crews continued to foster the same feeling of territorial supremacy, being 'almost always identified by their location of origin, even if that is now a city or a country rather than a city block'.[17] Hence, in order for the b-boy hierarchy and social status to remain intact, b-boys and their crews continued to battle for local recognition by 'claiming the streets with physical presence, using [their] body to publicly inscribe [their] identity on the surfaces of the city, to flaunt a unique personal style within a conventional format'.[18]

The format of these b-boy battles resembled improvised embodied dialogues between two dancers from opposing crews, who expressed themselves kinaesthetically through 'cartwheels, kicks, and feints'.[19] Attempting

11 Schloss, *Foundation*, p. 45.
12 Schloss, *Foundation*, p. 45.
13 Schloss, *Foundation*, p. 45.
14 Schloss, *Foundation*, pp. 84–85.
15 Schloss, *Foundation*, p 79.
16 Schloss, *Foundation*, p. 66.
17 Schloss, *Foundation*, p. 67.
18 Banes, *Writing Dancing*, p. 145.
19 Banes, *Writing Dancing*, p. 128.

to outperform each other with dance moves, b-boys typically maintained their social status by successfully managing 'to control the conduct of the others, especially their responsive treatment of him' (*PSEL*, p. 3). These kinaesthetic responses therefore followed an established structure.

A b-boy attack generally began with the dancer in an upright position performing fast and bouncy steps. These steps were influenced by a previous street dance developed by Latino gangs in Brooklyn called 'rocking'.[20] Hence, it is no coincidence that 'uprocking' or 'toprocking' have come to describe b-boying's introductory dance steps, which are also simply referred to as 'footwork'. 'Downrocks', on the other hand, are steps performed on the ground. These are commonly danced after a toprock sequence and include so-called 'power moves' and 'air moves' which have visible elements of the martial arts, acrobatics and gymnastics. The end of a b-boy routine is then concluded with a provocative freeze position, often embodying 'references to TV, *Playboy*, comic books, kung-fu films'[21] and directed in a boastful or insulting manner at the rival.

These battles occurred on designated 'firstspaces' such as local streets or at organized hip-hop jams. Here, the dancers presented themselves within a circle of people who formed the Goffmanian 'front'. This round, human formation became known as the 'cypher' and further served as 'a collective enterprise that mixes improvisation, competition, and mutual support'.[22] The cypher therefore heavily influenced the 'thirdspace' experience of a b-boy battle within the material 'firstspace'. Moreover, dance historian Sally Banes further claims that:

> b-boying's spatial level called to mind capoeira, the spectacular Brazilian dance [...] but the two were dissimilar enough in shape and timing that capoeira seemed at most only a distant relative, and certainly one the break dancers weren't acquainted with – at least on a conscious level.[23]

By comparing the b-boy cypher to the 'roda' in capoeira, Banes nevertheless touches upon a cultural similarity between the Latino-African martial arts dance and b-boying. She captures the two influential cultures that created the art of b-boying in the first place, namely African-American and, more importantly, Latino. The Latino influence on hip-hop dance has been most notably derived from dancing to Latino music. Bronx b-boy Pop Master Fabel elaborates on this relationship, explaining it is:

20 Schloss, *Foundation*, pp. 125–54.

21 Banes, *Writing Dancing*, p. 128.

22 Schloss, *Foundation*, p. 99.

23 Banes, *Writing Dancing*, p. 128. For a detailed overview of the dance styles and cultures that influenced the development and structure of b-boying in the Bronx, see Jorge Pabon, 'Physical Graffiti', in *That's the Joint!*, ed. by Forman and Neal, pp. 57–62.

> [j]ust like when you see someone doing real dope mamboing to mambo music, or a salsa dancer who's tight on. You know ... *it's the native of the dance* ... the old-timers did it and still love it and keep it alive, because, honestly, I think that it's part of the ritual.[24]

This *native* ritual further highlights a kinaesthetic relationship which is also 'intrinsic to understanding African and African-inspired musics'.[25] According to Chris Small, African-derived music 'hardly exists as a separate art from dance, and in many African languages there is no separate word for it'.[26] Hence, mambo or salsa can refer to the dance as well as to the specific musical genre. Similar to Rose's contrasting of African-American and European musical structures presented in the previous chapter, Greg Dimitriadis especially contrasts European musical norms to the African-inspired Latino music in which:

> [u]nlike composed 'classical' European forms (arts which are represented by some sort of written score), such musics are brought to life through live production and concurrent improvisation. Such arts often reflect a more flexible lyrical or musical aesthetic than do Western arts such as classical European music.[27]

Hence, while in African and Latino traditions a listener is engaged in the music by dancing to it, Dimitriadis concludes that in Western culture '[p]hysical engagement is, accordingly, downplayed in favour of polite listening'.[28] Thus, with regards to the 'thirdspace' of the Bronx, which was shaped by the sonic output of the hip-hop DJs' looped break beats of funk songs and salsa rhythms, Schloss asserts that 'b-boys and b-girls learn to feel history in their bodies through certain songs'.[29]

In addition to this aspect, the battle-attitude and provocativeness of the b-boy performance has been connected to an African-American background. Schloss, for instance, explains that '[c]reatively insulting one's opponent is a part of many competitive traditions across the African diaspora',[30] while Carla Huntington Stalling reads hip-hop dance performances as:

24 Pop Master Fabel, quoted in Schloss, *Foundation*, p. 25.

25 Greg Dimitriadis, 'Hip-Hop: From Live Performance to Mediated Narrative', *Popular Music*, 15 (1996), 179–94 (p. 180).

26 Christopher Small, *Music of the Common Tongue: Survival and Celebration in African American Music* (Hanover, NH: University Press of New England, 1987), p. 24.

27 Dimitriadis, 'Hip-Hop', 181.

28 Dimitriadis, 'Hip-Hop', 182.

29 Schloss, *Foundation*, p. 41.

30 Dimitriadis, 'Hip-Hop', 111.

> a physical form of playing-the-dozens in African American communities, where Signification and Signifyin [*sic*] are taken to a most elevated and intellectual level. Simply stated, in the danced text, the men competed with each other through dance moves that outperformed challengers in the physical conversation, which is similar to what they do in the verbal dozens, where men compete with each other in making verbal commentary.[31]

Hence, the historicality of b-boying can, on the one hand, be located within the 'thirdspace' experience of the Bronx with its Latino street-dancing tradition, its street-gang culture and hip-hop DJs while, on the other hand, it can reach much farther back in history by drawing upon Latinos' and African-Americans' 'common roots that they recognised in each other's cultures'.[32]

However, the hybridizing processes joining popular culture and local ethnic heritages did not stop in the Bronx. Eventually the West Coast funk style dances of, for example, popping and locking became incorporated into b-boying and hence into hip-hop culture as well. Popping emphasized isolated muscle contractions simulating robots or imitating the flow of water through the body. Locking became known as a dance that focused on swinging one's arms outwards and inwards, stopping in an abrupt 'lock' before continuing with the next movement. While it is commonly said that the 'old school' hip-hop dance styles comprise b-boying as well as popping and locking which led to the requirement of knowing a bit of every dance form in order to call oneself a b-boy,[33] 'new school' dance forms have been continually added to the umbrella term of 'hip-hop dance'. Consequentually, hip-hop dance has, according to Banes, become 'perhaps the quintessential form of popular dancing in the age of postmodernism, incorporating mixed allusions to the mass media and to high culture, and creating ironic narratives of personal and political identity'.[34]

The following analysis of hip-hop dance in Hamburg will engage with these danced narratives of personal identity, performed through b-boying, popping and 'hip-hop', a hybrid dance form which is also known as 'new style' as it fuses the choreographic conventions of jazz and the performative battle practices

31 Stalling Huntington, *Hip Hop Dance*, p. 40. 'Playing the Dozens' refers to a game that is culturally located in an African-American context. In it two opponents creatively insult each other and thus do battle with each other until one player wins. This game is often played in a circle of a cheering audience who also function as a jury.

32 Schloss, *Foundation*, p. 155.

33 Beat Boy Delles, interviewed by author, 21 May 2012.

34 Banes, *Writing Dancing*, p. xiv. For a comprehensive historical overview of all the dance styles which comprise hip-hop dance, see Eva Kimminich, 'Tanzstile der Hip Hop Kultur. Bewegungskult und Körperkommunikation', *KiF – Kulturen im Fokus*, Potsdamer Kulturanalysen, 2013, http://www.kulturenfokus.de/content/tanzstile-der-hip-hop-kultur [accessed 23 June 2014].

of b-boying. Despite the dance forms' different aesthetics and histories, they continue to abide by the dance norms established through b-boying's spatial, social and historical circumstances as outlined above. In order to offer a close reading of these dance forms' different kinaesthetics, the following section will introduce an approch that captures the openness and flexibility of hip-hop dance yet also allows the focus to be narrowed down to individual movements.

Reading the Choreographies of Hip-Hop

Anthropologist Jane C. Desmond understands any performed dance as being a universal bodily text through which knowledge of 'how social identities are signaled, formed, and negotiated through bodily movement' can be gained.[35] Detaching dance from any specific culture, genre or level of skill, Desmond suggests investigating danced texts by asking, amongst other things, the following questions:

> How does dance signal, enact, or rework social categories of identity?
>
> How do the meanings arising from the performance of various dance styles change as those styles migrate across national, racial, or class boundaries?
>
> How and what do we come to know through kinesthesia as a historically particular register of meaning?[36]

Relating Desmond's selected questions to a hip-hop dance context, the first inquiry touches upon the social aspect of hip-hop dance, namely on how social identity is managed, negotiated and presented through its performative norms and battle practices. The second question becomes relevant when looking at hip-hop dance in Germany, where it has migrated into new cultural spaces, either material or metaphorical, which are framed by different boundaries. The third question picks up on this cultural and spatial transition by identifying hip-hop dance's *historically particular* significance as a kinesthetic expression in the new culture.

In order to answer these questions, the movements constituting hip-hop dance need to be read as an adaptation of individual and collective identities which interact with other bodies in order to tell a narrative that is semantically situated in the world.[37] Such an approach to hip-hop dance will be facilitated

35 Jane C. Desmond, 'Embodying Difference: Issues in Dance and Cultural Studies', in *Meaning in Motion: New Cultural Studies of Dance*, ed. by Jane C. Desmond (Durham, NC: Duke University Press, 1997), pp. 29–54 (p. 29).

36 Desmond, 'Embodying Difference', p. 29.

37 Susan Leigh Foster, 'Choreographies of Gender', *Signs: Journal of Women in Culture and Society*, 24 (1998), 1–21 (pp. 8–9).

through a theoretical framework derived from dance historian Susan Leigh Foster and concerned with the choreography of dance. In her book *Reading Dancing: Bodies and Subjects in Contemporary American Dance*, Foster announces five choreographic practices that treat dance as a cultural narrative. These comprise *frame*, *style*, *vocabulary*, *syntax* and the *mode of representation*.[38]

Analysing the *frame* explains the way a dance performance is presented in contrast to other events. In b-boying this aspect relates to the battle tradition and to the cypher in which the battle unfolds. Moreover, the *frame* includes paratexts that refer to the performance. Examples include the title of the dance show, the venue or the advertising format of the event. Investigating the *style* indicates the dance's unique position and identity within its genre of dance and places its artistic expression in a social context. Thus, according to Thomas DeFrantz, an overarching, common *style* of hip-hop dance is defined by its 'explosive suddenness' when an 'array of interlocking rhythms, percussive accents of isolated body-parts pop out in unexpected phrasing'.[39] In this sense, the 'assertive angularity of body posture and an insistent virtuosic rhythmicity'[40] seem expressive of the controlled aggressiveness of b-boying fostered through its derivation from a particularly harsh socio-urban context.

The *vocabulary* of the dance refers to the names of the individual steps that make up a dance sequence or an entire performance. The rules that regulate the choice and sequencing of steps are called the *syntax*.[41] Foster elaborates on the fact that variation is the 'overriding syntactic principle of dance',[42] ranging from dance steps on the floor to dancing in an upright position or fully losing touch with the ground by leaping and jumping. In b-boying, the common *syntax* begins with toprocks, followed by downrocks and ending in a freeze position. While the freeze position often imitates a popular cultural figure or reference, analysing the *syntax* of a dance performance not only serves to describe movement but can also highlight a particular meaning through movement. As Foster explains, the variation of *syntax* can make references to the surrounding world by establishing 'harmonies, tensions, and counterpoints that give the dance both its meaning and energy'.[43]

Nonetheless, ultimately it is the spectator's task to connect the dance's *syntax* into a readable text in order to decode its signification. This interpretative process can be stimulated by the dance's *mode of representation* which forms

38 Susan Leigh Foster, *Reading Dancing: Bodies and Subjects in Contemporary American Dance* (Berkeley: University of California Press, 1986), p. 59.

39 DeFrantz, 'The Black Beat Made Visible', p. 77.

40 DeFrantz, 'The Black Beat Made Visible', p. 69.

41 Foster, *Reading Dancing*, p. 59.

42 Foster, *Reading Dancing*, p. 79.

43 Foster, *Reading Dancing*, p. 59.

the last choreographic practice identified by Foster. The *mode of representation* is not to be confused with the aforementioned *style*, for the difference is that '[w]here the representational mode of the dance alerts the viewer to a broad framework for signifying the world, style in dance clarifies this framework by adding references to cultural identity'.[44] Hence, in order to make sense of the outside events that influence a dance's narrative, Foster differentiates between four methods of movement: *resembling, imitating, replicating* and *reflecting*.[45]

By kinaesthetically *resembling* an item, a single movement or formation of dancers focuses on dancing a certain attribute or quality of the item. The identity of the danced element may therefore remain unclear to the viewer. Through *imitating* an item, however, the choreography will attempt to give an accurate danced version of it, leaving little doubt as to what is being danced. The viewer is left to judge whether the imitation is achieved successfully or not. Through *replication,* a movement does not intend to mimic the phenomenon as such but to dance the dynamic relationship that constitutes part of this element. Lastly, a *reflection* may only refer to a certain aspect or characteristic of a chosen item which could nevertheless also be interpreted as belonging to a completely different phenomenon to the one which initially served as an inspiration for the danced movement. The focus therefore remains on the dancer rather than on the item conveyed through dance. While all the aforementioned methods imply 'a stance toward the world that is crucial for the dance's meaning',[46] Foster asserts that usually only one of these methods dominates in a performance.[47]

Guided by Desmond's understandings and questions regarding hip-hop dance's cultural significance, as well as by the choreographic theory and kinaesthetic methods provided by Foster, the next section of this chapter will shift its attention from the development of hip-hop dance on the streets of the Bronx to its present manifestation in Hamburg. Taking into account the spatial, historical and social discourses that have shaped the norms and practices of this art form, the following analysis will introduce a brief historical overview of the way in which hip-hop dance has been adapted in West Germany before analysing the strategies undertaken by hip-hop dancers in Hamburg in order to make it meaningful within a contemporary German cultural context.

44 Foster, *Reading Dancing*, p. 77.
45 Foster, *Reading Dancing*, pp. 65–76.
46 Foster, *Reading Dancing*, p. 65.
47 Foster, *Reading Dancing*, p. 65.

The Beginnings of B-boying in West Germany

> Wann checken Politiker und Kulturleute in Deutschland, daß Hip Hop-Kultur zwar in New York geboren wurde, aber heute weltweit besteht und diese Zeitepoche, in der wir leben, bestimmt. 1984 hieß es Modetanz. Was sagen sie jetzt? [...] Vielleicht ist den Politikern Hip Hop zu undeutsch?[48]
>
> [When will these politicians and people in the cultural scene in Germany understand that hip-hop culture was born in New York but now exists worldwide and determines this era in which we live? It was called a trendy dance in 1984. What are they calling it now? [...] Maybe hip-hop is too *un*-German for the politicians?]

The 'Modetanz' of b-boying was initially introduced into Germany through the same media and feature films that had inspired German DJs and music producers during the early 1980s. German b-boy and former world champion Storm elaborates, saying that it was particularly the impact of *Beat Street* which became 'der Grund, warum viele Tänzer überhaupt erst angefangen hatten zu rocken. Wenn der Film in den folgenden Jahren im Fernsehen lief, kamen immer wieder neue Breaker zum Vorschein' [the reason so many dancers had started rocking. When the film was aired on television in subsequent years new dancers emerged time and again].[49] However, similarly to the German DJs' visual experience of hip-hop, the wave of emerging b-boys in Germany and their engagement in hip-hop's danced element were detached from the Bronx's 'thirdspace' experience, which surrounded the youth on screen. As a consequence, German b-boy champion Jango states that 'bis der Tanz B-Boying [in Deutschland] richtig verstanden wurde, das hat 20 Jahre gedauert. Ich glaube 20 Jahre, bis die Leute verstanden haben, dass eigentlich B-Boying nur B-Boying ist. Locking ist Locking. Popping ist Popping' [it took 20 years for the dance b-boying to be understood correctly in Germany. I think it took twenty years for people to understand that b-boying is just b-boying. Locking is just locking. Popping is just popping].[50] The delayed understanding and knowledge of hip-hop dance become evident in the example of Hamburg b-boy Metin, who began his hip-hop dance career by imitating steps:

> die man so aufschnappt aus dem Fernsehen oder so. Damals gab es ja kein YouTube und so weiter und so fort. Und dann hat mich jemand angesprochen was ich denn da tue. Ob ich weiß, was das ist. Und ich habe gesagt: 'Ich mache *Rap Dance*!' [*laughs*]. Und er meinte dann: 'Nein, das ist

48 Niels Robitzky, *Von Swipe Zu Storm: Breakdance in Deutschland* (Hamburg: Backspin, 2000), pp. 93–94.

49 Robitzky, *Von Swipe Zu Storm*, p. 24.

50 Jango, interviewed by author, 8 June 2012.

> kein *Rap Dance*, das ist *Break Dance*!'.[51] Und dann habe ich gedacht: 'Aha? *Break Dance*? Was ist das?'.[52]
>
> [that you just caught on TV or something. Back then there was no YouTube and so on and so forth. And then somebody came up to me and asked what I was doing. And I said: 'I'm doing *rap dance*'. [*laughs*] And he was like: 'No, that's not *rap dance*, that's *break dance*!'. And then I thought: 'Huh? *Break dance*? What is that?'.]

Metin's early lack of knowledge of context and content in the art of b-boying is what Banes considers to be a general consequence of the mediatization processes of b-boying. According to Banes, the production and dissemination of hip-hop feature films in cinema and television:

> changed both its form and its meaning. So to talk about breakdancing you have to divide it into two stages: before and after media. Before the media turned breaking into dazzling entertainment, it was a kind of serious game, a form of urban vernacular dance, a fusion of sports, dancing, and fighting whose performance had urgent social significance for the dancers.[53]

This analysis therefore concerns b-boying and hip-hop dance forms *after* the intervention of the media, when b-boying, according to Banes, gained 'a new meaning. It was no longer a battle for control of the streets, for neighbourhood fame'.[54] This does not mean that battles became obsolete, that dancing on the streets was not done elsewhere or that there was no aiming at fame anymore. Rather, without the 'thirdspace' experience of the Bronx, the dance's norms and practices became filled with other social agendas and cultural histories. In other words, the codes and signs of b-boying became representative of different cultural discourses in different national contexts.

In West Germany, b-boying initially unfolded as an imitation of the original kinaesthetic, yet soon transformed into a noticeable German style. Echoing Mirko Machine's distinction between American DJs who, in contrast to European DJs, scratched 'so amerikanisch *un*sauber' [in such an American-unclean way],[55] Jango explains that German b-boys performed 'schöne Kombination[en], schöne, saubere Sachen' [nice combinations, nice, clean things].[56] The clean, precise execution of dance steps eventually became known as 'straight German power'. While the label thus captures the straightness

51 'Break dance' is a term coined by the media and not by the hip-hop community.

52 Metin, interviewed by author, 4 May 2012.

53 Banes, *Writing Dancing*, p. 144.

54 Banes, *Writing Dancing*, p. 144.

55 Mirko Machine, interviewed by author, 10 May 2012.

56 Jango, interviewed by author, 8 June 2012.

and hence exactness of the movements, it also describes the other dominant feature of early German b-boying, which was 'mehr so powermäßig, mehr so viele Tricks, viele Powermoves, diese ganzen Akrobatiksachen' [more power-like, more like tricks, many power moves, all these acrobatic elements].[57]

This emphasis on acrobatics was no coincidence. Growing up in Hamburg, Jango remembers that 'damals [...] halt als Junge Tanzen nicht so cool [war] irgendwie. Wenn du getanzt hast, warst du eher nicht der coole Typ' [back then dancing for a boy just wasn't that cool somehow. If you danced, then you weren't really the cool kid].[58] In other words, an engagement in dance in West Germany did not re-enforce a statement of power or of masculinity, as it had done on the streets of the Bronx. This is because social dancing was not cultivated as a national tradition in which the art of b-boying could embed itself as a contemporary continuation. Rather, b-boying in West Germany became situated in another existing national narrative, namely gymnastics. Gymnastics, or *Turnen*, has formed a longstanding, popular German sports tradition since its institutionalization as a discipline by *Turnvater* Friedrich Ludwig Jahn in the early nineteenth century and has remained present in German schools' physical education classes and hence in everyday life up to this day.[59] Therefore, boys in West Germany seem to have made sense of the foreign kinaesthetic of b-boying by interpreting it as a form of *Turnen*. This does mean that this happened intentionally, but since most of the b-boys would have been exposed to gymnastics rather than to a culture of public participatory dance they only had gymnastics as a starting point for making sense of the movements comprising b-boying.

Nevertheless, despite engaging in a gymnastics-framed approach to this new dance form, German b-boys also expanded its *vocabulary*. This not only contributed to the development of new movements but also provided *vocabulary* with a German identity, for 'the power to name a dance movement represents a claim of authorship'[60] – be it personal or national authorship. Thus, an invented extension of the downrock move 'six-step' became the 'Brezel'. During the execution of the six-step the dancer takes six alternating steps around the axis of his body whilst remaining in a crouched position. Both hands are used for ground support in order to stabilize the upper body while the legs fulfil the movement. Hamburg hip-hop dancer Can explains that in performing a *Brezel*, 'man [...] das Gefühl [hat], dass man mit seinen

57 Jango, interviewed by author, 8 June 2012.

58 Jango, interviewed by author, 8 June 2012.

59 Gerald R. Gems and Gertrud Pfister, 'Germans, German *Turnen* and *Turner* Clubs as "Cradles of Ethnicity"', in Gerald R. Gems and Gertrud Pfister, *Understanding American Sports* (London: Routledge, 2009), pp. 69–73.

60 Schloss, *Foundation*, p. 76.

eigenen Füßen quasi die Brezel schlägt' [you have the feeling that you were turning a pretzel with your own feet].[61] While demonstrating the basic six-step, Can further explains:

> Storm hat sich dann gedacht: 'Okay, es gibt noch andere Wege'. [*Turns while doing the six-step*]. Und das war jetzt die erste Brezel zum Beispiel. [...] Nachher geht es dann noch weiter und dann hier noch rüber und dann drehen und das ist unglaublich. Und das ist alles choreographiert. Also es ist ganz klar: Es gibt die dritte Brezel, es gibt die fünfte Brezel.[62]
>
> [Storm then thought: 'Okay, there are still other ways'. [*Turns while doing the six-step*] That was the first pretzel, for example. [...] Then it goes on and on and you step over here and then turn and it's unbelievable. And it's all choreographed. So it's really clear: you have the third pretzel, you have the fifth pretzel.]

In other words, the step's *mode of representation* is achieved by *resembling* the abstract and contoured pretzel shape. Its *style* locates it in a hip-hop realm with the *vocabulary* further narrowing down its place of origin as German, with pretzels having been representative of German baking traditions both in and outside the country.[63] Expanding on German-derived hip-hop dance *vocabulary*, another example of a step is given by Hamburg popping dancer Azad. He explains that there exists:

> eine Bewegung, da macht man so, als ob man gerade das Auto anmachen würde. Und dabei gibt man so eine Bewegung von sich, dass es grad rütteln würde. Man nimmt ein Bein nach dem anderen nach oben. Das sieht immer ganz komisch aus, aber der Schritt kam aus Deutschland.[64]
>
> [a movement in which you, like, pretend to be starting the car. And then you do a move as if it was shaking. You take one leg up after the other. It always looks kind of funny but that step came from Germany.]

The movement Azad describes thus *replicates* the exaggerated and hence comical bodily performance of getting into a car. Incidentally, this German

61 Can, interviewed by author, 21 May 2012.

62 Can, interviewed by author, 21 May 2012. Storm has been Germany's most famous and successful b-boy, both nationally and internationally, since his involvement in b-boying in 1982.

63 While historical debates locate the origin of the pretzel in Italian, French and German monasteries, by the Middle Ages the pretzel had become a traditional Easter meal in Southern Germany and was subsequently exported to the United States by German immigrants in the seventeenth century (John Ayto, 'Pretzel', *The Diner's Dictionary: Word Origins of Food and Drink*, 2nd edn (Oxford University Press, 2012), http://www.oxfordreference.com [accessed 2 September 2013].

64 Azad, interviewed by author, 24 May 2012.

dance step has been termed the 'VW', re-signifiying yet another German cultural product in order to refer to its place of origin, with 'VW' moreover becoming metonymic for 'das Auto'. Just as these two examples demonstrate the cultural re-appropriation of German cultural symbols as new signs of hip-hop dance moves, they also show that they rely heavily on stereotypical items that characterize Germanness.[65] This perspective on self-stereotyping can further be applied to the 'straight German power' style, namely as an embodiment of the straight directness and skilled efficiency which continue to be attributed to the German national stereotype.[66] Taking these observations on b-boying's cultural adaptation into account, it could be concluded that the *Modetanz* has become something 'deutsch' after all.

However, despite these strategies of cultural appropriation, 'straight German power' was not necessarily understood as a positive adaptation and development of b-boying. Rather, it contradicted b-boying as a *dance* which was adorned with acrobatic elements by focussing solely on the latter aspect. The clean execution of the power moves further led the dancers to appear similar to each other and lacking 'so dieses gewisse Eigene' [a certain individuality].[67] Hence, German b-boys did not follow the b-boying norm and priority of 'defining one's identity through a superior dance style'.[68] The consequence of not having cultivated its dance element is made clear by Azad, who had never been:

> interessiert am Break Dance, weil ich fand es halt schön, was die da gemacht haben, aber ich habe da keine Ästhetik rausgesehen am Anfang. Weil ich habe immer nur Powermover gesehen. Ich habe nur Leute gesehen, die natürlich diese Riesenstunts gemacht haben. Ich habe nie das Tänzerische gesehen.[69]
>
> [interested in break dance because I thought it was nice what they were doing but in the beginning I never detected an aesthetic. Because I only always saw these power movers. I only saw people who were of course doing these massive stunts. I never saw the dance side of it.]

65 Similarly, a German scratch invented by world champion DJ Rafik from Dusseldorf was coined the 'Autobahn' scratch (Mirko Machine, interviewed by author, 10 May 2012).

66 In 2013, BBC 2 launched the programme 'Make me a German' which aimed at understanding German society's successful and supposedly efficient lifestyle. A critical review of this programme can be found at Emma Wallis, '"Make Me a German" | Europe | DW.DE | 08.08.2013', *DW.DE*, 8 August 2013, http://www.dw.de/make-me-a-german/a-17007958 [accessed 9 June 2014].

67 Jango, interviewed by author, 8 June 2012.

68 Schloss, *Foundation*, p. 66.

69 Azad, interviewed by author, 24 May 2012.

A reason for this is, according to Jango, because 'wenig deutsche B-Boys [...] sich für die anderen Tanzarten so [interessieren]. Dass sie mal ein bisschen ihren Horizont erweitern und gucken: "Okay, was kann man ein bisschen einfließen in seinen Tanz, um ein bisschen was zu verändern?"' [few German b-boys are interested in other dance forms. That they expand their horizons and see: 'Okay, what could I incorporate into my dance in order to change it up a bit?'].[70] A further reason can even be compared to DJ Ben Kenobi's refusal to play German hip-hop music since, according to him, the beats were not suitable for dancing. Indeed, Jango elaborates that 'in Deutschland [...] es teilweise immer noch sehr schwer [ist], dass die Leute wirklich so dieses Feeling zu der Musik haben' [in Germany it is still in part very difficult for people really to have this feeling for the music].[71] This observation also links to Samy Deluxe's statement which emphasized that there existed no cultural tradition which allowed German youth to experience German music as a meaningful marker of national identity. Hence, the struggle to *feel* music – a feature which was, furthermore, irrelevant in men's gymnastic routines – becomes a plausible consequence of the distorted historical relationship to music and disinterest in dance, especially compared to the Bronx's b-boys who felt and learned about their cultural heritage by specifically moving to the songs played by the DJs.

If the general consensus about dancing was therefore marked by disinterest and even by a dis-identification with this form of self-expression, the question remains of how b-boying could develop as a form of dance and at the same time as a German cultural practice. While DJs employed the techniques of turntabling and sampling which enabled them to re-discover German popular music and to situate themselves in a German historical narrative, how have b-boys 'Germanized' hip-hop dance without the opportunity to perform it as a present continuation of a national tradition that never really existed? The answers to these questions will be provided in the following section by looking at Hamburg hip-hop dancers such as Jango, whose 'Ding [...] immer schon ein bisschen mehr zu tanzen [war]. Bisschen mehr dieses Feeling, was eigentlich auch B-boying ausmacht so. [...] Allgemein dieses, dass B-boying auch Tanzen ist, wo man auf die Musik hören muss' [thing was always to dance a bit more. [To hone] a bit more of the feeling which constitutes b-boying. [...] In general, that b-boying is also a dance where you need to listen to the music].[72]

70 Jango, interviewed by author, 8 June 2012.
71 Jango, interviewed by author, 8 June 2012.
72 Jango, interviewed by author, 8 June 2012.

Hamburg and the German Identity of Hip-Hop Dance

> Wenn ich heute nach Hamburg gucke, sehe ich schon, dass Sonny mit dem, was er gemacht hat, sehr viel geprägt hat. Wir haben sehr viele Tänzer, die hier so ihren *eigenen* Charakter haben. So ihr eigenes Ding machen auf ihrer Art und Weise. Weil ich kenne andere Städte, da weißt du: 'Okay, der kommt aus Berlin, der kommt von da!'.[73]
>
> [When I look at Hamburg now, then I do see that Sonny shaped a lot with what he did. We have a lot of dancers who have their *own* character. Who do their own thing their own way. Because I know other cities where, you know: 'Okay, he is from Berlin, he is from there!'.]

Jango describes Hamburg's hip-hop dance community as a heterogeneous accumulation of characters and dance styles. However, he does so without mentioning Hamburg's 'secondspace' ideology, which had been the central focus for the identity and sound of its hip-hop musicians. Rather, Jango attributes the state of diversity to the city's first competitive b-boy, SonnyTee, who, in a way, can be seen as the personification of Hamburg's 'secondspace' since he grew up in St. Pauli as the son of a Javanese mariner and a Dutch mother.

Before hip-hop reached Hamburg, SonnyTee was first trained in kung fu. He remembers that 'dann [...] Breakdance [kommt] und natürlich [...] genau [passt], das perfekte Ding' [then came breakdance and of course it fitted exactly, the perfect thing].[74] SonnyTee thus concludes that he taught himself how to b-boy, 'eigentlich mit dem Know-How von Kung-Fu' [actually with the know-how from kung fu].[75] The pre-existing link between hip-hop dance and martial arts therefore parallels b-boying's original function in the Bronx, despite the media's supposed distortion of hip-hop culture's original meaning. By engaging in b-boying without perceiving it as aesthetically similar to German gymnastics, SonnyTee's personal knowledge and experience, as well as his status as world champion, have led him to be the local teacher and adviser for Hamburg's hip-hop dance community. This is a role common in b-boy culture, for Schloss explains that just as in 'Kung Fu, the b-boy

73 Jango, interviewed by author, 8 June 2012.

74 SonnyTee, interviewed by author, 29 August 2012.

75 SonnyTee, interviewed by author, 29 August 2012. The application of martial arts knowledge to b-boying was especially relevant for SonnyTee's battle tactics, since he explains that 'mein Trainer [...] immer gesagt [hat] früher: "Wenn du kämpfst, dann solltest du die anderen vorher nicht zeigen, was du machen willst. Die Moves. Und überraschen!". Und beim Tanzen ist [es] nix anderes' [my coach [...] always used to say: 'When you fight, then you should not show the others what you want to do. The Moves. And surprise!'. And it is the same when you dance] (SonnyTee, interviewed by author, 29 August 2012).

educational system not only offers a traceable educational lineage, but often a strong, accomplished mentor'.[76] Looking back at his local influence, SonnyTee explains:

> [W]arum ich auch auf Hamburg stolz bin ist, [...] dass jeder sich an seine[n] eigenen Style festgehalten [hat]. Und das ist, was ich erreicht habe aus den Hamburgern. So. Und das wollte ich schon immer, weil früher, als ich noch hier getanzt habe in Hamburg, habe ich anders getanzt und alle anderen tanzten, wie die Szene überall [in Deutschland].[77]

> [Why I am proud of Hamburg is [...] because everyone held onto their own style. And that is what I've achieved with the Hamburg crowd. So. And that is what I always wanted because in the past, when I still used to dance in Hamburg, I danced differently from everyone else, from the entire scene [in Germany].]

Reflecting upon the contemporary German b-boy scene, SonnyTee still claims that hip-hop dancers 'keinen nächsten Schritt zu machen [wagen]! Auch mit den Moves nicht! Das, was jemand schon mal gemacht hat, das machen die auch' [don't dare to take the next step! Not with moves either! What has been done before is what they keep on doing].[78] According to the local b-boy, the reason for this lack of courage is that 'wenn man was Eigenes macht, ist es immer fremd. Und alles, was fremd ist, muss man erst mal dran gewöhnt sein und dann heißt es immer: "Ihh, was ist das denn? Was machst du da? Ist das noch Breakdance? Oder nicht?" [whenever you do something individual it will always be something foreign. And you have to get used to everything foreign and then you hear: 'Eww, what's that? What are you doing? Is that still breakdancing? Or not?'].[79] SonnyTee's observation resonates with DJ Placeebo's claim that German DJs and music producers are not as open towards change as their French or British counterparts.

SonnyTee's success in developing and maintaining local diversity within hip-hop dance has also been facilitated by Hamburg's metropolitan cityspace, which offers many training and performance opportunities for its practitioners. Thus, urban 'firstspaces' remain relevant for the practice of b-boying, especially as spatial signifiers of hip-hop authenticity such as dancing on the raw surface material of the asphalt. However, these spaces also spur on territorial competition. An example of this delicate spatial discourse is presented by Jango, who remembers that in one account other local b-boys from Hamburg:

76 Schloss, *Foundation*, p. 52.

77 SonnyTee, interviewed by author, 29 August 2012.

78 SonnyTee, interviewed by author, 29 August 2012.

79 SonnyTee, interviewed by author, 29 August 2012.

> auf unsere Plätze [kamen] und meinten: 'Ey, könnt ihr bitte weggehen!'. So. So fing das an. Und jetzt immer mehr, immer mehr. [...] Weil, zum Beispiel, wir auch manchmal in die Europa-Passage kommen und dann sind die Jüngeren da. [...] [I]ch muss da mit denen diskutieren, dass wir jetzt kommen und sagen: 'Wir würden jetzt gern eine Streetshow machen'. 'Nee!' Ich mein, okay, uns gehört der Platz nicht und so. Aber die wissen überhaupt gar nicht, warum die das überhaupt machen.[80]

> [came to our spaces and said: 'Hey, could you please leave!'. Like. That's how it started. And now more and more, more and more. [...] Because, for example, we also go to the Europa Passage sometimes and then the younger ones are there. [...] [I] have to discuss with them that we have now arrived and say: 'We would like to do a street show'. 'No!' I mean, okay, we don't own the space and all that. But they don't even know why they are even doing it.]

While spatial territory remains equally important for contemporary German b-boys, it is not battled out in physical terms, such as used to be the case in the Bronx, but is instead negotiated through hip-hop knowledge. The issue is, therefore, based on adhering to a faithful engagement with the art form. This faithfulness is defined through performing on a cemented 'front' in a public environment as well as a thorough understanding of b-boying's norms. In this case, Jango touches upon the lack of respect by 'die Jüngeren' towards the elders of the art form.[81]

However, by conforming to this spatial priority, the adherence to the art form's norms and practices also keeps the hip-hop dancers local, since they are tied to the physical space. This contrasts with the global perspective of Hamburg adopted by the local DJs and music producers. While the city's 'secondspace' image served to support the mixing of musical knowledge and sounds into an innovative German hip-hop genre, the metaphorical spatiality of Hamburg does not carry the same significance in dance. Rather, Jango states that:

> Hamburg hat auf jeden Fall dieses typische Großstadtproblem, dass es viele Tänzer gibt, aber wenig Leute, die rauskommen, weil sie hier alles haben: Die haben hier Trainingsräume, die haben ihre Battles, die sie hier machen können. Sie können hier ihre Straßenshows machen.[82]

> [Hamburg definitely has this typical big city problem that you have many dancers but few people who get out because they have everything here: they

80 Jango, interviewed by author, 8 June 2012.
81 Klein and Friedrich, *Is this real?*, p. 41.
82 Jango, interviewed by author, 8 June 2012.

> have their training facilities, they have their battles that they can do here. They can do their street shows here.]

Hamburg's cityspace therefore becomes an arbitrary sign about its advancement and inhibition of hip-hop's art forms.

One of the few people who do go out of the cityspace is local popping dancer Azad. He leaves the northern German city in order to practise with his crew 'Baba Zula' in Berlin. The group includes the most skilled popping dancers in Germany and it is with them that Azad also represents Germany at international battles. However, despite their being national representatives, the crew's name does not reveal a German connection linguistically. Rather, it serves to portray the dancers' skills and the group's qualities by comparing these to the musical characteristics of the eponymous Turkish band Baba Zula. According to Azad, this music group plays:

> abstrakte Musik. Und die [Popping] Gruppe bestand eigentlich mehr nur aus Leuten, die aus dem Nahen Osten kamen. Das heißt, wir haben einen Türken, einen Kurden, einen Iraner, einen Araber. Ist halt ganz lustig. War halt eigentlich nie, dass wir das so geplant hatten, aber irgendwie hat es sich so zusammengeschlossen und [wir] dachten, wir nehmen uns auch einen orientalischen Namen, der uns auch irgendwo wiedergibt, weil wir sind auch irgendwo sehr abstrakt mit dem, was wir machen. In unserem Poppingstil. Und gleichzeitig ist es aber auch sehr orientalisch. So ein Touch. Und deswegen haben wir gesagt, das ist der Name: Baba Zula.[83]

> [abstract music. And the [popping] group only really consisted more of people who were from the Middle East. That means we have a Turk, a Kurd, an Iranian, an Arab. It's actually pretty funny. It was never really that we planned that but somehow it came together like that and [we] thought we should give ourselves an Oriental name that reflects us somehow, because we are also very abstract with what we do. Our popping style. And at the same it is also very Oriental. Like a touch. And that's why we said that's the name: Baba Zula.]

Baba Zula thus consists of an amalgamation of heterogeneous histories that collectively represent one holistic place, which in Bhabha's words becomes exemplary of the 'pluralism of the national sign, where difference returns as the same' (*LOC*, p. 221). Together, the members of popping crew Baba Zula open up a hybrid cultural space that situates Germany in a Middle Eastern cultural discourse. While signifying a united Orientalism, the dancers, however, do not see themselves as an 'other' juxtaposed to a German cultural sphere but treat their Oriental discourse as an enhancement of their dance genre. It provides them with diversity and uniqueness expressed as abstract dance styles. At the

83 Azad, interviewed by author, 24 May 2012.

same time, this intervention of cultural difference creates a common sense of belonging, held together through the crew's understanding and faithful practice of popping. In so doing, the union of Turkish, Kurdish, Arab and Iranian heritages under their shared German umbrella treats the Middle East as an imagined, holistic 'secondspace'. From a historical perspective, then, the 'third space' created by the popping crew Baba Zula destabilizes national boundaries and displaces Germany's historical present through their performances as culturally hybrid German dancers, even though the crew's heterogeneous cultural backgrounds were not an intended circumstance.

While Azad's participation in Baba Zula thus exemplifies the way in which dancers compete with dance crews outside their hometown, other hip-hop dancers in Hamburg rather accentuate their local connection. Indeed, despite hip-hop dance's spatial contrast to hip-hop music's urban identity, it does not eliminate hip-hop dancers' pride in and affiliation with Hamburg. Hip-hop dance crew 'Nordish by Nature' (NbN), for example, emphasize the importance of showing, 'dass Hamburg da ist. Das wollen wir auch machen so. Das ist unser Ziel, dass wir einfach auch zeigen, Hamburg ist da!' [that Hamburg is present. We want to do it like that. That is our aim, just to show that Hamburg is there!].[84] In this case Hamburg is represented as an imagined cityspace which is part of a wider 'Nordic' community. With Hamburg located in the northern region of Germany, and with its sea port having nurtured cultural exchange between other cities located on the coasts of Northern Europe, the dance crew's name refers to a geographic as well as cultural community of transnational 'Nordicness'. While appropriated as a name that captures the location where the paths of NbN's members crossed,[85] it also explicitly links them to Hamburg's hip-hop community, since the name originally referred to the title of a nationally successful hip-hop track by local rappers 'Fettes Brot' which will be elaborated on in the following chapter.

Although they are joined beneath the banner of Nordicness, member Can nevertheless states that, within the crew, every individual dancer is '*unique*. Man hat seine Persönlichkeit und man hat seine Skills' [*unique*. Everyone has his own personality and his own skills].[86] He exemplifies this by stating: '[I]ch habe einen ganz anderen Tanzstil als Franklyn oder Franklyn tanzt ganz anders wiederum als Andy' [I have a completely different dance style from Franklyn or Franklyn dances differently from Andy].[87] What is silenced in Can's emphasis on the dance crew's contrasting signs of uniqueness are the

84 Can, interviewed by author, 21 May 2012.
85 This statement comes from the dance crew's own explanation of the origin of their name.
86 Can, interviewed by author, 21 May 2012.
87 Can, interviewed by author, 21 May 2012.

various ethnic backgrounds of the dancers.[88] Hence, the phenotypical features that comprise NbN could also signify uniqueness in terms of the multiple cultures and ethnicities comprising its unity, for '[s]kin, as the key signifier of cultural and racial difference in the stereotype, is the most visible of fetishes, recognized as "common knowledge" in a range of cultural, political and historical discourses' (*LOC*, p. 112). Nonetheless, by representing a German city NbN challenge the visible stereotype of the supposedly 'natural' Northern German by deeming it irrelevant to determining a dancer's belonging. The physical attributes which are commonly identified as pertaining to a minority discourse do not come to signify a separation from the dominant German national narrative. Rather, through their slogan 'Stay Nordish! Stay Nature!', in which the natural, biological bodies and appearance become inclusive of a culturally constructed Nordic identity, NbN recognize that 'the split-space of enunciation may open the way to conceptualising an *inter*national culture, based not on the exoticism of multiculturalism or the *diversity* of cultures, but on the inscription and articulation of culture's *hybridity*' (*LOC*, p. 56). While hybridity has indeed already been manifested in Baba Zula's approach to hip-hop dance as a German-Oriental form of expression, in the case of NbN the hybridity serves rather to claim a local German identity and therefore presents a post-hybrid state of Germanness.

Can articulates his post-hybridity through a strategy in which his Turkishness is nurtured by the Nordish locality of Hamburg, stating: '[I]ch bin hier geboren und ich sehe mich als Deutscher' [I was born here and see myself as German].[89] This becomes especially evident in his presentation of himself as a German hip-hop dancer, for while it is 'unusual for b-boys and b-girls to dance under given names' – the same holds true for hip-hop dancers of other subgenres – the dancer 'will choose a name that suggests qualities they wish to project in their dance'.[90] Can not only dances under his official Turkish name, but his name and hence the quality of his dance are directly linked to his Turkish background. Thus, the hip-hop dancer points out: '[I]ch habe da auch türkische Tänze gelernt so in meiner Familie. Ich habe auch türkische Einflüsse. Ich meine, weiß ich nicht, irgendwo her muss das ja kommen, dass ich die ganze Zeit immer so rumzappel' [I also learned Turkish dances in my family. I also have Turkish influences. I mean, I don't know but it has to come from somewhere that I am constantly fidgeting around].[91] In other words, Can's passion for hip-hop dance seems to be motivated by his cultural access

88 The ethnic backgrounds include Middle Eastern, African, East Asian and Caucasian.

89 Can, interviewed by author, 21 May 2012.

90 Schloss, *Foundation*, p. 70.

91 Can, interviewed by author, 21 May 2012.

as provided by the 'other', namely his Turkishness, which embraces dance as a social form of expression with which he represents his local Hamburg identity.

This strategy of 'stigma' management is also adapted by Azad, who points out that, despite competing with Baba Zula, 'ich von erster Linie heraus so [sage]: "Ja, ich bin aus Hamburg." Und dann, wenn ich international vertrete, sage ich halt: "Ich bin aus Deutschland"' [I chiefly say: 'Yes, I am from Hamburg'. And then when I represent internationally I just say: 'I am from Germany'].[92] Like Can, Azad dances under his given Kurdish name, even though his official name is of Turkish origin.[93] Furthermore, although he had lived in Germany since the age of three, Azad's access to dance was similarly primed by his Kurdish heritage rather than by a German cultural context. The dancer explains:

> [M]eine Kultur, in der ich aufgewachsen bin, ist halt kurdisch. Kurdisch-deutsch. Und zum Beispiel bei Hochzeiten habe ich immer meinen Vater gesehen [...]. Man tanzt ja im Kreis, aber an den Händen. Also man kann das auch als *Halay* sehen. Und immer die ersten drei Tänzer vorne sind immer voll ausgerastet. Sie waren halt immer noch in diesem Schema, in dieser Bewegung, aber haben gegroovt. Das heißt, die waren immer voll locker, haben immer die Schulter mit dem ganzen Kopf und das war schon fast Trance-mäßig. Aber sie waren immer noch in der Musik und man hat das voll gespürt. Und dann habe ich schon als Kind meinem Dad wirklich zugesehen, wie er nach dem Tanz mit so einem glücklichen Gefühl, mit so einem Gefühl von Freiheit wiedergekommen ist, dass ich mir nur gedacht habe: 'Wow! Krass'. Also war ich schon immer damit irgendwo berührt.[94]

> [my culture in which I grew up is Kurdish. Kurdish-German. And, for example, I always saw my father at weddings. [...] You dance in a circle but hold hands. You could also describe it as a *halay.* And the first three dancers always went mental in the front. They were always in the same pattern, in this movement, but were grooving. This means they were always very loose and always moved their shoulders and entire head and it was almost trance-like. But they were still in the music and you could totally feel it. And then as a child I watched how happy my dad was when he came back from dancing, he had such a feeling of freedom that I just thought: 'Wow! Amazing'. So I was always somehow in touch with that.]

92 Azad, interviewed by author, 24 May 2012.

93 Azad was born in Syria. The Kurdish name 'Azad', chosen by his parents, was not permitted by Syrian officials, who forced Azad's parents to choose another name, one which reflects his mother's Turkish nationality (Azad, interviewed by author, 24 May 2012).

94 Azad, interviewed by author, 24 May 2012. A *Halay* is a festive traditional Turkish folk dance generally performed by men who hold on to each other's shoulders or hands in order to form a circle.

By experiencing the Kurdish culture practised in Germany, Azad has gained a feeling for music and an interest in dance which Jango had previously deemed lacking in most German b-boys. Moreover, this cultural experience fills the gap highlighted by Samy Deluxe, namely, that German youth were unable to experience and hence to identify with German music, which in the case of Azad and Can was substituted for by their access to their 'other' culture. In this context, Azad's personal experience of observing his father relates dancing to the feeling of happiness and, more importantly, to freedom. Incidentally, it is this attribute that is re-enforced through Azad's name, which means 'free' in Kurdish.

According to Azad '[war] Tanzen für sich selbst [...] schon immer mit dem Gefühl von Freiheit gebunden, weil, wenn du dich irgendwann nicht mehr frei fühlst beim Tanzen, dann ist es kein Tanz mehr' [Dancing for yourself has always been connected to the feeling of freedom because if you at one point no longer feel free when you dance then it's not dance anymore].[95] In hip-hop's dance genres, this freedom is created by the improvised practices of the dance and the ability to infuse *style, vocabulary* and *syntax* with an individual approach. Can contrasts this artistic freedom to the rigid framework of ballet, explaining that hip-hop dance is:

> freier als Ballet. Als ich in der Ballet Class stand, war es mir anfangs sehr unangenehm. Ich stand da und musste quasi irgendwie *pas-de-bourré, tendu* und sowas alles machen, und *piqué.* Und dafür gibt es so viele Begriffe, die man lernt und man kann sie alle tanzen! Das ist unglaublich! Also [mein Lehrer] hätte mir eine Vokabelliste geben können. Vier Seiten. Und ich hätte sie erst mal lernen müssen, ne? Und im Hip-Hop gibt es zwar auch gewisse Basics, die man auch nennen kann. Aber allein da fängt es schon an: Jeder tanzt diese Basics anders einfach, weil man sich im Hip-Hop freier fühlen darf, freier fühlen kann. Und gerade *das* macht den Tanz aus, dass er so frei ist. Dass jeder in den Tanz oder in die Musik etwas rein interpretiert und sich einfach darauf bewegt und dadurch entsteht einfach so unterschiedliches Material von Menschen. Das ist unglaublich. [*Pauses*] Freiheit. Ja. Ganz viel Freiheit.[96]
>
> [freer than ballet. When I stood in ballet class I felt very uncomfortable in the beginning. I just stood there and somehow had to do *pas-de-bourré, tendu* and *piqué* and stuff like that. And there are so many terms that you have to learn and you can dance them all! It's unbelievable! [My teacher] could have given me a vocabulary list. Four pages. And I would have had to learn it first,

95 Azad, interviewed by author, 24 May 2012.

96 Can, interviewed by author, 21 May 2012. *Pas-de-bourré, tendu* and *piqué* refer to specific dance steps in ballet which have also been adapted into jazz dance and hip-hop dance. While Can took ballet classes in order to broaden his knowledge of different dance styles, he now employs *pas-de-bourrés*, for example, in his hip-hop choreography.

> right? And yes, you also have certain basics in hip-hop that you can name. But it already starts right there: everybody dances the basics differently simply because you are allowed to feel freer in hip-hop, you can feel freer. And it is precisely *that* which makes up the dance, that it's so free. Everybody can interpret something into the dance or the music and move to it and that is how so much different material is created by people. It is unbelievable. [*Pauses*] Freedom. Yes. A whole lot of freedom.]

Thus, Can and Azad welcome hip-hop dance's open orality as opposed to ballet's fixed literacy. However, this open, free approach towards hip-hop dance also leads to the question of whether the creation of a specifically German hip-hop dance style is even achievable. While 'straight German power' was deemed an unfaithful approach to hip-hop dance, its rigid, clean execution, which made all dancers look similar, nevertheless identified the style as German. By altering this engagement in hip-hop dance the linear cultural historicality is distorted, since 'foreign' cultural inputs are applied to present a contemporary dance tradition pertaining to Germany. In other words, with hip-hop dance becoming treated as a free and democratic form of *dance*, this particular approach to the art form has been mobilized by a pluralism of forces beyond the German cultural realm which, in the end, seem to leave the kinaesthetic of German hip-hop dance identity-less.

A new strategy through which to provide German b-boying with a German identity was, therefore, to dance to a nationally identifying song. The song 'Ich liebe deutsche Land (De Det De Det De Dä)' (2001) by Verna Mae Bentley-Krause, for example, reached considerable popularity throughout the country after being promoted by the German comedian and television host Stefan Raab. A snippet from this German hit was in turn utilized in choreography by Hamburg's b-boy crew Muppets in 2004. They performed their dance at the national 'Battle of the Year' competition and Jango recalls that his brother Chris Rock:

> auf einer Hand gehüpft [hat] und da war dieses *Ich liebe deutsche Land* von Stefan Raab. *Ich liieebe deutsche Land.* [*Sings*] Und auf diesem Lied hat er halt so einen Sprungpart gemacht. Es war halt witzig, aber auch irgendwie voll krass, weil er [das] auf das Lied gemacht hat und das war halt so innerhalb von einem halben Jahr kannte es irgendwie ganz Deutschland mit dieser Show.[97]

> [jumped on one hand and there was this song *Ich liebe deutsche Land* by Stefan Raab. *Ich liieebe deutsche Land.* [*Sings*] And to that song he did this jumping part. It was funny but also completely crazy because he did [it] to the song and within half a year somehow the whole of Germany knew it with this show.]

97 Jango, interviewed by author 8 June 2012.

While 'Ich liebe deutsche Land (De Det De Det De Dä)' is indeed sung in German, the impact it had as a b-boy performance becomes more complex than the basing of its resonance on its previous commercial success. The first issue that arises in this context is the fact that Bentley-Krause is not herself German but became a German resident after having been stationed in West Germany with the US army in the 1980s.[98] Her foreignness was, moreover, immediately tied to the song as it was recorded as a home video, displaying Bentley-Krause's ethnicity as African-American. By presenting herself as the member of a German minority, the singer nevertheless praises, albeit in grammatically broken German, the positive attributes that she associates with Germany. Furthermore, Bentley-Krause's initial misspelling of the nation's name as 'deutsche Land' instead of 'Deutschland' remained the title of the song, for according to the singer it 'gave people something to laugh at, which made it an even bigger hit'.[99] In other words, the popularity of this German track is evidently influenced by racial parody, framing the black American singer as an exotic subject within a German cultural realm.

B-boy Chris Rock is half-Cameroonian and hence visibly defined as black, which inevitably makes his kinaesthetic interpretation of this song more compelling. Through the black embodiment of Bentley-Krause's song, the German b-boy engages in the continuation of a minoritized national narrative of Germany, and one particularly pertaining to the Afro-German experience. However, in both cases the performance of the song as well as its kinaesthetic interpretation claim a national affiliation which echoes Bhabha's observation that '"national" cultures are being produced from the perspective of disenfranchised minorities' (*LOC*, p. 8). It is thus intriguing to consider whether this statement of national affiliation would have succeeded if the singer of the same song and even the b-boy had been of 'white' German ethnicity. Perhaps it is only possible to express and even to normalize positive national feelings towards Germany through the use of a familiar shared language with a foreign tribal 'attribute'.

Shifting the focus to a different example of musical accompaniment as a strategy for national identification, it should also be mentioned that in 2010 the culturally heterogeneous, Berlin-based b-boy crew Flying Steps interpreted German classical composer Johann Sebastian Bach's music in their show 'Flying Bach'. While this example touches upon the employment of instrumental music, it is also another attempt to give hip-hop dance a national

98 Steve Mraz, 'European Spotlight: Verna Mae Bentley-Krause', *Stars and Stripes*, 14 July 2008, http://www.stripes.com/news/european-spotlight-verna-mae-bentley-krause1.80960 [accessed 3 September 2014].

99 Bentley-Krause, quoted in Mraz, 'European Spotlight'.

identity with the aid of German musical history and, in this case, through a social discourse of 'high culture' due to the choice of classical music. Moreover, by creating a b-boy show performed at indoor venues, Flying Bach not only elevates b-boying in a social context but in a spatial one as well, namely from the 'firstspace' of the streets onto the stage. This spatial aspect is particularly emphasized by Azad, who addresses hip-hop dance's social 'stigma' by stating that 'man [...] vor Balletttänzern so einen krassen Respekt [hat]! "Das ist der, der hat mit keiner Ahnung zusammengearbeitet und der ist halt in dieser Kompanie oder dies oder das." Und dann sagt man so: "Ja, man ist ein Hip-Hop Tänzer und man tanzt auf der Straße." [*Laughs*] Das war's' [ballet dancers get such enormous respect! 'That's so and so who works with I don't know who and is in that company and this and that.' And then you say: 'Yeah, I am a hip hop dancer and I dance on the streets'. [*Laughs*] That was it].[100]

With classical European dance performances such as ballet being traditionally performed in theatres where the audience engages in 'polite *viewing*', hip-hop dance's traditional *frame* of the streets within a participatory cypher evidently challenges the established performance norms familiar to a German audience. The consequence of this spatial discrepancy has already been lamented by Storm, who writes: '[S]o wie ich früher von Hip Hop-Jams träumte, auf denen es hunderte von Tänzern gab, so träume ich jetzt davon, daß [*sic*] unsere Tanzformen einmal genauso selbstverständlich in Theatern performt werden, wie die institutionalisierten Tanzkünste' [In the same way as I used to dream of hip-hop jams at which there were hundreds of dancers, so now do I dream that it will be just as normal for our dance form to be performed in theatres as it is for the institutionalized dance forms].[101] This statement can be compared to Das DJ Orchester's class discourse in terms of expressing social status through the appropriation of certain spaces and of certain codes of fashion. In order to counteract this same 'stigma' of hip-hop dance, Storm thus proposes to perform b-boying in spaces that are familiar to and respected by a German audience and which elevate the art form's social status.

However, conversely, the theatre stage remains a foreign *frame* for hip-hop dance. While SonnyTee has performed in 'Schmidt's Tivoli, Schmidt Theater, hier in Hamburg. Jeden Abend, jeden Tag. Oder beim Hansa-Theater' [Schmidt's Tivoli, Schmidt Theater, here in Hamburg. Every evening, every day. Or at the Hansa-Theater],[102] the b-boy concludes: '[D]a geht man auch kaputt. Da ist dieses *Feeling* nicht mehr da' [[I]t breaks you. The

100 Azad, interviewed by author, 24 May 2012.
101 Robitzky, *Von Swipe zu Storm*, p. 121.
102 SonnyTee, interviewed by author, 29 August 2012.

feeling vanishes].[103] Hence, while hip-hop dance may be better understood as pertaining to contemporary German culture through its performance to German-derived music and/or on elevated, indoor stages, such a change in 'firstspace' simultaneously distorts b-boying's norms and practices by losing its values and priorities. Unless the aim is indeed to fashion a hybrid spectacle which fuses hip-hop with German culture in order to create a completely new visual and aural experience such as 'Flying Bach', discerning the German identity of hip-hop dance may have to result in changing the perspective of what 'Politiker und Kulturleute' [politicians and people in the cultural scene] understand contemporary German culture to be, as previously criticized by Storm. The following close reading will exemplify this approach by looking at the spatial appropriations, social statements and historical awareness of Hamburg hip-hop dancers who bridge the original practice of b-boying with their contemporary representation of Germanness in a street show in Hamburg's city centre.

The *frame* of this street show is, first of all, a cinematic one, for the close reading is based on a camera recording of a performance by a conglomeration of local b-boys on 24 March 2012.[104] The performance took place at a 'firstspace' located in a public square between the Europa Passage and Karstadt in the Mönckebergstraße. Within this public 'firstspace' the stage or 'front' of the show is created by a cypher formed by passers-by and of which the camera's point of view forms part. The filming begins when a young man of East-Asian appearance, whose 'personal front' is defined by a white T-shirt, blue jeans and trainers, approaches the centre of the cypher. He announces the upcoming show in standard German (0:03). Behind him, the shot reveals the adjacent spectators of the cypher, as well as other young men standing within the circle. They are united by a similar choice of fashion, yet visibly include different ethnicities, such as Caucasian, African and Middle Eastern.

Following the welcoming address, Jango walks through the frame of the camera as he circles the audience shouting: 'Ich brauche alle Hände hier! Ein bisschen Stimmung, meine Freunde!' (0:08) [I need all hands here! Give us some cheering, my friends!]. At the same time, he briefly stops in front of the lens (0:10). During this moment the white letters on his black T-shirt become readable as 'Jango P.Nd Jackson'. His full artist name thus further consists of his initials P. Nd[105] and of a tribute to Michael Jackson, who was 'so die größte Inspiration. Ich glaube mit vier Jahren, fünf Jahren, hab' ich den so gesehen.

103 SonnyTee, interviewed by author, 29 August 2012.

104 '24. März 2012: Sonne', *Kanal von lizzarteos*, http://www.you-tube.com/watch?v=KdH895tVPHk [accessed 11 April 2012].

105 The letters 'Nd' form the first two consonants of Jango's Cameroonian last name.

Hab' das alles nachgemacht, was er gemacht hat' [like, the greatest inspiration. I think at age four or five I saw him. And I copied everything that he did].[106] After Jango continues walking onwards, a mash-up of the track 'Feel Good Inc' (2005) by the English trip-hop group Gorillaz is released from a ghetto-blaster off-screen. As soon as the music is heard, Jango and the remaining four dancers begin to animate the crowd by clapping to the beat.[107]

When the vocals of the song set in, the five b-boys transition from animating the crowd to performing a brief toprock sequence (0:32). This danced introduction immediately identifies the *frame* as a street show and the *style* of the dance as b-boying. Moreover, the b-boy formation can be treated as a Goffmanian 'team' similar to the DJ Orchester. From this social perspective, their dance routines can be read as a 'pre-established pattern of action which is unfolded during a performance and which may be presented and played through on other occasions' (*PSEL*, p. 16) and which, therefore, 'may be called a "part" or "routine"' (*PSEL*, p. 16). Thus, after the group choreography finishes, all dancers retreat to the back of the cypher with Jango remaining in the centre. His routine marks the first of a variety of pre-established patterns of actions performed within the human circle.

The first movement of Jango's performance begins with a quickly alternating left and right hand brushing through his hair whilst he remains otherwise immobile (0:40). As his hair has been grown into an Afro, this performative statement comments on Jango's hair as a racial signifier and as a marker of his b-boy identity, for his hair has been a defining attribute of his energy since childhood: 'Ich war als kleiner Junge schon so voll flippig und immer viel unterwegs und [mit] meine[n] Afrohaaren' [Already as a young boy I was totally way-out and out and about with my Afro].[108] Following the traditional b-boying *syntax*, Jango engages in his dance sequence with toprocks that are rapid and jagged, echoing the sound of the fast percussion beats in the song. His progression to the floor, to the raw environment of the asphalt, is initiated by a succession of rolls over his upper back with interval landings on his feet

106 Jango, interviewed by author, 8 June 2012.

107 The city of Hamburg does not officially support street shows, since, according to SonnyTee, 'Künstler [...] sich anmelden und genehmigen lassen [müssen], um da Straßenshow zu machen und das ist auch noch Gesetz, dass du nur [eine] halbe Stunde auf einem Platz verbleiben darfst' [Artists have to sign up and get official approval in order to do a street show there and it is also the law that you can only stay on one spot for half an hour]. He further emphasizes that 'mit Anlage darfst du normalerweise gar nicht. Es ist verboten in Hamburg mit einer elektronischen [Anlage] zu tanzen. [Man] darf nur mit Live-Instrumenten' [you are not normally allowed to have sound equipment. In Hamburg it is prohibited to dance with electronic equipment. You are only allowed live instruments] (SonnyTee, interviewed by author, 29 August 2012).

108 Jango, interviewed by author, 8 June 2012.

Figure 3: Jango posing on his toes

(Source: https://www.youtube.com/watch?v=KdH895tVPHk)

before he fully engages in downrocks and variations of six-steps. Shooting into an upright position, Jango lastly freezes in a pose *imitating* Michael Jackson (1:03). With a dance position frequently associated with the African-American pop star, Jango applies this choreographic *mode of representation* by rising to the tip of his toes and turning his knees inwards while looking downwards (see Figure 3).

Transitioning from his *imitation*, with which he pays personal tribute to his role model, Jango completes a full turn, landing with his legs over a hip-width apart. He then ends his routine with a final stroke through his hair, framing his Afro-Germanness as an inherent part of his presentation of self (1:04).

Following Jango's routine, local b-boy Crazy D enters the camera frame with a side flip (1:08). While he is wearing black trousers and a black t-shirt, it is his Middle Eastern phenotype that hints at his Afghan heritage. His name, however, serves to capture his energetic, aggressive and therefore 'crazy' dance style, with the letter D forming the initial of his official first name Dariusz. Returning to the centre of the cypher after his leap, Crazy D also follows the traditional b-boying *syntax* by engaging in a toprock sequence. However, midway through the routine he realizes that the crowd has ceased to clap to the beat. In order to re-animate the viewers and foster their participation in the cypher Crazy-D stops his movement and begins to clap instead (1:13). Although he succeeds in

Figure 4: Crazy D dancing salsa

(Source: https://www.youtube.com/watch?v=KdH895tVPHk)

bringing the audience to participate again, Crazy D does not, however, continue with toprocks but rather performs a brief salsa sequence (see Figure 4).

Comprising only four steps, his improvised choice of this particular *style* of dance momentarily links b-boying to its original socio-historical context of the street corner *salseros* of the Bronx. In this way Crazy D also emphasizes the nature of b-boying as a hybrid dance genre, and hence a genre in which salsa steps can be added as a viable movement within the *syntax* of b-boying. Crazy D subsequently proceeds to perform downrocks. When approaching the end of his routine, he rolls off over his shoulders before doing a mid-air 360° body turn in a horizontal position and landing flat on his back. After a brief pause, Crazy D jumps onto his feet and freezes in a handstand before giving Battle Buddha the lead to commence his routine (1:30).

Battle Buddha is the only ethnic German dancer performing in this street show as well as the only b-boy whose 'personal front' is adorned with a hat, besides his wearing a blue denim jacket over a white T-shirt and blue jeans with trainers. With an execution best described as flexible floppiness, Battle Buddha's artist's name serves to reflect his unique dance quality for he frequently knots his legs in the lotus position, *resembling* the image of Buddha. Hence, despite his ethnic German background Battle Buddha's personal *style* is not related to a clean and straight German power movement, but to Oriental religion instead.[109]

109 SonnyTee explains that Battle Buddha danced like the general German b-boy scene before the local mentor made him realize his unique strengths and creativity as a dancer (SonnyTee, interviewed by author, 29 August 2012).

Figure 5: Battle Buddha showing off his flexibility

(Source: https://www.youtube.com/watch?v=KdH895tVPHk)

Battle Buddha initiates his routine by running across the centre of the cypher with his hands held behind his back. He proceeds to reverse his steps whilst bringing his arms over his head to the front of his body without unlocking his hands (1:33). Moving directly into downrock sequences, his floor movements are filled with contortions showing off the flexibility of his back and legs (see Figure 5).

Remaining on the ground, Battle Buddha ends his performance with a ten-second-long balance on his right hand, whereby his right elbow is tucked into his rib cage in order to hold his own body weight in a horizontal position whilst he faces upwards (1:52). When he finally returns to his feet, Battle Buddha shares a final moment with the audience by clapping with them before walking to the back of the cypher, joining his fellow 'teammates'.

As these three routines provide sufficient insight into the way b-boys in Hamburg engage in hip-hop dance, the close reading of this street show concludes that a local performance of b-boying has the ability to re-evaluate contemporary visions and notions of Germanness. In terms of spatial appropriation, the b-boys adhere to the original *frame* of b-boying in which the 'front' and 'back' regions come to share the same space within the cypher. Its division is not marked by a visible material barrier, or by the appearance of the dancers, for their 'personal fronts' remain the same prior to and after the show. It is this observation which echoes hip-hop's norm of 'keeping it real' by re-presenting the same social identity, regardless of 'front' or 'back' region. Thus, the b-boys create a social 'third space' where 'front' and 'back' regions as well as their respective behaviour and appearance fuse into one for the sake of a faithful engagement in the art form. Having said this, it is the case that the dancers resort to a more distanced 'back' region for training purposes, just as the DJ Orchester practises in the *Lab*. These regions are primarily located in indoor youth centres. With training thus not happening on the streets, these public shows function primarily as a measurement for commitment and skill by employing the 'firstspace' materiality as the authentic spatial surface on which the art of b-boying must be performed.

The b-boys' performance in local public 'firstspaces' also contributes to the multicultural ideology of Hamburg's 'secondspace' by physically creating its 'thirdspace' experience through street shows which at the same time represent the pluralism of ethnicities. However, the dancers' 'making of geographies', to use Soja's term, does not reveal a specific Germanness about it, or a specific urban locality. While the *frame, style, vocabulary* and *syntax* all link to b-boying, the *modes of representation* incorporated by Jango (e.g., his *imitation* of Michael Jackson), Crazy D (*replicating* the danced relationship between salsa and b-boying as a dance) and Battle Buddha (e.g., *reflecting* a characteristic of the Buddha statue) serve rather to represent the dancers' personal life experiences, individual skills and b-boy identity instead of mirroring any stereotypically identifiable Germanness. As Battle Buddha is moreover the only ethnic German in the 'team' he can, rather, be understood as having a 'courtesy stigma' (*STGM*, p. 30) which provides 'a model of "normalization," showing how far normal could go in treating the stigmatized person as if he didn't have a stigma' (*STGM*, pp. 30–31). The cultural background of the b-boy performance would therefore presumably remain unknown to the viewer if it were not for the b-boys speaking German during their announcements.

In addressing the wider German society in their common language, the b-boys bridge the gap between their familiar verbal form of expression and their foreign bodily performance. Indeed, as Goffman notes, the 'information, as well as the sign through which it [the stigma] is conveyed, is reflexive and embodied; that is, it is conveyed by the very person in the immediate presence of those who receive the expression' (*STGM*, p. 430). In this sense, the dancers employ the strategy of emphasizing their supposed embodied difference while treating the 'receivers' of this expression as their equals, as an inclusive social category who are participating in their performance. Jango thus incorporates his African hair in his dance routine while at the same time addressing his German audience as '*meine* Freunde' [*my* friends]. His presentation of self through danced 'routines' therefore aims at presenting his German b-boy identity as a post-hybrid state of identity in which different ethnicities are inclusive of the contemporary concept of Germanness. His national patriotism is even expressed as a strong aversion to German b-boy fans who support a different nation at international b-boy battles:

> Du gehst halt zu *Battle of the Year* und auf einmal kommen die deutschen Leute mit einer Korea Fahne, wie beim Fußball. 'Korea! Korea!'. Wo ich mir denke: 'Cool, dass ihr die mögt, aber ... ist irgendwie kein Fußball so'. Es ist natürlich cool, dass sie so angefeuert werden und so, freut mich, aber, ey, da bin ich auch dann so ein bisschen patriotisch. Wo ich sage: 'Ey, wir sind doch Deutsche! Entweder wir feiern uns oder wir feiern gar keinen. So. Selbst wenn wir jemanden feiern, sind wir einfach ruhig'.[110]

> [You go to *Battle of the Year* and all of sudden German people arrive with a Korean flag, like at a football match. 'Korea! Korea!'. When I think to myself: 'It's cool that you like them but ... it's not really a football match'. It's cool, of course, that people cheer for them, it makes me happy, but then I am also a bit patriotic. When I say: 'Hey, we are Germans! Either we celebrate ourselves or we celebrate no one. And even if we celebrate someone, we just stay quiet'.]

Jango's statement shows not only that he and his 'teammates' fully accept post-hybrid identity concepts but that there is even an expectation amongst culturally hybrid German hip-hop dancers that they identify with Germany. In acknowledging that hip-hop dance creates and fosters a mono-national identification through multicultural practices, this art form allows its practitioners 'to define various aspects of their identity, develop strategies for integrating that identity into a larger social world, and then actually practice doing so'.[111] However, this integration of identity is not yet fully understood by German audiences. Rather, hip-hop dance is captured in its hybrid kinaesthetic presentation of self, which is not able to transmit this new perspective of Germanness to the common viewer. As this dance form will always look hybrid, it cannot resonate with familiarity when presented exclusively through danced movement.

Summary

Following the overview of the spatial, historical and social conditions that have created hip-hop's second element, this analysis has shown that, like DJing, b-boying in West Germany was initially practised as an imitation of

110 Jango, interviewed by author, 8 June 2012. By contrasting b-boying to football, Jango at the same time clarifies that b-boying follows different behavioural norms from those in Germany's national sport, despite its similar ability to represent and arouse national pride at sporting events.

111 Schloss, *Foundation*, p. 69.

its original. However, it soon became framed as a pseudo-continuation of an already established tradition of gymnastics and known for its 'straight German power' movement. It was suggested that this appropriation was due to the lack of previous German traditions of public participatory dance. Especially ethnic German male dancers rarely identified with a performative approach to dance, with the exception of, perhaps, ballroom dance or dancing in a darkened indoor dance club.[112]

In Hamburg, however, the majority of hip-hop dancers followed the approach of local role model SonnyTee, who rejected the nationally established style of b-boying. Hence, this analysis has highlighted the fact that Hamburg's hip-hop dance tradition is not discernable as a German art movement but as a diverse, individualistic performative art form. However, in contrast to the 'secondspace' ideology of Hamburg that influenced and authenticated a culturally diverse approach to hip-hop music, this chapter has established that spatial discourses are treated differently in hip-hop music and hip-hop dance. In dance, it is the 'firstspace' materiality of the urban surface that remains the marker of authenticity. This, in turn, makes the local hip-hop dancers seem parochial and inward-looking compared to their musical counterparts, as their spatial priorities do not support cultural exchange and mobility beyond urban borders. Nevertheless, the expression of an urban affiliation has remained important for dancers as well.

While the case studies presented in this chapter do not cover all dance crews that were active in Hamburg at the time, they do include relevant dancers whose groups have come to represent the city at a national level. Nordish by Nature, for instance, represent Hamburg as a multicultural cityspace through the amalgamation of different ethnicities within their dance crew. In so doing, NbN also allude to a post-hybrid state of identity in which multiethnicity is representative of contemporary Hamburg or even of Germany, depending on the location of the competition. Furthermore, NbN-member Can's access to other cultural dances has consciously or unconsciously mobilized him to engage in hip-hop dance. This was also the case with popping dancer Azad, whose passion to dance was primed by his Kurdish cultural and musical sensibilities. Similar observations, in which a hip-hop dancer's biography is relevant for his approach to and style of dance, are already found in the work of Arnd-Michael Nohl in an interview with Turkish b-boy Deniz from Berlin in the mid-1990s.[113] By competing with Baba Zula, Azad's abstract dance style serves, moreover, to represent a cultural hybrid space located between Germany and the Middle East which is shared with the cultural histories of his crew-members. NbN,

112 Cf. Klein and Friedrich, *Is this real?*, p. 181.
113 Nohl, 'Interkulturelle Bildungsprozesse im Breakdance', pp. 307–08.

on the other hand, rather represent a local German identity without direct ties to another, real or imagined, *Heimatland*, showing that different hip-hop dancers from Hamburg engage in different identity discourses. Nevertheless, in both cases Azad and Can emphasize the importance of experiencing music through dance – an approach that was enabled by their 'otherness' rather than their Germanness.

With these claims to representation and identity revealing the complexity of hip-hop dance as an expression of belonging, its freedom of movement has blurred its identification as German even further. The only strategy that provides hip-hop dance with a direct national identity is the employment of German music, in the form of either German lyrics or German classical compositions. An example of the former strategy presented in this chapter, however, challenged the danced message of the cultural acceptance and normalization of the Afro-German hybrid in a German context by interpreting a musical narrative that was based on a self-parody by an African immigrant living in Germany. The employment of classical music and the performance on theatre stages have, on the other hand, attempted to elevate the social status and acceptance of hip-hop dance as part of Germany's established dance culture, in a manner similar to the strategies employed by Das DJ Orchester. However, this spatiality also deconstructs the authentic experience and positive energy of hip-hop dance.

The close reading of the b-boy performance in Hamburg's city centre has, therefore, captured the way in which Hamburg's b-boys remain faithful to the dance form's spatiality while presenting the audience with a multicultural 'thirdspace' experience of Hamburg. This multiculturality is reflected in the dancers' physical appearance, for dance is strongly linked to the body of the artist. Ethnic differences therefore remain visible throughout hip-hop dance performances. At the same time, hip-hop dancers' engagement in this art form, especially at international battles, aims at participating in a mono-national discourse through their represention of their city or country. In this sense, hip-hop dancers institute a cultural concept of Germanness which includes cultural hybridity and which attempts to de-stigmatize visible or aural 'otherness' and make it a 'normal' German attribute.

While this concept of identity is accepted within hip-hop circles, the global adaptation of hip-hop dance, however, makes local performances in Hamburg difficult to read as an expression of Germanness for the wider public. Furthermore, while the German language is not needed as a form of communication amongst hip-hop dancers, it is required to relate hip-hop dance as a meaningful German practice to an audience. This highlights hip-hop dance's weak link to the German language compared to the performances and practices of hip-hop's music-making processes and reveals another problematic of the hybrid dancer and, in this case, of the kinaesthetic expression of a post-hybrid identity.

Nevertheless, the mentality and attitude fostered by the art form has provided tools with which SonnyTee and Can, for example, want to improve social exchange and an understanding of cultural differences in Hamburg. Can thus concludes that his goal as a hip-hop dancer is:

> den Austausch zu stärken. Zwischen den Leuten, die hier in Hamburg leben. Und einfach vielleicht auch mal so ein bisschen die Tänzerszene an sich zu verändern. Also auch damit quasi die Gesellschaft ein bisschen zu verändern, [...] im Umgang mit anderen Leuten. Zum Beispiel so Werte, wie Respekt. Toleranz. Und Freundlichkeit![114]

> [to strengthen exchange. Between the people who live here in Hamburg. And maybe just to change the dance scene itself a bit, as well. And almost to change society a bit, [...] in terms of social interaction. For example, values like respect. Tolerance. And friendliness!]

Whether the same aims can be achieved with hip-hop's lyrical element will be explored in the following chapter.

114 Can, interviewed by author, 21 May 2012.

CHAPTER 3

Rap

Rhyme Technicians and the Emergence of Rap

> When I started out as a DJ, MC-in' as an art hadn't been formulated yet. The microphone was just used for makin' announcements, like when the next party was gonna be, or people's moms would come to the party lookin' for them, and you would have to announce it on the mike.[1]

The statement by Bronx DJ Grandmaster Caz hints at the fact that the emergence of hip-hop's lyrical element is just as indebted to the DJs' neighbourhood parties as b-boying. While b-boys and b-girls initially danced to the musical break beats played by the DJs, over time the DJs' ambidextrous turntable skills became more sophisticated beyond the basic invention of 'looping' and 'scratching'. Consequentially, the party audience became focused on watching the DJs' manual acrobatics rather than moving to their beats.[2] In order to counteract this development, a new element was introduced at the DJ parties. Party hosts or 'Masters of Ceremony' (MCs) went on stage and 'filled a void – one created by the DJs – by bringing vocals and songs back into the spotlight'.[3] These MCs specifically connected to the audience in a way that was meaningful to them, namely by relying on the shared 'thirdspace' experience of living in the Bronx and by shouting 'little phrases and words from the neighbourhood that [they] used on the corner'.[4]

The successful addition of MCing eventually resulted in new crew formations consisting of the DJ and his hosts. This development can be compared to the previously mentioned local 'transition from gang-oriented affiliations (formed around their protection of turf) to music and break-dance affiliations that maintained and in some cases intensified the important structuring systems of territoriality'.[5] Within these crew formations it was DJ Grandmaster Flash and

1 Grandmaster Caz, quoted in Katz, *Groove Music*, p. 73.
2 Katz, *Groove Music*, p. 75.
3 Katz, *Groove Music*, p. 75.
4 DJ Kool Herc, quoted in George, 'Hip-Hop's Founding Fathers Speak the Truth', p. 51.
5 Forman, *The 'hood Comes First*, p. 70.

'The Furious Five' who became particularly influential in the establishment of hip-hop's lyrical element. Aside from shouting common phrases and words, Flash remembers that:

> Cowboy came up with a lot of phrases and had a powerful voice that just commanded action. 'Throw your hands in the air!' 'Clap to the beat!' 'Somebody scream!' all came from Cowboy. Kid Creole and his brother Melle Mel were the first to really flow and have a poetic feel to their rhymes. They were the first rhyme technicians. They were the first to toss a sentence back and forth. Kid would say, 'I', Mel would say 'was', Kid would say 'walking', Mel would say, 'down'. They just tossed sentences like that all day. It was incredible to watch, it was incredible to hear.[6]

While the audience animation thus began as an improvised practice of aural and visual entertainment, it eventually evolved into a 'form of rhymed storytelling accompanied by highly rhythmic, electronically based music'.[7] This form of storytelling became known as 'rapping'.

From the perspective of cultural history, Rose especially locates the art of rapping in an African-derived tradition. She bases her observation on a comparison of rap to the 'improvisational elements of jazz with the narrative sense of place in the blues; it has the oratory power of the black preacher and the emotional vulnerability of Southern soul music'.[8] Indeed, African-American preaching practices re-appear in the call-and-response tradition established at the DJs' block parties whereby the audience answered to the rappers' demands, such as to 'Say Ho! (Ho!), Say Hey, Ho! (Hey, Ho!) or I say Hip, you say Hop: Hip! (Hop!)'.[9] However, beyond the African-American cultures that defined the Bronx's 'thirdspace' rappers Melle Mel and The Kidd Creole were also of Cherokee descent, again showing that the new element of rap continued to foster the 'multi-ethnic nature of the founding community of hip-hop'.[10] Nevertheless, as with the DJs' fate, Ogbar again criticizes the fact that solely 'African American working-class, urban males emerged as the art's central representatives'.[11]

This specifically occurred when rap became detached from the performative stage of the DJ and the accompanying spatiality of the art form. Beyond rap's original performance as a live experience nurtured by the shared cultural knowledge and local traditions of the inhabitants of the Bronx, Rose

6 DJ Grandmaster Flash, quoted in George, 'Hip-Hop's Founding Fathers Speak the Truth', p. 51.
7 Rose, *Black Noise*, p. 2.
8 Rose, *Black Noise*, pp. 184–85.
9 Saied, *Rap in Deutschland*, p. 30.
10 Ogbar, *Hip-Hop Revolution*, p. 39.
11 Ogbar, *Hip-Hop Revolution*, p. 39.

highlights that it was also the socio-urban conditions of New York City's uptown boroughs which became influential for the 'shape and direction of rap'[12] as rappers started rhyming about 'the pleasures *and* problems of black urban life in contemporary America'.[13] The movement towards this lyrical re-orientation was again initiated by DJ Grandmaster Flash and the Furious Five with the release of their track 'The Message' in 1982.

Furious Five member Melle Mel lyrically portrays the 'fate of the individual spirit living within the parameters of the post-industrial urban landscape' and his song can be understood as an 'unmitigated and "authentic" portrayal of contemporary black urban life'.[14] In the chorus Melle Mel warns the listeners:

> Don't push me 'cause I'm close to the edge.
> I'm trying not to lose my head, ah huh-huh-huh.
> It's like a jungle sometimes it makes me wonder
> How I keep from going under.[15]

With the city of New York becoming a metaphorical 'jungle' encapsulating the chaotic, claustrophobic and animalistic fight for survival in this particular 'firstspace', this song initiated a new direction in rap that 'extended the genre's thematic boundaries, which up to this point had mostly been isolated in the conceptual loci of the party, night club, or roller rink'.[16] Rap became a lyrical art form which no longer narrated *in* particular urban spaces but *about* particular urban spaces, namely about 'stories that represent the creative fantasies, perspectives, and experiences of racial marginality in America'.[17] Moreover, Forman highlights that while 'The Message' established a rap sub-genre known as message, knowledge or reality rap 'all subsequent rap recordings dealing with sociopolitical concerns or spatially oriented themes relating to black cultural frames of experience owe a debt to "The Message"'.[18]

In terms of spatiality, rap was now an art form which was able to sustain itself with a 'secondspace' perspective on the city in which the 'cityspace becomes more of a mental or ideational field'.[19] Rappers went from being live entertainers to becoming 'producers of representational space and fictional narratives envisioned within actual environments and experiences'.[20]

12 Rose, *Black Noise*, p. 35.
13 Rose, *Black Noise*, p. 2 (my emphasis).
14 Mark Anthony Neal, 'Post-industrial Soul: Black Popular Music at the Crossroads', in *That's the Joint!*, ed. by Forman and Neal, pp. 476–502 (p. 486).
15 Grandmaster Flash and the Furious Five, *The Message* (Sugar Hill Records, 1982) [CD].
16 Forman, *The 'hood Comes First*, p. 83.
17 Rose, *Black Noise*, p. 3.
18 Forman, *The 'hood Comes First*, p. 83.
19 Soja, *Postmetropolis*, p. 11.
20 Forman, *The 'hood Comes First*, p. 93.

Consequentially, rappers further shifted from outdoor urban spaces into indoor recording studios, like the spatial transition of DJs who created beats for music production purposes. The paradox of this spatial shift, however, is highlighted by Forman. He states that while rap's content became further connected to street life, 'the music was actually moving away from the production and performance domains of the street at the time, and merging more consistently with the studios and executive spaces of the music industry'.[21]

Nevertheless, rappers maintained a link between the authentic practice of rap and its 'combined elements of geocultural and temporal locatedness'[22] by implying 'an intimate familiarity with the urban, working-class landscapes that gave rise to hip-hop in the 1970s'.[23] Hence, despite the transition of the art form's focus from being a 'thirdspace' experience to a 'secondspatial' reflection of a local cityspace, the spatiality of rap lyrics remained intrinsically based on the social components that characterized the 'thirdspace' of the Bronx. Thus, Forman concludes that the commercial success of 'The Message' 'shifted the rap form toward an incisive critical content, introducing what eventually became a standard and dominating rap discourse that maintained a pronounced ghettocentric sensibility'.[24]

Recorded rap could be disseminated easily via vinyl or airwaves. This meant that the notion of a ghettocentric sensibility rapidly spread to other national urban communities in the United States. The conditions of the Bronx remained paradigmatic for the overall conditions that defined the urban ghetto in its lyrical manifestation. Hence, specifically 'using the ghetto as a source of identity'[25] became the standardized urban 'secondspace' perspective and social discourse in commercial rap productions. More importantly, Forman emphasizes that these lyrical and hence 'fictional representations cannot be segregated from real places and practices, for in their symbolic forms they are recirculated into the social realm, taken up, and made meaningful in collective contexts through sophisticated social engagements'.[26] By the early 1990s, this spatial representation and social engagement culminated in the emergence of rap's most successful commercial genre, namely gangsta rap.

While the message-rap genre can be understood as a conscious lyrical 'engagement with interrelated issues of race, class, and cultural identity',[27] the new appearance of gangsta rap served rather to depict 'lifestyles of the

21 Forman, *The 'hood Comes First*, p. 124.
22 Forman, *The 'hood Comes First*, p. 87.
23 Ogbar, *Hip Hop Revolution*, p. 39.
24 Forman, *The 'hood Comes First*, p. 83.
25 Rose, *Black Noise*, p. 12.
26 Forman, *The 'hood Comes First*, p. 94.
27 Forman, *The 'hood Comes First*, p. 184.

young and edgy, replete with violent imagery of the steamy urban underside'.[28] Evolving in Los Angeles and its surrounding suburbs and counties, the descriptive imageries of the ghetto became the dominant 'secondspatial' discourse, whereby writing provocative lyrical stories about deviant social behaviours distorted rap's original emphasis on live performance skills and on being an outlet for channelling poetic creativity.[29] As Ogbar explains, a 'real' engagement in this lyrical art form was now being achieved by 'rappers who extol pathology (drug selling, gang banging, violence, pimping, etc)'.[30] Supporting this observation, Tickner points out that gangsta rap's:

> validation of aggressiveness successfully tapped into prevalent stereotypes concerning everyday life in the ghetto, albeit with perverse effects. Besides upholding values such as hedonistic consumerism and patriarchy, which ultimately reconfirmed the existing social order [...], many rappers, to prove their 'realness,' became accustomed to carrying weapons, doing jail time, and participating in occasional fights and shoot-outs.[31]

In consequence, Ogbar claims that this realness has been 'racialized as an extension of being black or brown'[32] while Forman also notes that 'the ghetto is elevated as the source of black authenticity'.[33] Indeed, the domination of gangsta rap and its socio-spatial discourses caused 'commercial rappers to eagerly declare their "real nigga" status',[34] meaning that these artists emphasized their 'tribal stigma' as a sign of ghetto-spatial authenticity. However, this status reveals a racial arbitrariness. While the first chapter touched upon black DJs being of Latino background, hip-hop scholar Samy H. Alim claims that the term 'nigga' is also 'used by females of all ethnicities in the San Francisco Bay Area to refer to each other in much the same way that males do'.[35] Moreover, with rap being hip-hop's *lyrical* element expressed in spoken language, its recorded state does not require a physical performance or the rapper's (black) body to communicate a 'nigga status'. Rather, rappers symbolize their 'tribal stigma' by articulating themselves in African-American Vernacular English

28 Forman, *The 'hood Comes First*, p. 184.

29 For an in-depth account of commercial gangsta rap's controversial influence on the image of hip-hop in the United States and beyond, see Tricia Rose, *The Hip Hop Wars: What We Talk about When We Talk about Hip Hop – and Why It Matters* (New York: BasicCivitas, 2008).

30 Ogbar, *Hip Hop Revolution*, p. 42.

31 Tickner, 'Aquí en el Ghetto', 124–25.

32 Ogbar, *Hip Hop Revolution*, pp. 65–66.

33 Forman, *The 'hood Comes First*, p. 94.

34 Ogbar, *Hip Hop Revolution*, p. 45.

35 Samy H. Alim, *Roc the MIC Right: The Language of Hip Hop Culture* (New York: Routledge, 2006), p. 78.

(AAVE) and 'ever-changing black slang'[36] which identifies them as 'members of the lower social class who quite noticeably bear the mark of their status in their speech' (*STGM*, p. 146).

However, even these linguistic social signifiers can become arbitrary, revealing the constructed racial authenticity of gangsta rap. While regional differentiation and dialects across black communities in the United States already have varying effects on the particular uses of AAVE,[37] American Latino rappers such as the members of Cypress Hill have also adapted AAVE pronunciation in their lyrical delivery. Ogbar claims that Cypress Hill's 'adoption of disparate cultural markers represents the group's attempt to affirm authenticity by conforming to popular notions of gangsta culture and "representing" their hood while adhering to the larger hegemonic forces in society that demand pan-Latinoism'.[38] Hence, despite the common understanding of the language variety as an inherent expression of African-American ethnicity, Cypress Hill represent rap's 'uncanny ability to absorb disparate styles while adhering to a definable and palpable hip-hop aesthetic'.[39]

Beyond gangsta rap's prevailing dominant influence on the art form's norms and practices, it should be noted that other rap styles and narratives have been established as well. Forman explains that the:

> aesthetic diversification contributed to a need for the genre distinctions [...] that were eventually implemented by the industry to identify the proliferation of new styles. These genre labels (knowledge rap, gangsta rap, reality rap, pop rap, etc) were eventually standardized in industry discourses and the media.[40]

Within these genre labels, AAVE has nevertheless remained the 'lingua franca' which has been 'used/borrowed and adapted/transformed by various ethnic groups inside and outside the U.S.'.[41] Hence, in order to examine rap beyond its commerciality, in which certain perspectives of spatiality, sociality and historicality have become the marketable status quo, rap's overall lyrical power needs to be the central focus of analysis. To this end, the following section will highlight four lyrical features which capture rap's aesthetic norms and lyrical practices regardless of its historical, spatial or social setting.

36 Rose, *Black Noise*, p. 3.
37 Alim, *Roc the MIC Right*, p. 78.
38 Ogbar, *Hip Hop Revolution*, p. 47.
39 Ogbar, *Hip Hop Revolution*, p. 53. For a contemporary, detailed account of Chicano rappers' negotiation of their *Latinidad* and 'real nigga status', see Amanda Martinez-Morrison, 'Black and Tan Realities: Chicanos in the Borderlands of the Hip-Hop Nation', in *The Voices of Latin/o American Hip-Hop*, ed. by Christopher Dennis (= *alter/nativas*, 2 (2014), http://alternativas.osu.edu/en/issues/spring-2014/essays1/martinez-morrison.html [accessed 17 August 2014].
40 Forman, The *'hood Comes First*, p. 165.
41 Alim, *Roc the MIC Right*, p. 71.

Reading the Orality of Rap as a Lyrical Text

Close readings of rap lyrics in this analysis will treat the art form as an oral tradition, and hence as a tradition that transfers knowledge through speech in contrast to literate cultures which employ the written word as the primary form of communication.[42] Rose defends rap as being directly influenced by African-derived oral traditions such as 'boasting, signifying, preaching, and earlier related black oral traditions'.[43] However, similar oral features have been identified in other cultural and historical contexts as well. The competitive and improvised nature of vulgar rhyming duels, for example, has been characteristic of the Scottish medieval tradition of 'flyting', which can be compared to the African-American ritual act of 'playing the dozens'.[44] Moreover, German hip-hop journalist Sascha Verlan claims that any of rap's supposedly African-derived oral characteristics can be found in any European or Asian cultures.[45] Hence, while rap should be understood as intrinsically linked to its emergence within the 'thirdspace' of the Bronx and therefore within an African-derived context, including its manifestation in Caribbean or Latino cultural backgrounds, there remains flexibility for other oral traditions to be incorporated or paralleled with rap when inserted into other cultural contexts.

Within these different cultural contexts, the aesthetics of rap remain distinguishable from other poetic art forms by the delivery of rhymes in synchronization with a musical beat. With a rapper's performance being defined and judged on his 'verbal mastery, mastery of delivery, creativity, personal style, and virtuosity',[46] this lyrical delivery is tied to a certain poetic feel called the 'flow'. According to Wu Tang Clan rapper Raekwon the flow does not refer to what you say, but '*how* you say it. Flow is like poetry goin' to the beat'.[47] While the flow can, therefore, only be detected aurally, German linguists Jannis Androutsopoulos and Arno Scholz have identified four

42 Michael Rappe, 'Rhythmus-Sound-Symbol: Struktur und Vermittlungsformen einer Oral Culture am Beispiel des Hip-Hop', in *Expressyourself! Europas kulturelle Kreativität zwischen Markt und Underground*, ed. by Eva Kimminich and others (Bielefeld: transcript, 2007), pp. 137–56 (p. 138).

43 Rose, *Black Noise*, p. 25.

44 Simon Johnson, 'Rap Music Originated in Medieval Scottish Pubs, Claims American Professor', *The Telegraph*, 28 December 2008, http://www.telegraph.co.uk/culture/music/3998862/Rap-music-originated-in-medieval-Scottish-pubs-claims-American-professor.html [accessed 22 April 2012].

45 Sascha Verlan, 'HipHop als schöne Kunst betrachtet', in *HipHop: Globale Kultur – Lokale Praktiken*, ed. by Androutsopoulos, pp. 138–46 (p. 141).

46 Rose, *Black Noise*, p. 163.

47 Raekwon in Alim, *Roc the MIC Right*, p. 95.

common criteria to help analyse and read rap lyrics closely.[48]

The first category that Androutsopoulos and Scholz identify comprises *song themes*, that is, the topics of the rapped messages. The German linguists stress that the appearance and repetition of certain topics depends on the particular sub-genre of rap as well as on national and cultural contexts, some topics becoming more relevant and meaningful than others. Androutsopoulos and Scholz summarize self-display, social critique, scene-specific discourse and more mundane themes such as drugs, partying, love and sex as the most iterated topics in rap narratives. The second category focuses on *ritualized speech acts*. This relates to the aforementioned practices of boasting and toasting as well as dissing. It also comprises the act of (re)presenting one's self in a specific geo-historical setting. Thirdly, Androutsopoulos and Scholz categorize *rap specific rhetoric*. This refers to the use and appearance of metaphors, simile, cultural references and acronyms as well as to the employment of homophonies and heterographs in rap lyrics. Lastly, *linguistic orientation* is the category in which rap lyrics are identified by their standardized and non-standardized linguistic appropriation as well as by the rapper's creative employment of different varieties and registers of language.

While Androutsopoulos employs the latter two categories for the investigation of global linguistic patterns in local rap lyrics,[49] this analysis will consider all four categories in order to identify their re-functioned signification in the linguistic and cultural context of Germany. By focussing on rap's appropriation in the hip-hop communities of Hamburg and Oldenburg, the comparative analysis will further reveal how hip-hop's lyrical element has been authentically integrated into the cities' social, historical and spatial structures, revealing that its 'realness is never static, thus allowing for continued shifts of expression in politics and race'.[50]

The Adaptation of Rap in West Germany

> Für mich hat Hip-Hop einfach die deutsche Sprache für die Leute in Deutschland wieder normal gemacht, dass sie sich dafür nicht schämen müssen. Dass es nämlich nicht ist, deutsch zu singen, oder wie man auch es immer mal nennen will, ist gleich Schlager. Oder deutsche Worte und Musik ist gleich Schlager.[51]

48 Jannis Androutsopoulos, 'HipHop und Sprache: Vertikale Intertextualität und die drei Sphären der Popkultur', in *HipHop: Globale Kultur – Lokale Praktiken*, ed. by Androutsopoulos, pp. 111–36 (p. 116).

49 Androutsopoulos, 'HipHop und Sprache', pp. 116–17.

50 Ogbar, *Hip Hop Revolution*, p. 53.

51 Mirko Machine, interviewed by author, 10 May 2012.

> [For me, hip-hop normalized the German language again for the people in Germany, so that they do not have to be ashamed of it. That it's not like singing in German, or whatever you want to call it, is the same as *Schlager*. Or German words and music equal *Schlager*.]

Mirko Machine emphasizes that hip-hop's lyrical element triggered a proud identification with German popular music by arguing that 'Schlager' was the only previous (and distasteful) German popular-music genre. However, within Mirko Machine's comparison lies another discourse, one that touches upon the relationship between popular music and the German language, a relationship that was normalized through the introduction of German rap, as this chapter will highlight.

The first official rap performance in German was aired on West German television in 1980, three years prior to the release of the first hip-hop films. This onetime spectacle was based on a parody of the internationally successful pop-rap track 'Rapper's Delight' (1979) put on by GLS United, which included TV host Thomas Gottschalk and his colleagues Frank Laufenberg and Manfred Sexauer. Their song 'Rapper's Deutsch', however, remained insignificant for the establishment of rap as a lyrical art form in Germany.[52] Without mentioning either GLS United or a German rap scene, Sleepwalker remembers that 'für uns waren ja alle Vorbilder Engländer oder Amis' [for us all of our idols were either English or American].[53] German youth who became interested in rap therefore expressed their affiliation to their role models by rapping in English as well.[54]

This linguistic imitation was, nevertheless, deemed an authentic and valid cultural re-production of rap. The favouring of a foreign language over a familiar one in early German rap becomes apparent in the following statement by Oldenburg graffiti artist Moe. After having listened to German-Turkish rapper Kool Savas's first attempts at rapping in German in the early 1980s, Moe admits that his graffiti crew were:

> begeistert von seinen Skills, also von seinen Fertigkeiten, aber [...] es unmöglich [fanden], dass er das auf Deutsch machte. Also es war wie so ein Tabubruch. Wir haben gesagt: 'Alter! Lern Englisch! Mach das auf Englisch und du hast eine große Zukunft. Vergiss das mit dem Deutschen. Das ist scheiße. Es hört sich einfach kacke an'.[55]

52 Hannes Loh and Sascha Verlan, 'die welle aus amerika spülte mich an land zurück', in Hannes Loh and Sascha Verlan, *25 Jahre Hip-Hop in Deutschland* (Höfen: Hannibal, 2006), pp. 134–39 (p. 134).
53 Sleepwalker, interviewed by author, 5 June 2012.
54 Sleepwalker, interviewed by author, 5 June 2012.
55 Moe, interviewed by author, 11 March 2012.

> [thrilled by his skills, in other words by his proficiency, but thought it was outrageous that he was doing it in German. It was like breaking a taboo. We said: 'Dude! Learn English! Do it in English and you will have a great future. Forget the German. It's shit. It just sounds like crap'.]

While Moe's dogmatic perspective on rap's anglicized form of delivery relates to the fact that German youth 'ja nur das [kannten]' [only knew it like this] when it came to their idols' *linguistic orientation*,[56] Sabine von Dirke links the initial relevance inscribed in the English language to a wider German national discourse. According to Dirke, the popularity of American and English rap in Germany was especially based on the fact that it was performed *in English*. In this way rap denied:

> German history, namely, that there were no untainted German folk traditions left after Nazism on which alternative popular music and youth culture could have been built. U.S. popular culture, especially those examples originating from African-American musical traditions, was the only valid tune that held the promise of liberation. In this context, the predominance of English within popular culture makes sense as a distancing device from the Nazi past.[57]

Moreover, the dis-identification with the German language expressed a refusal to value anything German when one considers that 'it is in and through language that the values of places are produced'.[58] It thus comes hardly as a surprise that it took a decade – and a united Germany – before rap in Germany began to emerge as a national musical genre in the commercial sector.

The reason for this linguistic shift is twofold. On the one hand, German rappers' 'insufficient knowledge of English'[59] inhibited the achievement of lyrical sophistication. On the other hand, Dirke explains that the 'switch to German made sense since rap wants to communicate with its audience. The desire to be understood by the audience, in terms of conveying a message and showing off one's rhetorical skills, became the primary motivating factor'.[60] In line with this observation, Hamburg freestyle rapper Stee, for example, became engaged in German rap specifically because of its familiar linguistic predisposition, explaining that 'als ich dann angefangen habe wirklich intensiver Musik zu hören, [...] mir einfach immer Inhalt wichtig [war]. Und ich kann so schlecht Englisch! [*Laughs*] Habe das alles nicht verstanden.

56 Sleepwalker, interviewed by author, 5 June 2012.

57 Sabine von Dirke, 'Hip-Hop Made in Germany: From Old School to the Kanaksta Movement', in *German Popular Culture – How "American" is It?*, ed. by Agnes C. Mueller (Ann Arbor: The University of Michigan Press, 2004), pp. 96–112 (p. 99).

58 Forman, *The 'hood Comes First*, p. 30.

59 Von Dirke, 'Hip-Hop Made in Germany', p. 102.

60 Von Dirke, 'Hip-Hop Made in Germany', p. 102.

Und deswegen höre ich auch hauptsächlich Deutschrap' [when I then started listening more intensely to music the content was always very important to me. And my English is so bad! [*Laughs*] I didn't understand anything. And that is why I mainly listen to German rap].[61] In other words, rap's emphasis on verbal aesthetics and lyrical content had the ability to outweigh the historical semantics attached to the German language by re-signifying it as a contemporary symbol of Germanness.

Thus the messages conveyed in early German rap also began to iterate contemporary *song themes* relevant to the German social landscape. Most notably, Heidelberg rap trio Advanced Chemistry began to express social critique in their track 'Fremd im eigenen Land' (1993). Directing their message at a German audience, the German-Haitian rapper Torch, German-Italian rapper Toni L, and Afro-German rapper Linguist addressed national topics of racism, already proposing a 'multicultural type of "Germanness"'[62] as a strategy with which to manage their 'tribal stigmata' as German citizens with foreign cultural backgrounds.

In the same year, rap group Fresh Familee from Ratingen commented on the discourse of Turkish migration in their track 'Ahmet Gündüz' (1993).[63] While Advanced Chemistry rapped exclusively from their personal points of view, Fresh Familee's lead German-Turkish rapper Tachiles alternates between rapping from the perspective of an imaginary Turkish *Gastarbeiter* [guest worker] named Ahmet Gündüz and of the son of such a *Gastarbeiter*. Moreover, in order to distinguish between these two viewpoints, Tachiles engages in two different *linguistic orientations*. For the former account he employs exaggeratedly broken German grammar articulated in a Turkish accent, while for the latter account he expresses himself in standard German. In this way he strategically supports his lyrical semantics through bi-lingual performances through which it is possible to differentiate between first and second generation migrants in Germany.

Tachiles' *linguistic orientation* therefore relates to the second reason for the German linguistic shift in German rap mentioned by Dirke, namely to the creative and playful employment of rhetorical skills. Indeed, early German rap became heavily judged by the rappers' use of 'vielsilbig, komplexe[n] Reime[n], viele[n] Wortspiele[n], geile[n] Stimme[n], gute[m] Flow. Also

61 Stee, interviewed by author, 26 July 2012.

62 Timothy S. Brown, '(African-)Americanization and Hip Hop in Germany', in *The Vinyl ain't Final – Hip Hop and the Globalization of Black Culture*, ed. by Dipannita Basu and Sidney J. Lemelle (London and Ann Arbor: Pluto Press, 2006), pp. 137–50 (p. 142); for more information on the content and impact of 'Fremd im eigenen Land' in Germany, see Saied, *Rap in Deutschland*, pp. 62–73.

63 Saied, *Rap in Deutschland*, p. 61.

irgendeine[r] rhythmische[n] Basis, die einfach Sinn macht' [diverse, complex rhymes, many puns, an awesome voice, a good flow. Any rhythmic foundation that makes sense].[64] Rappers thus began discovering the characteristics and linguistic possibilities of their German language by adhering to the same lyrical aesthetics that had defined rap since its emergence in the Bronx. This is best captured by the label chief of Rattos Locos Records Blacky White's description of Samy Deluxe as being 'ein Typ, der kann *echt* rappen. So. Das kann man schon messen mit dem Ami-Scheiß, bloß halt auf Deutsch. Der flowt, der kann langsam, schnell, *boom boom*, der geht ab! Der ist nicht neben dem Takt' [a guy who can really rap. Like, it really measures up to that American shit, but just in German. He flows, he can do it slow, fast, *boom boom*, he is on fire! He is not out of synch with the beat].[65] The 'realness' of German rap therefore continued to be based on rhythm and the delivery of a lyrical flow. Nonetheless, while German was re-discovered as a viable and valued language for the production of German popular music, its use did not transmit the same social discourse as that expressed by the German rappers' American or English role models.

While African-American and Latino rappers denoted their socio-racial identity through their rhetoric in the form of AAVE and black slang, Samy Deluxe explains that 'am Anfang […] es schon noch so ein bisschen [war], [dass] man erwartet, dass du jedenfalls "Vernünftiges", in Anführungszeichen, Deutsch sprichst als Deutschrapper' [in the beginning it was still a bit the case that, as a German rapper, you were expected to speak, in quotation marks, "proper" German].[66] Hence, despite the fact that *song themes* written by culturally 'foreign' rappers touched upon internal socio-political topics like racism and ethnic segregation, Samy Deluxe explains that 'die ersten türkischen Rapper, [die] so auf Deutsch [gerappt haben] […] so Boulevard Bou aus Heidelberg [waren], der eben so *mega* eloquent und eigentlich total der Deutsche ist' [the first Turkish rappers who rapped in German […] were like Boulevard Bou from Heidelberg who rapped so *uber* eloquently that he really is totally German].[67] Indeed, even Cheesman notes in his analysis of Tachiles' German lyrics that the rapper:

> exemplifies a delight in linguistic play which characterizes the best contemporary German rap. And this kind of text conveys at least as effectively

64 Samy Deluxe, interviewed by author, 29 July 2012.
65 Blacky White, interviewed by author, 10 July 2012.
66 Samy Deluxe, interviewed by author, 29 July 2012.
67 Samy Deluxe, interviewed by author, 29 July 2012.

> as any explicit message that 'typical Turks', regardless of their legal status, are full participants in contemporary German culture.[68]

In other words, German rap did not become symbolic of a lower social class, since German rappers' 'tribal stigmata' were silenced through their enunciation of 'proper' German.

A reason for the lack of this symbolic translation can be deduced by comparing the spatiality of American rap *song themes* to German ones, with Oldenburg rapper K-Four explaining that:

> we don't have no ghetto in Germany, man. Everybody gets money from the welfare. [...] We've got a social net. [...] So, you cannot talk about a ghetto like: 'It's necessary for me to hustle to survive'. You might be that greedy, like 'I'm not satisfied with this 300 euros or whatever they give me. I want more. That is why I sell drugs'. You might say *that*. But it's *not* necessary for you to survive. So. It's just one sort of luxury. Gangster by choice![69]

While K-Four touches upon lyrical content rather than on linguistic signifiers, the fact that ghettoes are said to be non-existent in Germany implies that they do not become urban spaces with a specific social and racial discourse representable in German rap. This, however, does not mean that different urban spaces were irrelevant in German rap. Instead of reflecting their social perspective through language, rappers' linguistic distinctions related to their regional geography.

The flexibility of this spatial re-orientation in rap's linguistic semantics becomes ironically evident with the example of Frankfurt-born rapper D-Flame. He initially claimed that '*wenn* jemand auf Englisch rappen darf, dann wohl ich! Wenn ich irgendwie da [in den USA] auch Wurzeln hab' und nicht irgend 'nen Peter Schmidt' [*if* anyone has the right to rap in English than of course it's me! Since I have roots [in the USA] and not some Peter Schmidt].[70] However, when rapping in German D-Flame's German identity was challenged as his producers insisted: 'Du darfst nicht zu viel Hessisch reden, das kommt nicht an! Also du musst mit i*ch*, di*ch*, mi*ch* [rappen]' [You can't talk so much Hessian, that won't pull. You have to rap with i*ch*, di*ch*, mi*ch*].[71] D-Flame clarifes that 'in Frankfurt da gibt's ja kein C.H. Da sagt man i*sch*, di*sch*, mi*sch*' [in Frankfurt there is no C.H. There you say i*sch*, di*sch*, mi*sch*],[72] hence the 'stigma' of his Germanness was not linked to his dark skin

68 Cheesman, 'Polyglot Pop Politics', 213

69 K-Four, interviewed by author, 9 February 2012.

70 D-Flame, interviewed by author, 26 July 2012. As previously mentioned, D-Flame's father was an American citizen of Jamaican and Cherokee-Indian descent.

71 D-Flame, interviewed by author, 26 July 2012.

72 D-Flame, interviewed by author, 26 July 2012.

or to his Polish-Caribbean ethnicity but to his regional German dialect. While regional dialects have featured most prominently in German folk music and in *volkstümliche Musik*, German rap altered the relationship between regional dialects and folk traditions by allowing these forms of speech to be attractive and approved as a statement of contemporary German urban lifestyles. Remembering a rap recording session with Jan Delay in Hamburg, D-Flame talks about listening to his verses, exclaiming:

> 'Nee! Oh! Zu viele S.C.H. wieder! Zu viele S.C.H.! Lass uns noch mal aufnehmen. [...] Ich will diese *chh-chhh* mehr.' Und er [Jan Delay] so: 'Nein! Das bist du dann nicht mehr! Wie du redest, so will ich das auch gehört haben auf dem Song!'. So. Und ich so: 'Hä? In Frankfurt sagen die mir die ganze Zeit in Hamburg fährt keiner drauf ab, wenn ich dieses Frankfurterische ....' Er so: 'Nee! Genau darauf fahren Leute ab, die aus anderen Städten kommen!'.[73]
>
> ['No! Oh! Too much S.C.H. again! Too much S.C.H.! Let us record again. [...] I want more of this *chh-chhh*.' And he [Jan Delay] was like: 'No! That won't be you anymore! The way you talk, that is how I want to hear it in the song!'. And I was like: 'Huh? In Frankfurt they tell me that nobody in Hamburg likes this Frankfurtian ....' He was like: 'No! That is exactly what people from different cities like.']

Thus, the language use in early German rap represented not only social or racial discourses but geo-cultural ones, as well. This linguistic perspective on spatial representations will be further explored in the following analyses.

Hamburg and the Metropolitan Performances of German Rap

Rap in Hamburg began as a live art form, similar to its original performance and 'thirdspace' experience in the Bronx. However, as rappers in West Germany lacked the shared conditions of sociality, spatiality and historicality that framed American rap, the performances of rap in Germany became re-located from the outside, public, neighbourhood blocks into indoor and private 'firstspaces'.

One popular local rap location, for instance, was a basement in Hamburg's district of Eimsbüttel. Here, the art of 'freestyling' was practised, meaning the creation of improvised rhymes over an instrumental beat. The practice of this rap tradition transformed the local, underground 'firstspace' into 'eine Kreativschmiede des Grauens' [a creative smithy of horror][74] as

73 D-Flame, interviewed by author, 26 July 2012.
74 DJ Ben Kenobi, interviewed by author, 3 July 2012.

'die Sprachbegeisterteren unter uns' [language aficionados amongst us][75] exchanged and perfected their rhetorical skills. The relevance of this particular 'thirdspace' experience for Hamburg's rap community is emphasized by Samy Deluxe, who writes that the basement became the 'Heimat des Hip Hop aus Hamburg, d[as] Epizentrum des Labels, des Clans, der Familie namens "Eimsbush Entertainment"' [home of hip-hop from Hamburg, the epicentre of the label, of the clan, of the family named 'Eimsbush Entertainment'].[76] Characterized as Hamburg rap's epicentre, the basement also became a hybrid space as the name 'Eimsbush' fused the name of its German 'firstspace' location with the idealized hip-hop identity of the New York City borough Flatbush into a cultural 'third space' pertaining to local hip-hop.[77]

A similar spatial adaptation of rap was also unfolding in the south of Hamburg. Freestyle rapper Nan-D recalls the scheduled 'Mittwochstreffen, die fünf Jahre in meinem Keller mit Schlechta Umgang stattfanden, um zu üben' [meetings on Wednesdays that were held in my basement for five years with Schlechta Umgang in order to practise].[78] Nowadays, Nan-D and the members of Schlechta Umgang have relocated their domestic freestyle sessions to a local club. Sharing the same district as the DJ Orchester's *Lab*, the move to Hamburg's Schanzenviertel has allowed the practice of rap to remain a live 'thirdspace' experience and even 'umsonst und für jeden zugänglich' [free and open to the public].[79] Furthermore, Nan-D emphasizes that 'bei uns [...] der Conscious Rap [regiert]' [conscious rap reigns at our events],[80] in other words anti-commercial rap that delivers 'positive, uplifting messages, often delivered over smooth, ear-grabbing beats'.[81] While Schlechta Umgang has, therefore, remained commercially underground, Eimsbush chose a different path.

By 1994, the local basement meetings at Eimsbush had led to the establishment of the aforementioned rap label 'Eimsbush Entertainment'[82] – coinciding with the time at which German rap became normalized as a German form of expression. While rappers were indeed improving their

75 Samy Deluxe, interviewed by author, 29 July 2012.

76 Samy Sorge, *Dis wo ich herkomm* (Reinbeck: Rohwolt Verlag, 2009), p. 81.

77 Many commercially successful rappers were from Flatbush, including Talib Kweli and Busta Rhymes (Jennifer R. Young, 'Brooklyn Beats: Hip Hop's Home to Everyone from Everywhere', in *Hip Hop in America: A Regional Guide*, ed. by Mickey Hess (Santa Barbara, CA: Greenwood Press, 2010), pp. 75–106.

78 Nan-D, email to author, 4 July 2012.

79 Nan-D, email to author, 4 July 2012.

80 Nan-D, email to author, 4 July 2012.

81 Henry Adaso, 'What is Conscious Rap?', *Rap/Hip-Hop* (About.com, n.d.), http://rap.about.com/od/genresstyles/p/ConsciousRap.htm [accessed 30 October 2013].

82 Rappers and DJs who were members of or affiliated with Eimsbush Entertainment include Samy Deluxe, Jan Delay, D-Flame, Das Bo and DJ Ben Kenobi.

rhetorical skills, Samy Deluxe regards Eimbush's commercial evolution as being inextricably linked to Hamburg's urban conditions and hence to forces beyond mere lyrical talent. The existing structures and establishment of professional music businesses provided the local rappers with 'direkte Vorbilder nicht nur zum Hören, sondern mit denen wir reden konnten' [firsthand idols not only to listen to but to talk to].[83] Hence, despite rap being a newly evolving German musical genre, the artists could rely on previous local knowledge regarding the commercial circulation of music. Samy Deluxe specifically contrasts this aspect to other German cityspaces, explaining that:

> das hatten Leute in anderen Städten teilweise einfach nicht gehabt und das ist auch nicht so ein Vorwurf deshalb oder so ein Ding deswegen sind wir Hamburger geiler, aber es war irgendwas, was einfach kulturell hier schon verankert war. Das war so ein Nährboden auf dem einfach *independent* Musik wachsen konnte und sich aufbauen konnte.[84]
>
> [some people from other cities just did not have it and this is not an accusation or supposed to mean that we Hamburgers are more awesome or anything like that, but it was simply something that was already culturally anchored here. It was a nutritious ground on which *independent* music could simply grow fast and establish itself.]

Over time, the professional as well as spatial conditions in Hamburg allowed local rap to flourish in various directions which, according to Blacky White, nowadays include the:

> Street Ding. Dann gibt es andere Crews, die richtig auf *gangsta rapper* machen. Dann gibt es halt so Freestyletypen. Und verschiedene Intentionen. Die einen wollen irgendwie Echo und *100-million-dollars*. Die anderen wollen einfach nur rappen und Spaß haben.[85]
>
> [street thing. Then there are other crews who really want to be *gangsta rappers*. Then there are freestyle guys. And different ambitions. Some somehow really want the Echo and *100-million-dollars*. The others just want to rap and have fun].

Within all these variations, rappers still engage in social, spatial and historical discourses particular to their intentions. Thus, Sleepwalker remembers:

83 Samy Deluxe, interviewed by author, 29 July 2012.

84 Samy Deluxe, interviewed by author, 29 July 2012.

85 Blacky White, interviewed by author, 10 July 2012. The *Echo* is an annual German music award that honours artists' achievements in the national and international pop music industry.

> [F]rüher konnte man noch über sich selber Witze machen und all so einen Schnick Schnack. [Man] hat das noch mit mehr Humor genommen. Man muss auch sagen natürlich war der Hip-Hop damals, gerade der Hamburger [war] mehr in so einer Wohnzimmerlaune. [Rap] ist aus dem Wohnzimmer entstanden, sage ich mal, oder aus dem Keller.[86]

> [[B]ack then you could joke about yourself and all that jazz. [You] took it with more humour. Of course you have to acknowledge that hip-hop back then, especially the Hamburg variety, was in more of a living room mood. [Rap] was created in the living room, or out of the basement.]

He further contrasts this spatially-related mood and style to other rap traditions, explaining: '[W]enn der Rap von der Straße kommt, natürlich ist er auch aggressiver' [[W]hen rap comes from the street it is of course more aggressive].[87] Hence, the 'firstspace' in which rap is practised, or the imagined 'secondspace' the rapper seeks to represent, influences rap's lyrical sound. This observation echoes Forman's previous statement about the 'undeniable effect of spatial variation that facilitates or encourages different practices within each separate domain.'[88] In Hamburg, rap's spatial variation and its accompanying practices have established themselves in three spatial, or rather geographic, categories. These comprise urban, regional and national narratives, which are all based within the cityspace of Hamburg and, despite their different spatiality, all serve to affirm a local German identity. Hence, in order to frame their lyrical messages according to their intention and purpose, rap artists have communicated different social, spatial and historical perspectives on Hamburg.

While already having touched upon the regional differentiation in early German rap represented through a regionally defined *linguistic orientation*, Gizmo describes the locals of Hamburg as having 'schon einen krassen Hamburger Schnack!' [a crass Hamburg *Schnack*].[89] *Schnack* refers to a particular sort of humerous utterance which imitates the sound of Low German. DJ Ben Kenobi specifies that 'mit bestimmten Leuten [...] man so [redet], wenn du erst mal auf den Pegel gehst' [you talk like that to specific people when you've had enough to drink].[90] This situational appearance of Hamburg's characteristic form of informal communication is iterated by Hamburg rapper CB, who explains that whenever 'irgendeiner auf einmal auf voll betrunken Platt schnackt ist es derbe *nice*' [somebody just starts

86 Sleepwalker, interviewed by author, 5 June 2012.
87 Sleepwalker, interviewed by author, 5 June 2012.
88 Forman, *The 'hood Comes First*, p. 109.
89 DJ Ben Kenobi, interviewed by author, 17 July 2012.
90 Gizmo and DJ Ben Kenobi, interviewed by author, 17 July 2012.

drunkenly talking *Platt* then that is really cool].[91] CB's mentioning of 'Platt' in the context of the Hamburg *Schnack* serves, moreover, to frame the historical side of this type of local communication.

With the regional language of Low German, *Plattdeutsch,* becoming nearly extinct by the eighteenth century,[92] it nowadays remains mostly as a pseudo-regional dialect, namely in fixed expressions or utterances in which standard German is pronounced with a Low German accent. CB explains that 'man [...] halt so alte Sachen mitzunehmen [versucht], so von unseren Eltern oder von unseren Opas' [you try to pick up old things, like from our parents or grandparents],[93] a remark which highlights the contemporary generation's attempts to retain knowledge of this regional language and hence of this local identity. In this sense, the contemporary appropriation of *Platt* as a regional symbol and the use of a humorous *Schnack* have become local signs of Hamburg and further appropriated in local German rap productions as well.

In 1995, rap trio Fettes Brot made use of this regional linguistic identity in their party rap track 'Nordish by Nature'.[94] While the title already hints at a northern geography, it is also an allusion to the African-American rap trio Naughty by Nature. By keeping the n-alliteration intact, the substituted word 'Nordish' serves rather to define an imaginative pan-Northern European identity, touched upon in the previous chapter on hip-hop dance. In this case, the widely encompassing category of identity is reflected through the inclusion of multiple Nordic languages in the rap track. The song's *linguistic orientation* therefore includes Danish and Dutch rapped by international colleagues, apart from Low German and standard German verses rapped by Fettes Brot and Der Tobi & Das Bo. However, the edited radio version and the video clip to 'Nordish by Nature' only feature Der Tobi & Das Bo as additional rappers, omitting the Danish and Dutch lyrics.[95] This does not distort the message of the song for the track begins in Low German, immediately communicating its regional identity to the listener. A close reading of this first stanza will highlight the way Fettes Brot engage in spatial, historical and social discourses

91 CB, interviewed by author, 24 August 2012.

92 Nils Langer, 'Low German', in *Germanic Standardizations – From Past to Present*, ed. by Ana Deumert and Wim Vandenbussche (Amsterdam: John Benjamins, 2003), pp. 282–302 (p. 285 and p. 292).

93 CB, interviewed by author, 24 August 2012.

94 Since 2009, rap trio De Fofftig Pens from Bremen have been exclusively rapping in Low German, albeit in a regional dialect from Hamburg's neighbouring city-state. Their name is, furthermore, a parodic allusion to American gangsta rapper 50Cent and engages in a similar hybridized hip-hop discourse to Fettes Brot's song title 'Nordish by Nature'.

95 For a detailed close reading of the video clip to 'Nordish by Nature', see Klein and Friedrich, *Is this real?*, pp. 117–19.

in order to represent Hamburg's regional identity through hip-hop's norms and practices.

After an aural introduction over the first bars of the beat, consisting of sampled seagull sounds and ocean waves which sonically allude to Hamburg's maritime geography, Fettes Brot member Schiffmeister initiates the song by counting:

> Een, twej, een, twej, drej.
> Sech mol: 'Hey' (Hey!), sech mol: 'Hoo' (Hoo!)
> Dat is Fettes Brot op Platt inne Disco.
> Jo, ick bün de Jung achtern Plattenspeeler.
> Un so deel ick op as Störtebeker sine Likedeeler.
> Dor is for jeden wat dorbi, wat ik speel.
> Bi uns in Norden heet dat nich 'Disco', sondern 'Dans op de Deel'.
> Ik krakehl veel Platt in dat Mikrofon.
> Büst nich unt'n Norden is dat schwer to verstohn.
> Wohn' anne Waterkant, dohn wi all.
> Un da schnackt man nu ma so.
> Hör mal 'n beeten to.
> 'Hummel Hummel' ('Mors! Mors!').[96]
>
> [One, two, one, two, three.
> Say, 'Hey!' (Hey!), say: 'Ho!' (Ho!)
> This is Fettes Brot in Platt in the disco.
> Yo, I'm the boy behind the turntables
> And I deal like Störtebeker dealt his Likedeeler.
> There is something for everyone, what I play.
> For us from the North it's not called 'disco' but 'Dans op de Deel'.
> I yell a lot of Platt into the microphone.
> If you're not from the North then it's hard to understand.
> I live near the water, as everyone does
> And there you just talk this way.
> Listen up a bit.
> 'Hummel Hummel' ('Mors! Mors!').]

While adhering to the same sentence structure as standard German, Schiffmeister's attempt at Low German does not evolve organically but becomes a word-by-word translation of standard German. The 'Lowness' becomes identifiable through his choice of vocabulary, as well as through phonetics such as the lack of diphthongs, the harsh-sounding alveolar vibrant [r] and the sharp [s] preceding a [t] or a [p]. Through this pseudo *linguistic orientation*, which nevertheless symbolically communicates a regional

96 Fettes Brot, *Nordish by Nature* (Alternation (2), 1995), maxi-single [CD].

identity, Schiffmeister proceeds to address his imagined audience through the employment of *rap specific rhetoric* in the form of the traditional hey/ho call-and-response pattern in the first couplet.

In the second couplet, Schiffmeister broadens the cultural references pertaining to a hip-hop discourse by mentioning his *Plattenspeeler*. Metaphorically standing behind his turntables, Schiffmeister engages in rap's *ritualized speech acts* by boasting about his diverse musical selection. In so doing, Schiffmeister compares his musical situation to the *Likedeeler*, the brotherhood of pirate-leader and local legend Störtebeker: just as the *Likedeeler* distributed their share of stolen goods equally amongst themselves, so is DJ Schiffmeister able to cover all the musical tastes of his audience members. From the rhetorical use of a simile to the geographical relocation of hip-hop DJ parties in Northern Germany, Schiffmeister further emphasizes that partying in his maritime region 'anne Waterkant' [near the water] is called 'Dans op de Deel' [dancing together]. *Dans op de Deel* was also the name of a regional television programme at the time when this rap song was released. The programme specifically featured Low German folk music and its name became a common synonym for regional dance music and identity.

By the end of the verse, Schiffmeister engages in another local discourse by re-functioning the oral tradition of the call-and-response 'Hummel, Hummel – Mors, Mors', turning it from a local greeting tradition into a *ritualized speech act* of rap. The verbal exchange rests on the story in which a water carrier by the name of Hans Hummel supplied water to the inhabitants of Hamburg who lived further away from the water sources. In the process he was frequently harassed by children who yelled 'Hummel, Hummel'. Not being able to react under the heavy weight of the water buckets resting on his shoulders, Hans Hummel merely replied 'Mors, Mors',[97] meaning 'arse arse', presumably like the colloquial expression: 'Ihr könnt mich mal am Arsch lecken!' [You can kiss my ass!]. Thus, the appearance of this call-and-response tradition in a rap track rests exclusively on the audience's awareness of how to respond 'correctly' to this call.

The entire excerpt from this verse therefore only becomes meaningful through access to Northern German cultural knowledge as well as through insight into rap's norms and practices. Schiffmeister creates a lyrical 'third space' in which knowledge of hip-hop culture *and* knowledge of Hamburg depend on each other in order for the *song theme* to resonate meaningfully amongst the audience. From a spatial perspective, Schiffmeister represents Hamburg's regional maritime 'secondspace' through a historical linguistic discourse, Low German also having been the official language of the Hanseatic

97 Douglas Amrine, *Hamburg* (London: Dorling Kindersley, 2012), p. 67.

League.[98] The *linguistic orientation* of the rap track therefore captures a regional identity which is inextricably linked to the city of Hamburg. Moreover, with *Platt* appearing more commonly in contemporary contexts of inebriated and entertaining occasions, the *song theme* suitably mirrors the everyday expression of this local language, which at the same time continues to treat rap as an oral tradition. As well as the culturally ambivalent incorporation of *ritual speech acts*, Schiffmeister succeeds in drawing upon discourses concerning spatiality and historicality in order to embed rap in a regional narrative.

Yet another 'third space' opens up in terms of the song's social perspective. While the remaining rap parts that make up 'Nordish by Nature' are performed in standard German by the other members of Fettes Brot, as well as by Tobi and Das Bo, the latter challenges the Nordic category by being of Bosnian-Herzegovinian ethnicity. Like the members of hip-hop dance crew 'Nordish by Nature', Das Bo's identification with and representation of this Northern Germanness 'contests genealogies of "origin" that lead to claims for cultural supremacy and historical priority' (*LOC*, p. 225). In this particular rap context, Das Bo manages his 'stigma' of foreignness by demonstrating that having a different ethnic heritage is irrelevant for identifying with a transnational (Nordic) region. Moreover, as Hamburg DJ Vito recounts, the presence of Das Bo at freestyle sessions left his fellow Eimsbush rappers 'relativ angespannt, [weil er] diese Doppelreime oder so zweideutige Sachen schon damals rausgehauen hat' [relatively tense because even then he was able to knock out these double-rhymes and ambiguous things like that].[99] Hence, as with Samy Deluxe's mentioning of Boulevard Bou's perfect mastering of the German language, Das Bo further shows that a foreign cultural background is insignificant when cultivating a sophisticated command of the German language.

However, whilst this light-hearted engagement with rap provided linguistic strategies with which to manage social and racial 'stigmata', by the turn of the millennium rap's commercial character had slowly begun to change. As with the rise in popularity of America's West Coast gangsta rap, commercially oriented rappers in Germany began positioning their narratives in deviant urban spaces as well.[100] Thus, despite K-Four and DJ Ben Kenobi claiming that rappers in the United States have 'ganz andere Probleme [...], als die hier. So: "Hier ist das Ghetto". In Deutschland gibt es das in dem Sinne so nicht' [completely different problems [...], from the people here. Like: 'Here is

98 Langer, 'Low German', pp. 285–88.

99 DJ Vito, interviewed by author, 21 June 2012.

100 German gangsta rap was not new in Germany, having already enjoyed success through hip-hop duo Rödelheim-Hartreim Projekt in the mid-1990s. However, this sub-genre did not overshadow the German rap scene to the extent that gangsta rappers did after 2001.

the ghetto'. It doesn't exist like that in Germany],[101] rappers from Germany's capital presented a different perspective on their city.

In 2001 the rap label Aggro Berlin was established in Berlin. Saied explains that 'erst mit dem Erscheinen von Aggro Berlin [...] unter Jugendlichen ein derartig hoher Identifikations- und Aneignungs-Boom entstanden [ist], der die urbane Stadt beziehungsweise Stadtquartiere, in denen die Jugendlichen leben, als Hauptthema fokussiert' [only starting with the appearance of Aggro Berlin did such a major boom in identification and appropriation develop amongst young people, with a main theme that focused on the urban city or, rather, city districts in which the young people lived].[102] In other words, Aggro Berlin promoted German gangsta narratives with an emerging focus on outdoor urban 'firstspaces'. This new orientation was especially advanced through the success of rapper Sido and his neighbourhood-centred track 'Mein Block' (2004):

> Spätestens seit Sido's 'Mein Block' ist das vermeintlich deutsche Ghetto in den Mainstream importiert worden. Danach folgten jede Menge weiterer Visualisierungen von Quartieren, die in der Politik sowie in der sozialen Arbeit ehemals als sozialer Brennpunkt und nun als Stadtteil mit besonderem Erneuerungsbedarf gelten. Der Anknüpfungspunkt an die lokalen Quartiere geht mit einem teilweise Zelebrieren und Glorifizierung dieser einher.[103]
>
> [Ever since Sido's 'Mein Block' the supposed German ghetto has been imported into the mainstream. Then followed a number of further visualizations of districts which, in politics and in social work, used to count as social hotspots and which now count as city districts especially in need of renewal. The point of connection to the local districts is partly accompanied by their celebration and glorification.]

Hence by shifting rap's narratives into 'firstspaces' which became framed as ghetto-centric 'secondspaces' rappers began to address the fact that German cityspaces 'nicht nur Innovationen, Kreativität, wirtschaftliche Entwicklung [generier[en]], [sie] bring[en] auch zusätzlich Hierarchien, Ungleichheit, soziale Polarisierung und Ungerechtigkeit hervor' [not only generate innovation, creativity [and] economic development but also produce additional hierarchies, inequality, social polarization and injustice].[104] Consequentially, this spatial perspective influenced German rap's social discourse, for Samy Deluxe explains that, 'das soziale Spektrum [...] aufgegangen [ist]. Es ist noch

101 DJ Ben Kenobi, interviewed by author, 3 July 2012.
102 Saied, *Rap in Deutschland*, p. 108.
103 Saied, *Rap in Deutschland*, p. 81.
104 Soja, 'Vom "Zeitgeist" zum "Raumgeist"', p. 242.

weniger Mittelstand und [...] jetzt auch irgendwie eine offizielle Sprache für die Unterschicht, [...] jeder kann es sich irgendwie zutrauen' [the social spectrum has broadened. It's even less middle class and [...] now also somehow an official voice for the lower class, [...] everyone can somehow trust themselves to do it].[105] In other words, newly emerging German gangsta rappers represented their socially fragmented urban lifestyle by reflecting this fragmentation linguistically through broken grammar and a 'Straßenüberslang, der eigentlich nicht eindeutig deutsch für jeden ist' [street-uber-slang that is not clearly German to everyone].[106] However, in contrast to the relationship between the urban ghetto and the 'real nigga status' which had been nurtured in American gangsta rap, the German ghetto did not automatically become a racial extension of belonging to an ethnic minority. With Sido of ethnic German origin on his father's side, the gangsta rappers' *linguistic orientation* was rather a means to add socio-economic authenticity to their *song themes* and to distinguish their narratives from previous German rap, while the overall German rap community remained as multicultural as it had been since the 1980s.

While the wave of commercial gangsta rap thus flourished in Berlin, its impact and commercial success were felt in Hamburg as well. Here, however, this new subgenre of rap opened up a commercial niche for local street rappers.[107] Hamburg's rap community had been mostly identified through its 'Wohnzimmerlaune' [living room spirit], yet by 2008 a different perspective on the Northern German metropolis was emerging. This was primarily initiated through the rap label Rattos Locos Records.[108] The Germanized Spanish name serves to personify the rappers who are signed under this label as dirty urban creatures rejected by the dominant society due to the specific urban spaces they inhabit. At the same time, Rattos Locos identify with the cleverness of rats as they learn to survive regardless of attempts to eliminate them.[109] The direction of rap promoted by the label therefore adheres to the street as a 'marketing utility that was alternately derogatory and romantic [while] in the minds of many rap artists "the street" became the official source of the music's authenticity and cultural value'.[110] Nate57 explains that by not engaging in a

105 Samy Deluxe, interviewed by author, 29 July 2012.
106 Samy Deluxe, interviewed by author, 29 July 2012.
107 While street rap was always practised in Hamburg, the local rap image of the city did not reflect this sub-genre but rather represented solely the living room rap movement (Sleepwalker, interviewed by author, 5 June 2012; cf. Blacky White, interviewed by author, 10 July 201).
108 Blacky White, interviewed by author, 10 July 2014.
109 Blacky White, interviewed by author, 10 July 2014.
110 Forman, *The 'hood Comes First*, p. 112.

lyrical glorification of the deviant social behaviour which is central to gangsta rap narratives, Hamburg's local street rappers aim to become the commercial voice for those inhabitants 'die auf jeden Fall eine andere Sicht auf die Welt haben, als wenn es dir finanziell gut geht, glaub ich so. Ja und das will ich den Leuten erklären. Einfach *unsere* Welt erklären!' [who definitely have a different perspective on the world compared to being financially well-off, I think. Yeah and that is what I want to explain to people. Just to explain *our* world!].[111]

Nate57 has also explained (see Chapter 2) that his music reflects Hamburg's socio-spatial history since he creates his beats using the same approach as local pirates did in the past by collecting knowledge about and insight into different cultures. In a similar context, this identification with pirates has also come to define Rattos Locos' adaptation of rap. Member Telly Tellz, for instance, states that 'diese Störtebeker Mentalität, damit kann ich mich identifizieren! [...] Seemänner sind offen für andere Kulturen in meinen Augen. Und das ist Seefahrt und das ist diese Piratenkultur! Damit kann ich mich identifizieren. Weil das sind Outlaws' [this Störtebeker mentality, I can identify with that! [...] In my eyes, sailors are always open towards other cultures. And that is seafaring and that is pirate culture! I can identify with that. Because they are outlaws].[112]

By referring to Störtebeker, Telly Tellz draws upon the same signifiers of locality as employed in the rap track 'Nordish by Nature'. However, Telly Tellz simultaneously re-frames this historical perspective in accordance with his intentions and his image as a contemporary street rapper linked to Hamburg's lower social class. He also shows how rappers are able to 'compose opposing narratives of the very same urban space; sometimes they use the same references and images for conflicting political purposes',[113] as observed by Stehle in her analysis of German gangsta rap. Thus, the juxtaposing appropriation of Hamburg's pirate legends, which previously served to express a regional Nordic identity, is re-signified to represent Hamburg's urban outcast. More specifically, this urban outcast is located in the particular neighbourhood of St. Pauli. According to Blacky White, the reason for this specific urban identification is to show:

> wo du herkommst. Und ich finde, dass es das auch in Deutschland gibt, aber es gab nicht immer so viele Viertel, die wirklich so *boom!* So wie Queens oder Brooklyn [...]. Hier gab es Eimsbush. Im Aggro Berlin Zusammenhang gab es

111 Nate57, interviewed by author, 21 August 2012.
112 Telly Tellz, interviewed by author, 22 August 2012.
113 Stehle, *Ghetto Voices*, p. 4.

> auch ein paar Viertel. Dieses Märkische Viertel oder so. Aber wir sind die St. Pauli *Hustler*.[114]
>
> [where you are from. And I find that you also have that in Germany too but there weren't always as many boroughs that really like *boom!* Like Queens or Brooklyn [...]. Here we had Eimsbush. We had some quarters in the context of Aggro Berlin. This Märkische Viertel and the like. But we are the *hustlers* from St. Pauli.]

In representing their 'hood' Rattos Locos engage in rap's practice of being 'contextually linked to conditions in a city comprised of an amalgamation of neighbourhoods and boroughs with their own highly particularised social norms and cultural nuances'.[115] As St. Pauli is, furthermore, located in close geographic vicinity to the port which justifies and authenticates the rappers' association with pirate mythology, it is also home to the city's red-light district, providing it with an anti-normative 'secondspatial' identity beyond its multicultural nuances. By comparing St. Pauli to Queens or Brooklyn, Blacky White moreover iterates Forman's observation that '[a]lready fully acknowledged as the source of the expanding hip-hop scene, New York was frequently cast as the backdrop or setting for much of the lyrical and thematic content'.[116] This acknowledgement becomes evident in Nate57's and Telly Tellz's track 'Nur die Starken überleben' (2010), which re-interprets the rap song 'Survival of the Fittest' (1995) by New York City's rap duo Mobb Deep.

With a title that addresses the constant competition and tension that defined the 'thirdspace' experience of living in Queens, Mobb Deep express their perspective on urban 'culture as an uneven, incomplete production of meaning and value, often composed of incommensurable demands and practices, produced in the act of social survival' (*LOC*, p. 247). This is summarized in their hook 'We living this 'til the day that we die. Survival of the fit, only the strong survive'.[117] The same 'thirdspace' experience is iterated by Nate57, who explains that growing up in St. Pauli 'einen *stark* [macht]' [makes you strong].[118] Thus, in contrast to the indoor 'firstspaces' which defined Hamburg's early rap sound and where Eimsbush eventually existed solely as a hybrid 'secondspace', Rattos Locos treat their urban 'secondspace' as a reflection of the actual 'thirdspace' experience in which 'the imagined geography tends to become the "real" geography, with the representation coming to define and order the reality' (*THSP*, p. 79). Employing Mobb Deep's

114 Blacky White, interviewed by author, 10 July 2012.
115 Forman, '"Represent": Race, Space and Place in Rap Music', 67.
116 Forman, *The 'hood Comes First*, p. 99.
117 Mobb Deep, *Survival of the Fittest* (Loud Records, 1995) [CD].
118 Nate57, interviewed by author, 21 August 2012.

original musical beat as an aural representation of Hamburg's urban reality, Nate57 initiates the track by inviting the listeners on a lyrical excursion round St. Pauli:

Komm, wir machen eine Tour durch die Gegend.
Neben Burger King siehst du wie die Huren da so stehen.
Vergebens!
Wenn ich unterwegs bin,
Sieht man nur Probleme.
Viele schwach!
Mir kommen die Tränen.
Guck, Kunststudenten fragen mich immer nach Ot.
Ich bleibe lieber misstrauisch,
Vielleicht ist er ja ein Cop.[119]

[Come, we'll take a tour around the area.
You'll see the whores just standing next to Burger King.
In vain!
When I am out
You just see problems.
Many weak!
I'll start to cry.
Look, art students are always asking me for ot.
I rather stay sceptical
Maybe he is a cop.]

The melancholy atmosphere that arises throughout Nate57's descriptive verses is embedded in impure rhyme patterns and in *rap specific rhetoric* that relies on words connoting sadness and desperation. This bleak socio-spatial ambience is further communicated in the accompanying video clip, which, using black and white, manifests the rappers' 'sense of locale, visually representing the places of significance which they inhabit and delineating different social settings and different regions'.[120] As problems become visible when Nate57 is underway, these problems are especially located in the outside urban 'firstspace', namely on the streets. His allusions to the regular use of recreational drugs and to the consequent presence of undercover police in this area are, moreover, verbalized by rhyming the colloquial Turkish term for weed (*ot*) with the common Americanism for police officer. Similar hybrid *linguistic orientation* appears in Telly Tellz's following verses as well. In imitating a conversation between a clerk and himself, he raps:

119 Nate57, 'Nur die Starken überleben', *Verrückte Ratten* (Rattos Locos Records, 2009), http://deutscher-hip-hop.com/?path=download&contentid=2282 [accessed 9 June 2016].
120 Forman, *The 'hood Comes First*, p. 245.

Figure 6: Rattos Locos Records logo

(Copyright: Rattos Locos Records)

> Geh mal hier hin, geh mal da hin,
> Hol das Papier für dein Parra.
> Hol mal dies, hol mal das für Hartz IV.
> Drei hundert im Monat?
> Digga, woll'n die mich verarschen?[121]
>
> [Go here, go there.
> Get that paperwork for your parra.
> Get this, get that for Hartz IV.
> Three hundred a month?
> Dude, are you kidding me?]

In describing the iterative and unsatisfying process of bureaucracy, the second verse is created by a 'pa'-aliteration constructed through the use of German and Turkish words. While *parra* signifies money in Turkish, it is through the mention of the *Hartz VI* reform, the German state benefit of three hundred Euros a month that can be claimed by unemployed citizens, that Telly Tellz specifically situates his rap narrative in a social discourse pertaining to a German context. While he does not describe his 'thirdspace' experience in spatial terms as Nate57 did, Telly Tellz's local affiliation nevertheless becomes apparent through his use of the term 'Digga'. This form of address can be understood as the German equivalent of 'mate' or 'dude' and is primarily heard in, and associated with, Hamburg. Its etymology is related to the German word

121 Telly Tellz, 'Nur die Starken überleben'.

'Dicker' [fatty]. Pronounced with a Hamburg accent, the velar stops of the [k] approximate the common sound of a [g]. Moreover, through the substitution of an '-a' for the written suffix '-er' the word parallels the spelling of 'nigga' despite their etymological unrelatedness.

These two brief lyrical excerpts thus illustrate the way in which a previously established *song theme* about socio-urban criticism can be (in)fused with cultural content pertaining to St. Pauli. In this way, Nate57's and Telly Tellz's rap track creates a 'third space' which shows 'that even the same signs can be appropriated, translated, rehistorisized and read anew' (*LOC*, p. 55). While Mobb Deep's beat is appropriated as the musical signifier of urban and social desperation, the *song theme* is translated culturally and linguistically in order to become meaningful within a Hamburg context and re-historicized as a contemporary socio-urban narrative. However, this means Telly Tellz and Nate57 also challenge the Germanness of their lyrical product. While their *linguistic orientation* supports Telly's and Nate57's local street credibility as rappers who employ the language used in the lower social class, neither rapper is of Turkish descent.[122] This aspect widens their production of a 'third space' even further.

Nate57's and Telly Tellz's appropriation of *ot* and *parra* proves that language is not a fixed sign of culture, or of nationality. Rather, it highlights the ambivalent 'process of language that is crucial to the production of meaning and ensures, at the same time, that meaning is never simply mimetic and transparent' (*LOC*, p. 52). The 'thirdspace' experience of St. Pauli is thus lyrically represented as a 'secondspace' through the use of local as well as multilingual signifiers. Indeed, Blacky White specifically claims that Rattos Locos 'wären nicht wie wir wären, wären wir nicht hier groß geworden. Weil das ist echt so ein Multikulti Hot Spot immer gewesen [...] und das prägt dich. Das zeigt sich in der Musik' [wouldn't be the way we are had we not grown up here. Because this has always really been a multicultural hot spot [...] and that shapes you. It shows in the music].[123]

Beyond musically and lyrically representing the local multiculturalism of St. Pauli, this 'thirdspace' experience is portrayed in the logo of Rattos Locos Records as well (see Figure 6). Without creating a logo 'genau wie St. Pauli mit einem Totenkopf' [just like St. Pauli with one skull] Rattos Locos present

122 Turks comprise the largest ethnic minority in Germany (Anonymous, 'Ausländische Bevölkerung in Deutschland 2011', in *Statistisches Jahrbuch Deutschland und Internationales* (Wiesbaden: Statistisches Bundesamt, 2012), https://www.destatis.de/DE/Publikationen/Statistisches Jahrbuch/StatistischesJahrbuch2012.pdf?__blob=publicationFile<20.2.2012. [accessed 21 April 2014].

123 Blacky White, interviewed by author, 10 July 2012.

themselves as a trio of skulls situated in front of a set of crossbones.[124] The largest skull, the one in the centre, is characterized by a streaked pattern on its head. The left one is defined by a dark patch of hair, whereas the right skull is merely portrayed with a faint shade of grey on its head. Together, the three skulls serve to present St. Pauli as an urban borough where:

> verschiedene Kulturen zusammenkommen. Das sieht man ja auch auf dem Logo. Der eine hat *Cornrows*, der andere hat so eine Kanakenfrisur[125] und der dritte hat so 'ne Glatze, Kurzhaar. Das soll die Deutschen, die Niggas und die Kanaken alle zusammen darstellen.[126]
>
> [different cultures come together. You see that in the logo. One guy has corn rows, the other has a kanak hair style and the third is, like, bald, has short hair. That is supposed to represent the Germans, the niggas and the kanaks all together.]

Thus, according to Rattos Locos, two thirds of St. Pauli's population are made up by ethnic 'others',[127] a claim which echoes Bhabha when he writes that the post-modern city 'has been altered by mass migration and settlement' (*LOC*, p. 316). However, the compelling aspect of Blacky White's statement is that the migrants and multicultural settlers in St. Pauli do not necessarily seek to alter their national affiliation with Germany. Rather, the tri-culturality presented by the stereotypically self-representative trio of skulls is also able to represent one person's national identity. Blacky White thus pursues German rap because he is 'halb Afrikaner, das ist schwarze Musik' [half African, this is black music][128] yet adds that by becoming a rap-label manager in Hamburg he now resembles

124 Blacky White, interviewed by author, 10 July 2012. 'Genau wie St. Pauli' refers to the flag of local football team FC St. Pauli, whose skull-and-crossbones symbol became representative of the entire district and a sign for its local patriotism.

125 The German term *Kanake* is, according to Cheesman, often 'used of brown-skinned people. It has been appropriated by some racialized Germans, notably hip hoppers of color, as a group self-ascription. This combative usage goes back to the late 1980s in urban hip hop circles, where it is compared with US rappers' "niggah," though closer connotative equivalents are "spick" or, in the UK, "Paki"' (Tom Cheesman, 'Talking "Kanak": Zaimoglu contra Leitkultur', in *Multicultural Germany*, ed. by Göktürk and Wolbert, pp. 82–99 (p. 85).

126 Blacky White, interviewed by author, 10 July 2012.

127 St. Pauli is one of the districts in Hamburg with the highest number of immigrants or Germans from a different cultural background, as well as the highest unemployment rate (Anonymous, 'Germany. Statistisches Amt für Hamburg und Schleswig-Holstein', *Hamburger Stadtteilprofile 2013*, 15th edn (Hamburg: Anstalt des Öffentlichen Rechts, 2013), http://www.statistik-nord.de/uploads/tx_standocuments/NR15_Statistik-Profile2013.pdf [accessed 1 April 2014].

128 Blacky White, interviewed by author, 10 July 2012.

a 'Business Kanak' [business kanak].[129] Being German, African and a *Kanake* therefore composes a fluid identity category without any component excluding the others.

This inclusive cultural statement also transcends the street rap genre and the specific urban space of St. Pauli. Former Eimsbush member Samy Deluxe, for instance, visually manifests his Africanness through his cornrows in the music video to 'Weck mich auf' [Wake me up] (2001),[130] employing a racial 'attribute' that recalls Jango's emphasis on his Afro in his dance performance. However, Samy Deluxe also claims that he is 'mit Abstand der verrückteste Kanake' [by far the craziest Kanake][131] and 'ein deutscher Mann, so steht's in meinem Pass' [a German man, that's what it says in my passport].[132] Hence, by expressing a German identity through German rap, both Rattos Locos and Samy Deluxe challenge the:

> debates on multiculturalism [which] are generally preoccupied with determining the degrees of compatibility or conflict between cultures. What is obscured by this perspective are the porous boundaries between groups, the diffuse notions of identity, the deterritorialized links between members of groups, the globalizing patterns of communication and the hybrid process of cultural transformation.[133]

In this case one might even talk about a post-hybrid process of cultural transformation since the multiple cultural identifications and racial appearances serve to represent a German identity rooted in Hamburg. Telly Tellz, for instance, refers to himself as a contemporary German 'Mischlingskind' [mongrel child], provocatively appropriating this label of identity in the *song theme* of his first single and as the title of his first mix tape.[134] In this context, the rapper re-introduces this 'tribal stigma' as a valid and real contemporary state of identity, despite its historically-tainted racialized use in Germany (see Herzog).

Samy Deluxe engages in a similar *linguistic discourse*, sharing the same

129 Blacky White, interviewed by author, 10 July 2012.

130 'Samy Deluxe – Weck Mich Auf', *SamyDeluxeVEVO*, http://www.youtube.com/watch?v=yiWd14IoN2Y [accessed 12 May 2014].

131 Samy Deluxe, 'Reimemonsta 2011', *Schwarz Weiß* (EMI, 2011) [CD].

132 Samy Deluxe, 'Dis Wo ich Herkomm', *Dis Wo ich Herkomm* (EMI, 2009) [CD].

133 Papastergiadis, *The Turbulence of Migration*, p. 105.

134 Telly Tellz, *Mischlingskind* (Rattos Locos Records, 2010), https://www.youtube.com/watch?v=efvmTzuGF3U [accessed 9 June 2016]. For an analysis of Telly Tellz's track 'Mischlingskind' see Marissa K. Munderloh, '*Heb die Fahne hoch, Santa Pauli Patriot!*: A Case Study of Urban Place-Making in Rap Music', in *Place-Making in urbanen Diskursen – Interdisziplinäre Beiträge zur Stadtforschung*, ed. by Beatrix Busse and Ingo H. Warnke, Diskursmuster – Discourse Patterns, 7 (Boston/Berlin: de Gruyter, 2014), pp. 421–42.

fate as Telly Tellz since both were born and raised in Hamburg by a German mother yet without their African father. In his song 'Schwarz Weiß' (2011), Samy Deluxe rhymes:

> Ich bin 'ne Mischung, aber nenn mich nicht Mischling.
> Nenn mich 'Baby', weil ich so frisch kling.
> Oder nenn mich Samy, weil ich so Deluxe bin.[135]
>
> [I'm a mixture but don't call me a mongrel.
> Call me 'baby' because I sound so fresh.
> Or call me Samy because I am so deluxe.]

The verse playfully engages with labels and descriptions of 'tribal stigmata', whereby Samy Deluxe manages his African identity by rejecting the label *Mischling*, thus revealing a mixedness in terms of positive and negative understanding of the contemporary use of the term. Rather, Samy Deluxe describes himself through the way he sounds: deluxe. Indeed, this last aspect is directly captured in yet another song, in which Samy Deluxe raps: 'Hör, wie elegant ich diese Sprache hier spreche, als ob ich diese dunkle Hautfarbe nicht hätte' [Listen to how elegantly I speak this language, as if I didn't have this dark skin colour].[136] While characterizing his rhetoric as elegant, Samy Deluxe also touches upon the supposed relationship between a poor command of the German language and being stigmatized as a minority or a foreigner – a relationship often emphasized in German gangsta or street rap. However, by not adhering to the urban practices, social norms and forms of linguistic articulation that are tied to gangsta or street rap, Samy Deluxe challenges this assumption as his rhetorical skills, on the contrary, enable him to become spatially, socially and racially transient. Taking advantage of this condition, Samy Deluxe continues to engage in a German cultural discourse through rap's lyrical aesthetic; however, he does so by re-framing the dominant commercial focus of German rap from its negative gangsta sub-genre to a positive and hence relevant art form for German national culture. In an excerpt from the track 'Poesie Album' (2011),[137] Samy Deluxe, for instance, raps that he is:

> So Schiller, so Goethe, so bitter, so böse.
> Noch immer der größte
> Poet, der hier lebt.
> Wenn ihr jetzt noch mehr wollt,
> Fütter' ich euch deutschen Dichtern Reime

135 Samy Deluxe, 'Schwarz Weiß', *Schwarz Weiß* (EMI, 2011) [CD].

136 Samy Deluxe 'Hände Hoch', *Schwarz Weiß* (EMI, 2011) [CD].

137 In 1996, Bremer hip-hop duo Zentrifugal also released a track called 'Poesiealbum' which touched upon the lyrical sophistication of German rap.

Bis ihr alle brecht wie Bertolt.
Das ist für mich echter Erfolg.
Wenn der Text noch mehr rollt.
Und ich schein' wie der Morgenstern.
Hoffe, dass ihr alle
Aus den Reimen und den Worten lernt.
Meine Damen und Herren,
Was würde ich bloß tun hier, wär' ich nicht Rapstar?
Wahrscheinlich wär' ich der neue Erich Kästner.[138]

[So Schiller, so Goethe, so bitter, so angry.
Still the greatest
Poet who lives here.
If you want more
I will feed you German poets with rhymes
Until you all vomit like Bertolt.
In my eyes that is real success.
When the text rolls even more.
And I shine like the morning star.
Hope that you all
Learn from my rhymes and words.
Ladies and Gentlemen,
What would I just do if I weren't a rap star?
I'd probably be the new Erich Kästner.]

Through an alternating 'i' and 'ö' assonance, Samy Deluxe starts his stanza by comparing his rap skills and persona to the grandeur of past German lyric poets Schiller and Goethe. Claiming his status as Germany's greatest living poet, he continues with the use of similes in reference to German authors Bertolt Brecht and Christian Morgenstern. By engaging in the practice of signifying, Samy Deluxe employs the second person plural present tense of the verb 'brechen' [to vomit], which results in the homophone and hence ambivalent word 'brecht' alluding to the German poet's surname. In the latter example, Samy Deluxe employs the literal meaning of Morgenstern's surname in order to boast about the way he shines like Venus, the morning star.

Following these comparisons Samy Deluxe utilizes rap's original function as an oral tradition in which 'sämtliche oral kommunizierte Inhalte ihrer Gestalt nach flüchtig und zeitgebunden sind, [und] nur im Moment des kommunikativen Aktes von den an diesem Akt Teilhabenden wahrgenommen werden' [the form of all orally communicated content is fleeting and temporary and such communication is only realized as such at the moment

138 Samy Deluxe, 'Poesie Album', *Schwarz Weiß* (EMI, 2011) [CD].

of this communicative act by those who are participating in this act].[139] Since the album on which 'Poesie Album' features was published without a song book, Samy Deluxe acknowledges his imaginary listeners by addressing them formally as 'Meine Damen und Herren' [Ladies and Gentlemen] and hopes that they are able to acquire knowledge from his words and rhymes. Then, in a final comparison, he equates his rap star status and skills to those of the award-winning German author of children's books Erich Kästner, who died in 1974.

This lyrical excerpt thus serves to show how Samy Deluxe fuses knowledge of Germany's literary history with rap's *ritualized speech act* of signifying and a *rap specific rhetoric* iterating the traditional 'braggadocious style'[140] of rap's lyrical delivery. This strategy has not been uncommon in German rap, with Cheesman noting that German rap 'increasingly sets itself in German lyric traditions; but this tendency is in productive tension with its continuing sense of indebtedness to American forebears, and its ear for new developments in American and other international hip hop'.[141] By engaging in this productive tension Samy Deluxe not only equates blackness with Germanness, but also alters the social status of rap. The Afro-German rapper blends rap's lyrical practices with a historical discourse that re-signifies rap as an art form for those with a literary education due to his clearly pronounced standard German.

Gizmo further describes Samy Deluxe as 'der beste Rapper Deutschlands' [Germany's best rapper].[142] This status therefore allows the rapper further to manage his 'stigma' by becoming a 'speaker' – a role that Goffman relates to socially stigmatized individuals who appear:

> before various audiences of normal and of the stigmatized; they present the case for the stigmatized, when they themselves are natives of the group, provide a living model of fully-normal achievement, being heroes of adjustment who are subject to public awards for proving that an individual of this kind can be a good person (*STGM*, pp. 24–25).

In this way, however, Samy Deluxe does not present his 'tribal stigma' from a minority perspective but rather as a national and hence authoritative cultural sign, revealing:

> how, in signifying the present, something comes to be repeated, relocated and translated in the name of tradition, in the guise of a pastness that is not

139 Rappe, 'Rhythmus-Sound-Symbol', p. 139.

140 Ogbar, *Hip Hop Revolution*, p. 70.

141 Cheesman, 'Polyglot Pop Politics', 210. German hip-hop crew Anarchist Academy had, for example, released a track called 'Brecht goes HipHop' in 1996 which even quoted Brecht, amongst other German lyricists (Cheesman, 'Polyglot Pop Politics', 209).

142 Gizmo, interviewed by author, 17 July 2014.

> necessarily a faithful sign of historical memory but a strategy of representing authority (*LOC*, pp. 51–52).

This strategy ultimately rests in Samy Deluxe's post-hybrid lyrical presentation of identity, in which his 'tribal stigma' becomes representative of contemporary German culture expressed through an engagement with rap.

As an interim summary of the first analysis of rap's manifestation in Hamburg, the exploration of hip-hop's lyrical art form illustrated the variety of strategies inherent in rap's social, spatial and historical components, features with which rappers have been able to establish rap as a meaningful cultural practice and with which they are able to express their regional, urban and national identity. While German rap in Hamburg started as a live performance and hence as a 'thirdspace' experience unfolding in domestic 'firstspaces', part of this tradition transcended into the commercial realm. Enabled by the structures and conditions of Hamburg's metropolitan cityspace, commercial German rap, on the one hand, transitioned from the initial spatial manifestation of rap into a 'secondspatial' discourse. With the body no longer being tied to a rap performance, language became the most prominent substitution and signifier for the imagined 'secondspaces'. Three examples served to analyse the commercial manifestation of local rap, with lyrics becoming the focus of close readings and, at the same time, being treated as direct citations of the rappers. These selected close readings highlighted the ways in which differing perspectives of sociality, historicality and spatiality in Hamburg are implemented as lyrical representations of a German region, neighbourhood or nation and expressed through the targeted use of the German language. However, even beyond these lyrical examples and close readings of rap as 'secondspace' imageries, hip-hop's lyrical art form continues to be practised as a 'thirdspace' experience in Hamburg. Thus, rapper Stee concludes that, 'wenn du auf gute Hip-Hop Veranstaltungen gehen willst und dich ein bisschen auskennst, kannst du das auf jeden Fall mindestens einmal die Woche machen! Und ich glaube, das hat im Moment nicht jede Stadt' [if you want to attend good hip-hop events and you know your way around, then you can definitely find at least one a week! And I don't think that is possible in every city at the moment].[143] In line with this observation, the following analysis will now turn to the German rap community of Oldenburg.

143 Stee, interviewed by author, 26 July 2012.

Oldenburg and the Provincial Performances of German Rap

Rap in Oldenburg established itself in the same fashion as it did in Hamburg, namely, as a live and non-commercial practice performed in indoor private 'firstspaces'. K-Four adds that Oldenburg's overarching rap sound can be described as 'the backpacker sound'[144] – a synonym for the aforementioned conscious rap sub-genre which reigned at the freestyle sessions in the basement of Schlechta Umgang. Indeed, this link between indoor spatiality, anti-commerciality and freestyle rap is addressed in the rap track 'One Love' (2007), in which Oldenburg rapper Jordan MC rhymes:

> Guter Untergrund.
> Ich versprech', du kannst ihn hier finden.
> Hungrige MCs.
> Ich sag' nur: 24 Linguisten.[145]
>
> [Good underground.
> I promise you can find it here.
> Hungry MCs.
> I'm just saying: 24 linguists.]

The term 'Untergrund' refers to a spatial as well as to a non-commercial rap discourse in which Jordan MC claims that Oldenburg's underground rap community comprises twenty-four rappers or, in this case, linguists. Their identification as language scientists expresses the early German approach to rap, treating it as an art form for German language aficionados as described by Samy Deluxe. However, Jordan MC in particular addresses one local freestyle crew named Linguisten 24 in which the number's original purpose is to symbolize the location where the linguists engage in rap.

While the rappers of Eimsbush represent their locality by appropriating the first syllable of their district Eimsbüttel, Oldenburg's rap crew base their spatial identification on flat number 24. Inhabited by three members of the crew, it is not the 'firstspace' of the basement but rather of the living room which has become the epicentre of local freestyle rap. The domestic spatial discourse thus reflects a *Wohnzimmerlaune* in which the rappers primarily focus on honing their rhetorical skills and on creating improvised rhymed stories. The lyrical and linguistic priorities of this domesticized 'backpack' rap genre become even more evident when it is acknowledged that the 'firstspace' of the '24' is located in Oldenburg's small, but nevertheless well-known, red-

144 K-Four, interviewed by author, 9 February 2012.

145 Jordan MC, 'One Love' (2007), https://www.youtube.com/watch?v=rBp6gWIqiQs [accessed 9 June 2016].

light district. Hence, while Rattos Locos have based their local identity in St. Pauli, the same urban 'secondspace' of pimps and prostitutes in Oldenburg becomes irrelevant for its linguists, as their rap genre and practices do not aim at mirroring the particular socio-urban discourses through *song themes* or *linguistic orientation*. Rather, Moe compares Oldenburg's rap community to the 'Künstler-Boheme der 20er' [Bohemian artist society of the 20s].[146] When talking about attending the indoor freestyle sessions, the local graffiti artist explains that:

> so eine elektrisierende Geschichte habe ich lange nicht mehr erlebt. Dass das Donnerstagsabends immer offene Tür ist. Jeder kann reinkommen, jeder kann rappen, jeder kann was beitragen. Und ich habe da Dinge erlebt, wo mir die Tränen gekommen sind. Wo Jungs da drüber erzählt haben, wie sie ihren Vater zum ersten Mal hier über Facebook gefunden haben. Und dann interagiert haben. Jeder hat seinen Seelenstriptease betrieben in Reimform. Und das war eine Atmosphäre, wo dir die Tränen einfach gekullert sind, weil die Menschen ganz authentisch waren.[147]
>
> [I have not experienced such an electrifying thing in a long time. Open door every Thursday evening. Anyone can enter, anyone can rap, can contribute something. And I have experienced things which brought tears to my eyes. Where boys have talked about how they found their father for the first time through Facebook. And then they interacted. Everybody did their soul striptease in rhyme form. And that was an atmosphere in which tears just started streaming down your face because people were so authentic.]

Moe's description of authenticity is thus defined by the interrelatedness of an electrifying 'thirdspace' experience created through the rappers' 'interaction (that is, face-to-face interaction) [which] may be roughly defined as the reciprocal influence of individuals upon another's actions when in one another's immediate physical presence' (*PSEL*, p. 15). In other words, by engaging in freestyle rap the practitioners present their social self by means of improvised yet nevertheless personal *song themes* as they convert the living room of the '24' into a Goffmanian 'front'.

The relevance of the domestic 'firstspaces' for local rappers becomes apparent even beyond the reciprocal freestyle sessions. As Oldenburg, unlike Hamburg, does not have the structures that enable the commercial development of rap,[148] rappers and music producers build their recording

146 Moe, interviewed by author, 11 March 2012.

147 Moe, interviewed by author, 11 March 2012.

148 It should, however, be mentioned that nowadays it is possible to become commercially successful by uploading songs onto the Internet, such as onto YouTube, regardless of one's urban location. In that way, rappers judge their success by counting the number of views in

studios in living rooms, basements or bedrooms. Furthermore, the specific living room of the '24' remains a Goffmanian 'front' even for recorded rap productions by becoming a designated 'setting' for accompanying rap video clips. This is the case for local rapper Juiz's rap track '4x4' (2013), which features linguists Jordan MC, Starchild and Macentosh.[149]

While the entire cinematic narrative unfolds in the flat '24', the *song theme* chosen for this recorded rap track connects the contemporary appropriation of rap in Oldenburg to the past performative tradition of rap in the Bronx. A close reading of a lyrical excerpt of '4x4' will provide a closer insight into the way Oldenburg's rappers authenticate their artistic performance, as Macentosh claims that they are:

> Oldenburg City's Master Chiefs.
> Für Peeps,
> Die richtig Bock drauf haben.
> Die Hip-Hop auch noch spüren und nicht in Form von Klamottenmarken.
> Hip-Hop auch noch verstehen
> Ohne billiges Bumsgepose.
> Inszenierte Beefgeschichten gesetzt als schlechte Promotion.
> Wo sind die wahren Heads von früher?
> Fast keiner mehr zu sehen.
> Wir tragen gerne euer Erbe,
> Bis es in anderen lebt.
> Für die nächsten, die es lernen
> Ist die Zeit noch nicht zu spät.
> Begreift Rap in seiner Reimform
> Und ihr könnt Rap verstehen.[150]
>
> [For peeps
> Who are really keen for it.
> Who still feel hip-hop and not just in the form of clothing brands.
> Who still understand hip-hop
> Without cheap sexual posing.
> Staged beef stories framed as bad promotion.
> Where are the true heads from the past?
> Almost nobody left to be seen.
> We gladly carry your legacy
> Until it lives in others.
> For the next ones who will learn

---

terms of clicks that their track or video has received.

149 Juiz feat. Starchild, Jordan MC und Macentosh, '4x4', *JuizySupport*, http://www.youtube.com/watch?v=XxdfdcjR3n0 [accessed 12 February 2014].

150 Macentosh, in Juiz feat. None aka Starchild, Jordan&Macentosh, '4x4', *Eigenregie* (Cubetribe Studio, 2014) [CD].

It is not yet too late.
Comprehend rap in its rhyme form
And then you will understand rap.]

The rap stanza consists of the common rap verse structure of sixteen bars, captured further in the title of the song along with the division of four rappers and four rap parts. Macentosh's part closes the track with a continuation of the *song theme*'s boastful self-display and *rap specific rhetoric*, such as referring to hip-hop aficionados as 'heads' in order to show knowledge of and affiliation with hip-hop culture. More specifically, Macentosh places hip-hop's norms and practices within a historical discourse which is represented by his and his colleagues' engagement in hip-hop culture's 'true' and hence original narrative. While the *linguistic orientation* is manifested in standard German infused with English slang, Macentosh frames the true narrative of rap as a 'thirdspace' experience, as an art form to be felt or sensed beyond visible fashion statements, images and commercial marketing strategies. In stating this, Macentosh touches upon Tickner's argument that while rap 'came alive on the streets of the ghetto' it was subsequently 'exported to the rest of the world by capitalist music industry which influenced its development by creating certain notions of authenticity detached from hip-hop culture's original social and political roots'.[151]

By emphasizing the importance of hip-hop's roots and by teaching and passing on the art form to the following generation, Macentosh situates himself in rap's historical continuity, albeit spatially re-located to Oldenburg, Germany. Nonetheless, as Macentosh ultimately concludes, the location remains irrelevant for a faithful engagement in rap as one needs to understand its lyrical aesthetics. This perspective liberates the art form from any social discourses or particular urban spaces and cultural histories. Hence, by proudly identifying themselves as 'Oldenburg City's Master Chiefs' the rappers who feature on '4x4' provide a fitting example of the way hip-hop culture can indeed be 'ein Kleinstadtphänomen [und] [...] nicht zwangsläufig mit der für Großstädte charakteristischen Erfahrung des sozialen Bruchs, der Heterogenität und Dichte verbunden sein [muss]' [a small-town phenomenon [which] does not necessarily have to be connected to the characteristic experience of the social rupture, heterogeneity and density of the metropolis].[152]

The positive affiliation with Oldenburg can be detected in other recorded rap tracks as well. Stylez-Tyson, for instance, begins his track 'OneLove' (2012), by claiming:

151 Tickner, 'Aquí en el Ghetto', 126.

152 Klein and Friedrich, 'Populäre Stadtansichten. Bildinszenierungen des Urbanen im HipHop', p. 87.

Oldenburg, 261,
Ihr seid meine Stadt.
Jeder einzelne von euch, weil ihr sie einzigartig macht.[153]

[Oldenburg, 261,
You are my city.
Each and every one of you because you make it unique.]

While Oldenburg's urban uniqueness is created by its inhabitants, Stylez-Tyson expresses his identification with the cityspace by referring to it in the 'secondspatial' code '261'. This number comprises the first three digits of Oldenburg's postcode. Such urban signification is not uncommon in rap, being an adaptation of American rappers' original practice of referring to 'particular streets, boulevards and neighbourhoods, telephone area codes [and] postal service zip codes'.[154] Similarly, Nate57 expresses his urban affiliation through the number 57, which represents his St. Pauli neighbourhood, the *Karolinenviertel*, with its postcode terminating in 57.[155]

However, in the case of Oldenburg, the combination '261' signifies the city in its entirety. The last two digits are decisive in determining the city's districts and their omission allows '261' to refer to Oldenburg as a holistic cityspace. The numerical code therefore provides a metropolitan feel to this average-sized Northern German city, as Friedrich and Klein point out that 'global zirkulierenden Symbole des Urbanen im Lokalen ein urbanes Lebensgefühl her[stellen]' [globally circulating symbols of the urban create a sense of urban life on the local level].[156] Stylez-Tyson elaborates on the consequence of this all-encompassing 'secondspace' perspective on Oldenburg when he continues to rap:

Ich kenne jeden Straßenzug,
Wie meine Westentasche.
Ein Haufen Bräute,
Weil ich jede zweite schon im Bettchen hatte.
Tausend Leute,
Weil ich mit jedem dritten Geschäfte mache.
Und nicht zuletzt,
Weil jeder vierte mit jedem fünften hier verwandt ist.[157]

153 Stylez-Tyson, 'OneLove' (2012), single, https://www.youtube.com/watch?v=i8jCkOfYy_Q [accessed 30 June 2016].
154 Forman, *The 'hood Comes First*, p. xvii.
155 Nate57, interviewed by author, 21 August 2012.
156 Klein and Friedrich, 'Populäre Stadtansichten. Bildinszenierungen des Urbanen im HipHop', p. 87.
157 Stylez-Tyson, 'OneLove'.

[I know every street
Like the back of my hand.
A bunch of brides
Because I've bedded every second one.
A thousand people
Because I do business with every third one.
And not least
Because here every forth one is related to every fifth one.]

By employing *rap specific rhetoric* in his use of simile, Stylez-Tyson expresses his profound acquaintance with Oldenburg's 'firstspace' and its inhabitants. While engaging in the *ritualized speech act* of boasting in order to state the nature of his local relationships, Stylez-Tyson's knowledge of and insight into Oldenburg's cityspace are ultimately due to the inhabitants' supposed genetic relatedness, an allusion to the city's small-scale 'firstspace' and hence intimate 'thirdspace' experience. Nevertheless, the positive identification with Oldenburg is captured in the title of the track where 'One Love' acts as a synonym for Oldenburg's hip-hop community.

The term's scene-specific signification was established by Jordan MC's rap track 'One Love'. While the concept of an all-encompassing love was adopted into hip-hop terminology via Jamaican cultural influences in the Bronx, it became symbolic for the unity of hip-hop's four main artistic elements.[158] Tickner even highlights the fact that 'the local, everyday absorption of dominant cultural commodities such as music changes the commodities' significance but does so in a myriad ways, depending on the place and time in question'.[159] Jordan MC exclusively inscribes hip-hop's one love into Oldenburg's local hip-hop community. He re-interprets the first letter of both words as a synonym for Oldenburg since 'OL' represents the city on national vehicle registration plates.

However, Oldenburg's hip-hop community is also represented through Jordan MC's targeted use of lyrically coded messages. Thus, Jordan MC's discursive strategy creates an imagined bond between him and the listener since, as Berns and Schlobinski point out in their analysis of German rap, 'to decipher [a] line is thus a sort of privilege, as listeners are made to feel that they share a special knowledge'.[160] In line with this observation, Jordan MC, for example, raps:

158 For more information on the religious and spiritual origins of the concept of 'one love' in Jamaican culture, see Robert Roskind, *Rasta Heart: A Journey into One Love* (Blowing Rock, NC: One Love, 2001).

159 Tickner, 'Aquí en el Ghetto', 126.

160 Jan Berns and Peter Schlobinski, 'Constructions of Identity in German Hip-hop Culture', in *Discourse Constructions of Youth Identities*, ed. by Jannis Androutsopoulos and Alexandra Georgakopoulou (Amsterdam: Benjamins, 2003), pp. 197–219 (p. 208).

Danke für die Stunden im Keller,
Sbek.
Ich vergess' nichts.
Gute Momente!
Das Leben ist oft 'Arm und Hässlich'.[161]

[Thanks for the hours in the basement,
Sbek.
I'll forget nothing.
Good moments!
Life is often 'poor and ugly'.]

The name Sbek only makes sense if one knows that he is a local graffiti artist and member of the local hip-hop community; while Jordan MC's description of life simultaneously comes to signify a life which is positively affected by the 'thirdspace' experience of rival freestyle rap crew Arm und Hässlich. Together with Macentosh's and Stylez-Tyson's lyrics, the brief rap excerpts therefore present ways in which Oldenburg's local hip-hop community is able to engage in rap as a meaningful, authentic practice within a small German town without the same spatial and social conditions as Hamburg.

At the same time, the spatial appropriation of rap in Oldenburg can be more clearly divided into 'the micro and the macro, with neither inherently privileged, but only with the accompanying recognition that no city – indeed, no lived space – is ever completely knowable no matter what perspective' (*THSP*, p. 310). The micro is located in the 'firstspaces' of selected domestic rooms that encapsulate the 'thirdspace' experience of local rap as an improvised, rhetorical form of the presentation of the self. This appropriation of rap is therefore comparable to the original tradition of rap in the Bronx prior to the commercial turn of hip-hop's lyrical element. The macro, on the other hand, is captured in the small cityspace of Oldenburg as it is symbolically 'enlarged' by treating it lyrically as a holistic urban 'secondspace', a treatment enforced through the use of distinct codes such as 261 or One Love. These two spatial perspectives also have an influential effect on rap's social discourse, since neither the standard German *linguistic orientation* nor the personal or locally based *song themes* communicate a particular or a deviant social status. Rather, the general use of language mirrors K-Four's statement that Oldenburg's rap community comprises 'normal people who are living their normal lives'.[162] From Goffman's point of view this refers to 'unstigmatised' people, in contrast to the lifestyles promoted by gangsta or street rappers (*STGM*, p. 5).

Indeed, with none of the members of the Linguisten 24 being of an

161 Jordan MC, 'One Love'.
162 K-Four, interviewed by author, 9 February 2012.

ethnicity other than German, the use of language does not serve to manage 'tribal stigmata' or 'blemishes of character', in contrast to the lyrical messages in the majority of contemporary German gangsta rap. Rather, by belonging to a middle-class, white German hip-hop community, Oldenburg's rappers adapt rap according to the spaces and social structures available to them in Oldenburg: as an underground, communal practice centred on fostering local interaction and creative engagement with the German language. Hence, in order for rap to function as a communal local practice, 'lyrics and rhythms must achieve success on the home front first, where the flow, subject matter, style and image must resonate meaningfully among those who share common bonds to place'.[163] While the overall approach to rap in Oldenburg is not driven by commercial success, local rappers who do attempt to become marketable choose to alter the common subject matter and style of rap that had previously resonated meaningfully amongst its local rappers. This, for example, is the case with NewMan on the Block. According to K-Four:

> Oldenburg is not that big that you can say it is a gangsta town like Hannover or Hamburg where a lot of crime does happen. We are not in New York or L.A. [*laughing*] where people get shot by drive-by.[164]

Although Oldenburg cannot provide 'thirdspace' experiences relevant for creating gangsta rap or street rap narratives, Oldenburg rapper NewMan on the Block nevertheless insists that his local rap is 'Gangsta!'.[165]

NewMan was introduced to German rap whilst in prison, since '*da* haben die zur Zeit alle Bushido gehört' [at that time everyone in there listened to Bushido].[166] With German-Tunisian gangsta rapper Bushido signed to Aggro Berlin, NewMan's understanding of German rap was instantly framed by ghetto-centred narratives about Berlin's socially deviant lifestyles. In order to adhere to the norms and lyrical messages of this commercial sub-genre of rap, NewMan has strategically re-functioned his local urban district of Nadorst into 'das kleine Ghetto' [the little ghetto].[167] NewMan bases this 'secondspace' perspective on the supposed fact that 'wenn da zwei dicke Hochhäuser stehen, dann hast du ein Ghetto. [*Laughs*] Geht ja immer ganz schnell, dass man irgendwas als Ghetto bezeichnet. Wenn man irgendwo eine Gegend hat, wo viele sozial schwache Leute hingehen und viele Ausländer' [whenever there are two fat tower blocks standing there, then you have a ghetto. [*Laughs*] It doesn't ever take very long for something to be described as a ghetto.

163 Forman, '"Represent": Race, Space and Place in Rap Music', 73.
164 K-Four, interviewed by author, 9 February 2012.
165 NewMan on the Block, interviewed by author, 11 February 2012.
166 NewMan on the Block, interviewed by author, 11 February 2012.
167 NewMan on the Block, interviewed by author, 11 February 2012.

Whenever there is any sort of area where many socially disadvantaged people and many foreigners go]. While describing Oldenburg's ghetto from a particular 'firstspace' as well as from a 'thirdspace' perspective defined by the lived experience of its socially stigmatized inhabitants, NewMan even identifies with this ghetto imagery 'weil ich im Block groß geworden bin' [because I grew up on the block].[168] This socio-spatial discourse is ultimately represented through his artist's name, which fuses the literal translation of his German surname with the name of the commercial American rap boy group NewKids on the Block.[169]

However, despite creating and identifying with a 'secondspatial' urban ghetto in Oldenburg NewMan does not represent his imaginary home in linguistic terms. With German gangsta rap's common articulation based on a 'Straßenüberslang' (as described by Samy Deluxe), NewMan's *linguistic orientation* is, rather, manifested in his use of standard German. His lyrical aims are, moreover, to 'hin und wieder mal in einer Zeile jemanden zum Lachen bringen. Coole Sprüche, auch *Punch Lines* genannt. So was finde ich gut. So was feier ich selber. So, wo man erst richtig hinhören muss. Wortspiele, Metaphern' [make someone laugh with a verse now and again. Cool lines, also called *punch lines*. That is what I like. That is what I celebrate myself. Where you really have listen. Puns, metaphors].[170] NewMan lyrically emphasizes his authoritative status as an ethnic German. In other words, he engages in a deviant socio-spatial discourse that does not aim at re-framing minority discourses but at supporting his German nationalist perspective. He explains that due to 'meine Vergangenheit mit Hooligans und solchen Konsorten [...] [...] ich auch manchmal YouTube-Einträge [kriege], so: "Seit wann Nazis denn rappen?"' [my past with hooligans and the like [...] I sometimes get YouTube comments like: 'Since when do Nazis rap?'].[171]

According to German hip-hop scholar Murat Güngör, such politically and socially discordant narratives have become a common feature. In an interview with Bushido, Güngör, for example, explains that German youth:

> denken ja nicht mehr in Kategorien wie Links und Rechts. Für die ist es kein Widerspruch, Bushido zu hören und NPD zu wählen. Sie picken sich raus, was ihnen gefällt. Aus deinen Stücken nehmen sie sich eben die aggressive Härte. Das Gefährliche an eurer Musik ist doch, dass Jugendliche plötzlich ganz

168 NewMan on the Block, interviewed by author, 11 February 2012. The term 'block' has become a signature location within German street rap to describe a ghetto, especially since Aggro Berlin rapper Sido referred to his neighbourhood as *mein Block* in his eponymous track in 2004.

169 NewMan on the Block, interviewed by author, 11 February 2012.

170 NewMan on the Block, interviewed by author, 11 February 2012.

171 NewMan on the Block, interviewed by author, 11 February 2012.

> selbstverständlich mit nationalistischen, sexistischen und extrem aggressiven Metaphern spielen.[172]
>
> [no longer think in categories like left and right. For them it's not a contradiction to listen to Bushido and vote for the NPD. They pick out whatever they like. From your pieces they take the aggressive hardness. What is dangerous about your music is that all of a sudden young people start playing with nationalistic, sexist and aggressive metaphors as if that were perfectly normal.]

Such split political statements can also be found in NewMan's *song themes*, which, for example, include 'patriotische Songs für Deutschland' [patriotic songs for Germany].[173] In his track 'Ich bin Deutschland' (2011) NewMan raps that he has:

> Blaue Augen, weiße Haut.
> Ich bin Deutschland.
> Ich bin kein Nazi und Faschist,
> Doch ich bin Deutschland.
> […]
> Und dieser Araber hier ist mein Freund, man.[174]
>
> [Blue eyes, white skin.
> I am Germany.
> I'm no Nazi and no Fascist
> But I'm Germany.
> […]
> And this Arab here is my friend, man.]

While, on the one hand, NewMan creates his gangsta image in the 'thirdspace' of the blocks of Nadorst, a close reading of this lyrical excerpt shows how he expands his spatial identity discourse to encompass a national Germanness. The 'secondspace' of the ghetto provides a juxtaposing historical perspective as it 'conjures images from the past: Jewish ghettos, genocide, and Nazi racism'.[175] Through his represention of his national identity by stereotypical 'attributes' that denote 'Aryan purity' and hence Nazi racism, NewMan's self-reflection as 'being Germany' also re-negotiates the past political and racial messages

172 Alex Rühle and Dirk Peitz, 'Interview mit Bushido, Loh, Güngör – Harte Texte und die Härte der Nazis', *Sueddeutsche Zeitung – Kultur*, 11 May 2010, http://www.sueddeutsche.de/ kultur/ interview-mit-bushido-loh-guengoer-harte-texte-und-die-haerte-der-nazis-1.425538-2 [accessed 30 May 2012]. For more information regarding the relationship between German nationalist movements and gangsta rap music, see Güngör and Loh, *Fear of a Kanak Planet*, pp. 278–315.

173 NewMan on the Block, interviewed by author, 11 February 2012.

174 NewMan on the Block, 'Ich bin Deutschland', *Kategorie Gangsta* (2011) [mixtape, CD].

175 Stehle, *Ghetto Voices*, p. 12.

behind these disturbing cultural signifiers: not only does he deny a Nazi affiliation despite his physical description of himself but he also affirms his friendship with an Arab. However, the rapper does not specify whether 'dieser Araber' [this Arab] refers to a foreigner in Germany or to a local inhabitant who is described as being of Middle Eastern descent by NewMan. Indeed, his supposed friend may understand his phenotype as a marker of Germanness.

NewMan's paradoxical narratives and contradictory presentation of himself in his rap lyrics thus expose the limits of rap's representation of reality, with NewMan admitting that 'zu mir [...] auch alle [sagen], ich bin nicht authentisch [*laughs*], weil ich zu viel übertreibe und nicht echt ist, was ich rappe' [everyone also tells me that I am not authentic [*laughs*] because I exaggerate and because what I rap is not real].[176] The reason for this lack of perceived authenticity lies in the fact that his imagined 'secondspace' and the narratives positioned in this space do not resonate meaningfully in Oldenburg and amongst its rap community. NewMan therefore provides an example of the way an engagement in rap can be contested through a mismatch of spatial discourses.

The following example relates to a different discordance concerning rapper K-Four. K-Four – mentioned above as a local rapper – was actually born and raised in Harare, relocating to Oldenburg as a child. At the time of the interview he was Oldenburg's only black rapper and his *song themes* have been inspired by 'my life, the people around me, my environment'.[177] Disseminating stories which are framed by his local 'thirdspace' experience in Oldenburg, the African rapper further elaborates on the importance of representing one's urban community for 'who else is gonna be proud of you, if not your city? That is where your friends is [*sic*]. That's your hometown'.[178]

However, K-Four's *song themes* are delivered in a *linguistic orientation* that does not resonate meaningfully amongst his local rap community, for he expresses himself in English. While his language choice could serve to reflect his Zimbabwean nationality, K-Four rejects the employment of his native form of English since 'they all mix it up with Shona when they speak in my country'.[179] Instead, K-Four chooses to appropriate AAVE in order to 'keep it international so [that] anybody can understand'.[180] Nevertheless, K-Four's employment of AAVE includes 'slang words. Like, words which are even hard to identify if English is your native language. [...] I would say *gwop*. They say

176 NewMan on the Block, interviewed by author, 11 February 2012.

177 K-Four, interviewed by author, 9 February 2012.

178 K-Four, interviewed by author, 9 February 2012.

179 K-Four, interviewed by author, 9 February 2012. Shona is a Bantu language spoken by the Shona people of Zimbabwe.

180 K-Four, interviewed by author, 9 February 2012.

skrilla. All words for money. [*Laughs*] [...] That's New York slang'.[181] Thus, in the introductory track to his mix tape *The Beginner* (2012) K-Four raps:

> This is the story of my life.
> The story of a winner.
> [...]
> I'm a killer.
> Fuck them like a bad bitch,
> For the skrilla.[182]

With K-Four beginning his lyrical journey by re-living his life in Germany, it remains questionable whether the appearance of New York slang is easier to understand than Shona within K-Four's otherwise standard-English narrative. Thus K-Four's linguistic codes do not reflect his personal story as they relate to neither his Zimbabwean nor German identity; he instead employs AAVE as a strategy of cultural camouflage which enables him to be (*mis*)understood as an African-American rapper.

In line with this observation, local rapper Henry the First admits that 'wenn man seine [K-Four's] Musik hört und seine Raps hört, dann klingen die auch echt amerikanisch so. Wenn mir das jetzt jemand zeigt und ich kenne den nicht, würde ich denken das ist jemand aus Amerika' [when you listen to his [K-Four's] music and his raps then they really do sound American. If someone showed him to me and I didn't know him, I would think that he was someone from America].[183] Hence, K-Four manages his 'tribal stigma' in order to claim the status of a 'real nigga'. K-Four's mimetic *linguistic orientation* combined with his physical 'attributes' equips him with the necessary tools to conform to the image of a commercial African-American rap artist. According to Bhabha, such a negotiation of identity 'proposes a social subject constituted through cultural hybridisation, the overdetermination of communal or group differences, the articulation of baffling alikeness and banal divergence'.[184] By presenting a 'baffling alikeness' to an African-American rapper, K-Four equally presents a 'banal divergence' from German rap. While this strategy may have resonated successfully in Germany, during the early 1980s, it is now understood by some listeners as an unfaithful practice of rap. Henry the First explains further: '[W]enn ich 50Cent hören will, dann höre ich 50Cent. Und nicht einen Schwarzen aus Deutschland, der auch so rappt wie 50Cent. Ne? [...] Ich meine gibt es einen amerikanisch-sprechenden Musiker *aus* Deutschland

181 K-Four, interviewed by author, 9 February 2012.

182 K-Four, 'The Beginner', *The Beginner* (Str8 Team Ent., 2012), http://www.datpiff.com/K-Four-The-Beginner-mixtape.371741.html [accessed 9 June 2016].

183 Henry the First, interviewed by author, 25 January 2012.

184 Bhabha, 'Culture's In-Between', 168.

im Rap, der erfolgreich geworden ist? – Nein!' [[I]f I want to listen to 50Cent, then I will listen to 50Cent. And not to a black guy from Germany who raps just like 50Cent. You know? [...] I mean is there an American-speaking musician from Germany in the rap scene who has become successful? – No!].[185] The issue that Henry the First highlights is thus not related to K-Four's being a Zimbabwean living in Germany but to the latter's targeted *linguistic orientation*, which does not reflect his position within a German cultural context. While K-Four nevertheless states that his *song themes* are 'influenced by my life over here so when you listen to some of my songs, I'm not saying most of my songs, but some of my songs, you can hear I am influenced by German culture',[186] his *linguistic orientation* creates a rupture in the mirroring effect of his 'thirdspace' experience in Oldenburg.

A last example of the way Oldenburg's rap tradition is altered in order to pursue commercial goals can be compared to K-Four's relationship to Germany, for local rappers MicFire and his former colleague Roulette[187] moved to Germany as young teenagers as well. However, they previously belonged to:

> the Germanic diaspora, who had been dispersed across Eastern Europe, and may no longer speak the German language, or have had any contact with the state for generations, [yet] are entitled to full citizenship and are offered welfare packages to encourage their 'return' to the motherland.[188]

Having thus returned to his motherland of Germany, Roulette states that he is from 'Kasachstan, weil die Mentalität ist geblieben' [Kazakhstan because the mentality has stayed].[189] This becomes apparent in his and MicFire's use of Russian as their designated language in rap. The reason, according to MicFire, is 'weil ich mich da am wohlsten fühle [wenn ich] auf Russisch rappe halt, ne? Auf meine Heimatsprache' [because I just feel most comfortable when rapping in Russian, right? In my native language].[190] Similarly, although he has returned to his motherland of Germany, Roulette states: '[I]ch habe sofort auf Russisch geschrieben, weil mein Deutsch war nicht so weit und ist immer noch nicht so weit' [I immediately started writing in Russian because my German wasn't that good and still isn't that good].[191] Hence, MicFire and Roulette do not take advantage of the post-gangsta-rap language discourse in which, as Samy Deluxe explains, rappers are able to admit to themselves:

185 Henry the First, interviewed by author, 25 January 2012.
186 K-Four, interviewed by author, 9 February 2012.
187 Roulette died on 1 December 2013.
188 Papastergiadis, *The Turbulence of Migration*, p. 60.
189 Roulette, interviewed by author, 14 February, 2012.
190 MicFire, interviewed by author, 14 February 2012.
191 Roulette, interviewed by author, 14 February, 2012.

'[I]ch muss jetzt nicht so gut deutsch sprechen können, wie Samy oder Torch, um deutsch rappen zu können' [I don't have to speak such good German as Samy or Torch in order to rap in German].[192] Instead, MicFire and Roulette engage in a Russian *linguistic orientation* as a sign of cultural nostalgia. At the same time, however, this *linguistic orientation* displaces the rappers' physical spatiality, which is evidently that of Germany. As they record and perform in Germany, a 'third space' emerges in terms of MicFire's and Roulette's identity as artists. This becomes evident in the following dialogue:

> MicFire: 'Also ich würde "Künstler, der aus Deutschland berichtet" sagen [*laughing*]. So würde ich es nennen! Aber jetzt kein deutscher Künstler. Oder ich *weiß* auch nicht, Alter. Im normalem Pass steht ja auch ich bin ja Deutscher, ne?'
>
> Roulette: 'Ja.'
>
> MicFire: 'Was würdest du sagen?'
>
> Roulette: 'Ja, also theoretisch so ... hmm...' [*Thinking*]
>
> MicFire: ' [...] Ich würd einfach sagen: "Ich bin Deutscher, weil es in meinem Pass steht und weil ich mich auch sehr wohl hier fühle und das Land ist gut zu mir." Und ich versuch dem Land auch das zu geben, was es mir gibt so.'
>
> Roulette: 'Ja.'
>
> MicFire: '[...] wie gesagt, ich bin ein Künstler, der aus Deutschland berichtet'. [*laughs*]
>
> Roulette: 'Ja, würd' ich auch so sagen.'
>
> MicFire: '[...] Ich habe viele deutsche Freunde. Ich fühle mich hier zuhause. Ich fühle mich *echt* hier zuhause. [*Thinking*] Aber weiß, wo meine Wurzeln sind. Ich glaube das können wir so stehen lassen. Für mich, von meiner Seite aus.'
>
> Roulette: 'Ja ich würde sagen: "Ich bin russischer Künstler", [...] aber sonst würde ich auch sagen: "Ich bin einer, der aus Deutschland berichtet".'[193]
>
> [MicFire: 'I would say "an artist who reports from Germany" [*laughing*]. That's what I would call it! But not a German artist. Or, I don't know either, dude. It says I am German in my normal passport, too, right?'
>
> Roulette: 'Yes.'
>
> MicFire: 'What would you say?'
>
> Roulette: 'Yeah, so theoretically ... hmm...' [*Thinking*]

192 Samy Deluxe, interviewed by author, 29 July 2012.
193 MicFire and Roulette, interviewed by author, 14 February 2012.

MicFire: '[…] I would just say: "I am German because that is what it says in my passport and because I feel good here and the country is good to me". And I try to give to the country what it gives to me.'

Roulette: 'Yes.'

MicFire: '[…] as I said, I am an artist who reports from Germany.' [*Laughs*]

Roulette: 'Yeah, I would say that too'.]

This 'third space' specifically opens as MicFire and Roulette re-negotiate the 'dominant assumption on the relationship between traditional authenticity and contemporary culture'.[194] One the one hand, MicFire raps in his traditional, authentic Russian *Heimatsprache*, while on the other hand he feels *zuhause* [at home] in contemporary Germany. This dialectic is ultimately summarized by MicFire when he explains that 'wenn ich nach Russland komme so sage ich: "Hier sind meine Wurzeln, hier sind meine Leute". Ne? Und: "Ich komme aus Oldenburg, Deutschland". Fertig' [when I arrive in Russia I say: 'Here are my roots, here are my people.' You know? And: 'I come from Oldenburg, Germany'. Done].[195]

The German spatiality is instead captured in MicFire's and Roulette's *song themes* since they reflect 'was das Leben ist um uns herum so' [how life is around us].[196] As in K-Four's lyrical content, the cityspace of Oldenburg provides 'the social contexts and raw resources for lyrics'[197] although they rap in Russian. Therefore, Roulette and MicFire also create a 'third space' on a 'secondspatial' level as *song themes* relate to a German national sphere, yet are expressed through *rap specific rhetoric* and *ritualized speech acts* embedded in a Russian *linguistic orientation*. This is, for example, illustrated in the rap track 'Made in Germany' (2013),[198] in which MicFire places himself and his rap productions in a bi-national discourse: 'Eto made in Germany – quality! | Russkii rap kak zhiguli [This is made in Germany – quality! | Russian rap is like Zhiguli].[199] By infusing Russian lyrics with English terminology manifested in bilingual rhymes similar to Nate57's and Telly Tellz's German-Turkish discourse, MicFire distinguishes his Russian rap sound produced in Germany from the Russian rap produced in Russia. Through the use of simile, he compares the stereotypically high-quality production of German goods to the

194 Papastergiadis, 'Hybridity and Ambivalence', 40.
195 MicFire, interviewed by author, 14 February 2012.
196 MicFire, interviewed by author, 14 February 2012.
197 Forman, '"Represent": Race, Space and Place in Rap Music', 71.
198 In February 2015, rapper BOZ, who at the time was still signed to Rattos Locos Records, also released a rap track and album called 'Made in Germany' which presents his perspective as a German-Pakistani street rapper from Hamburg.
199 MicFire, 'Made in Germany', *Made in Germany* (Mafyo & Star Trip Loopers, 2013), https://www.youtube.com/watch?v=VCv7mgNLhRI [accessed 9 June 2016].

Figure 7: 'Made in Germany' EP cover

(Copyright: MicFire)

low-quality production of cars in the former Soviet Union. In other words, MicFire enhances his Russian rap sound through his access to German culture and hence to German work ethics, as his producers are ethnic Germans from Oldenburg. Thus, while being of German ethnicity as well as having German citizenship, MicFire reverses his identity discourse by employing his access to German culture to empower his Russian identity – and hence in the opposite manner to the way Germanness has been negotiated by Hamburg's hip-hop dancers, who instead use their foreignness as a contribution to and enrichment of their semi- or non-ethnic Germanness and their belonging to Hamburg. This identity strategy is visibly manifested on the cover of MicFire's EP 'Made in Germany' (see Figure 7).

MicFire is seated at a table with a knife and fork in his hand. The plate in front of him is overflowing with Russian food varieties with traditional cuisine represented by sliced sausages, potatoes and *pel'meni* dumplings, amongst other items. MicFire therefore nurtures himself with Russian food and hence Russian traditions even though the image was taken in a 'firstspace' located in Germany. With his national identity officially manifested in the Russian passport (despite MicFire's previously statement that he is registered as a German citizen), MicFire's social status is further framed from an upscale perspective as he symbolically surrounds himself by financial wealth emanating from his German environment. This is represented through the fifty-Euro notes resting in his Russian passport, as well as through the key to his Mercedes-Benz, setting a contrast between this German car manufacturer and the Soviet Zhiguli.

Despite producing rap music in Germany, MicFire's *song themes* do not address a German audience. Rather, the 'Schwerpunkt liegt komplett [auf] Russland' [the focus is completely on Russia] since MicFire explains that 'wenn wir irgendwas ausdrücken wollen, dann muss man das auch verstehen' [if we want to express something, then it has to be understood].[200] In order to overcome this problem in Oldenburg, MicFire and, previously, Roulette have based their local performances in a particular 'firstspace' whose 'secondspace' identity is a Russian nightclub. While this nightclub is materially in Oldenburg, neither its 'secondspace' image nor its 'thirdspace' experience iterates the actual national location of this 'firstspace' as party-goers are almost exclusively of Russian ethnicity. Therefore, the language of communication inside the club is Russian, while its selection of bar snacks even includes Russian foods such as *shashlik* or *kielbasa*. Hence, with Russian culture being lived in this German geographic space, the dance club becomes a cultural 'third space' in its 'thirdspace' experience in which Russian rap lyrics are able to resonate meaningfully and successfully amongst a portion of the Oldenburg audience. This aspect therefore is in contrast to NewMan and K-Four's socio-cultural rap messages and images as rappers from Oldenburg, especially since MicFire also participates in the aforementioned freestyle sessions in the living room of the '24', thus keeping the local tradition of improvised rap practices alive as well.

Summary

The comparative analysis of rap's manifestation in Hamburg and Oldenburg has provided insights into the ways in which rap has become a meaningful practice in two different German urban locales, with the two cityspaces allowing a distinct local development of hip-hop's lyrical art form. In both case studies, rap was initially appropriated as a freestyling practice through which rappers

200 MicFire, interviewed by author, 14 February, 2012.

began discovering the linguistic possibilities of their languages. In so doing, they also experienced rap as a live 'thirdspace' located in material domestic 'firstspaces'. Detached from the social, spatial and historical components that shaped the art of rap in the Bronx, the two German communities thus exemplified the idea that 'the way its [rap's] cultural symbols and language are appropriated, localized, and hybridized is intimately linked to how specific social actors experience the world as lived reality'.[201]

Oldenburg's underground rap tradition has remained tied to its initial spatial practices, while Hamburg's cityspace has provided the conditions and structures for rappers to pursue this lyrical art form commercially. This latter intention on the part of rap altered the rapper's relationship to the cityspace, as this became expressed as a mediated imagined 'secondspace'. With this urban differentiation in mind, the 'assertion of Spatiality opens the Historicality and Sociality of human lifeworlds to interpretations and knowledges that many of its most disciplined observers never imagined, while simultaneously maintaining the rich insights they provide for understanding the production of lived space' (*THSP*, p. 72). In Oldenburg, the acknowledgement of rap's spatiality has shown how ethnic German rappers manage their authentic engagement in rap, despite living in a particularly small provincial cityspace. The spatial conditions do not allow for much variation in terms of distinct representations of urban attributes, with the conscious or backpack rap genre of freestyling becoming the most viable form of local rap. In this way, the rappers treat their city as a homogeneous whole without nuanced neighbourhoods and particular boroughs in which other rap genres can flourish. Moreover, as rap is not primarily pursued with commercial intentions, Oldenburg's rappers do not need to provide their rap productions with a local identity or style of genre often expressed in *linguistic orientations* and *song themes*. Rather, rappers such as Stylez-Tyson, Macentosh, Jordan MC and Juiz engage in rap in their personal spare time, with this lyrical art form becoming an artistic, almost therapeutic form of communication within their local German lifestyle.

However, some rappers from Oldenburg do seek a commercial route and want be known beyond local boundaries. Ethnic German rapper NewMan, for example, engages in a provocative, nationalist discourse by identifying himself as a local gangsta rapper from the imagined 'secondspace' of the ghetto. K-Four chooses to participate in an imagined cultural-historical discourse by presenting himself as an African-American rapper using AAVE in order for his rap to be understood and consumed at an international level. However, both strategies put the rapper at risk of not being deemed

201 Tickner, 'Aquí en el Ghetto', 128.

authentic, as the rap productions do not reflect the actual 'firstspace' and 'thirdspace' experiences of Oldenburg.

The only exception to the established local approach to rap is provided by MicFire. He partakes in Oldenburg's rap-freestyling tradition and, at the same time, participates in a commercial Russian rap discourse. Due to the number of German citizens sharing MicFire's bi-cultural identity, his Russian-framed 'secondspace' perspective on Oldenburg is able to resonate meaningfully amongst German consumers of Russian heritage. MicFire does not attempt to affirm his German ethnicity through rap but rather aims at improving his Russian rap music and image through his contact with German culture, thus reversing any claim towards a post-hybrid German identity.

In Hamburg, on the other hand, the cityspace's structures have been able to accommodate different sub-genres and their practices. Commercially oriented rappers can, therefore, represent different social, spatial and historical perspectives on their cityspace. Fettes Brot, for instance, employed the Northern German linguistic signifier of *Platt* as an identifier of their Northern German region, with lyrics engaging in a historical discourse that relied on local knowledge as well as on insights into hip-hop's practices. The mainly ethnic German rappers thus hybridized their regional culture, while the understanding of transnational Nordic codes and traditions also enabled the inclusion of other ethnicities and cultural backgrounds into this consciously fabricated identity category.

Moving into a more current manifestation of local rap after the wave of gangsta rap dominated the commercial image of German hip-hop, Rattos Locos have presented their social background by reflecting Hamburg's lived streets in their lyrics through their use of unsophisticated, bilingual German. By situating themselves in a historical and spatial narrative of St. Pauli, the culturally hybrid rappers further emphasize their social deviance by belonging to a neighbourhood that perpetuates anti-normative behaviour. They frame themselves as the current local outlaws in the tradition of the Hanseatic pirates. St. Pauli, however, is home to numerous ethnic and cultural minority groups – which Rattos Locos nevertheless represent as a contemporary reality of Hamburg through their stereotyped images of Afro-German, *Kanaken* and ethnic German skulls on their label logo. In this sense, Rattos Locos do not treat their multicultural neighbourhood as an 'other' but as part of the German cityspace and hence of the lived Hamburg experience, claiming a post-hybrid German identity.

From the streets of St. Pauli this statement of local post-hybridity has been spatially expanded by Samy Deluxe. Embedding himself and the art of rap in a German national narrative, Samy Deluxe orally mimics the German literary tradition through his sophisticated and articulated rhetoric. Moreover, by strategically framing his rap as 'deutsche Hochkultur' [German high culture][202] Samy Deluxe engages in a social discourse which elevates rap's status within German culture beyond regional folk traditions or deviant urban lifestyles and revives the connection between rap and '"Reim", "Lyrik", "Dichter", "Poet,"' ['rhyme', 'verse', 'writer', 'poet'][203] which, as Cheesman observes, have loomed 'very large among the names of hip hop crews and recordings' in the early stages of German rap.[204] With this strategy, the Afro-German rapper thus attempts to show that rap and culturally hybrid identities are part of contemporary Germanness.

With rap therefore enabling the lyrical dissemination of many different socio-cultural identity discourses and claims of belonging, this comparative analysis has shown that, with the exception of MicFire, rap's implementation as a culturally meaningful German art form relies on the rapper's German *linguistic orientation*, regardless of personal intention and strategies of 'stigma' management. In line with Mirko Machine's introductory statement, hip-hop's lyrical element has thus, according to Mark Pennay, spurred on:

> independence and confidence among young Germans that they can create music in German for Germans – the most positive development within postunification Germany of a renaissance within the local music scene, and within which the transmuted and initially contested genre of Rap has played a key role.[205]

Whether this artistic independence and confidence are also shared by graffiti artists in Germany will be analysed in the following and final chapter.

202 Samy Deluxe, 'Hände Hoch', *Schwarz Weiß* (EMI, 2011) [CD].

203 Cheesman, 'Polyglot Pop Politics', 209.

204 Cheesman, 'Polyglot Pop Politics', 209.

205 Mark *Pennay*, 'Rap in *Germany*: The Birth of a Genre', in *Global Noise*, ed. by Mitchell, pp. 111–33 (p. 128).

CHAPTER 4

Graffiti Art

The Origins of Graffiti Art and Hip-Hop Culture

I was into graffiti. That's where Kool Herc came from.[1]

As this chapter turns to the last art form that constitutes one of the four main elements of hip-hop culture, the introductory statement by DJ Kool Herc addresses the fact that graffiti existed before the art of DJing and hence prior to the establishment of local block parties. Indeed, the term graffiti goes back even further as it has served to describe ancient etchings and drawings 'since man encountered his first stone wall'.[2] Nonetheless, despite the time lapse between the first stone wall and the post-industrial New York City of the 1970s, the spatiality of graffiti has remained inextricably linked to vertical, material 'firstspaces'. Moreover, the historicality of graffiti and the artist's sociality become evident through the etchings and drawings on these 'firstspaces', as Nelson George concludes that contemporary knowledge of the 'world's early history comes from pictures and symbols scrawled centuries ago'.[3] Since hip-hop-related graffiti are framed by the same trialectics, this analysis will distinguish between ancient mural writings and the contemporary visual artistic element of hip-hop culture by referring to the latter as 'graffiti art' throughout this chapter.

Graffiti art's earliest beginnings are rooted in Philadelphia. During the 1960s, the local tradition of using aerosol spray cans to leave traces on the city's material 'firstspaces' 'took shape as an aesthetic response to changes in

1 Kool Herc, quoted in George, 'Hip-Hop's Founding Fathers Speak the Truth', p. 45. According to David Ley and Roman Cybriwsky, the adjective 'cool', when applied to graffiti art, 'denotes confidence, style, suavity, a mastery of the intricate signal language of street life' (David Ley and Roman Cybriwsky, 'Urban Graffiti as Territorial Markers', *Annals of the Association of American Geographers*, 64 (1974), 491–505 (p. 494). Herc is an abbreviation of Hercules, describing Kool Herc's body size (Castleman, *Getting Up*, p. 72).

2 Nelson George, *Hip Hop America* (New York: Penguin Books, 1998), p. 11.

3 George, *Hip Hop America*, p. 11.

the common experience of the modern urban environment'.[4] Spray-painting certain codes mainly functioned to set distinct territorial markers with which local street gangs communicated group membership and a specific urban affiliation.[5] Eventually, however, the repeated appearance of the word 'Cornbread' re-functioned the tradition of using spray-painted symbols as territorial indicators. They became anonymous presentations of the writer's self, independent of particular street gang practices.[6] Cornbread's spatial ritual eventually reached New York City as well, where graffiti art's appropriation of 'firstspaces' would be treated as 'a set of materialized "spatial practices" that work together to produce and reproduce the concrete forms and specific patternings of urbanism as a way of life'.[7]

According to Rose, in this new cityspace 'the writer credited with inspiring the movement, Taki 183, is a Greek teenager named Demetrius who lived in the Washington Heights section of Manhattan'.[8] Graffiti scholar Craig Castleman further explains that 'Taki was an unemployed seventeen year old with nothing better to do than pass the summer days spraying his name wherever he happened to be'.[9] Moving through the metropolitan city of New York and its particular boroughs and neighbourhoods, Taki disrupted the rhythms of citylife by writing 'his name all over the subway cars and stations'.[10] Hence, while the emergence of graffiti art in New York City was deeply tied to the architectonics of the human built environment (*THSP*, p. 75), it was detached from the exclusive built environment of the Bronx and hence from a cultural-historical discourse pertaining to African-American and Latino inhabitants which was previously deemed the driving cultural force behind DJing, rapping and b-boying.

Furthermore, the expression of graffiti art existed without the presence of the artist's body, unlike b-boying or DJing. In other words, the sprayer's racial attributes became invisible in the visual consumption of this art form, with emerging graffiti artists presenting their selves as spray-painted traces and hence as written identities.[11] In so doing, hip-hop's graffiti artists diverge from Goffman's observations on people's presentations of self since their art

4 Joe A. Austin, 'More to see than a Canvas in a White Cube: For an Art in the Street', *City*, 14 (2010), 33–47 (p. 35).

5 Ley and Cybriwsky, 'Urban Graffiti as Territorial Markers', 492.

6 Ley and Cybriwsky, 'Urban Graffiti as Territorial Markers', 493.

7 Soja, *Postmetropolis*, p. 10.

8 Rose, *Black Noise*, p. 42.

9 Craig Castleman, 'The Politics of Graffiti', in *That's the Joint!*, ed. by Forman and Neal, pp. 14–34 (p. 14); Rose, however, writes that Taki 183 worked as a messenger (Rose, *Black Noise*, p. 42).

10 Rose, *Black Noise*, p. 42.

11 MacDonald, *The Graffiti Subculture*, p. 215.

form allows their identities to be managed without face-to-face interaction in the presence of others. Thus, Taki 183 presented his self through the repetitive written pseudonym 'Taki 183', which laid the foundation of 'the most basic and simplest form of graffiti',[12] namely 'tagging'.

The practice of tagging refers not only to spreading one's 'tag' but also to identifying the artist through the targeted use of personally stylized letters. With the establishment of this practice, local imitators of Taki 183's materialized spatial ritual 'began to develop elaborate individual styles, themes, formats and techniques, most of which were designed to increase visibility, individual identity, and status'.[13] This development also spurred the creation of distinct spray-painted fonts, such as the '"bubble letter", or fat, rounded letters that were designed and named by Phase II; the "3D letter", or block letters with a three-dimensional appearance, first used by Pistol 1; and "wild style", a name used to describe almost an "unreadable" style'.[14]

The employment of such fonts also led to newly evolving formats in graffiti art. Thus, the successor of the simple tag became the enlarged 'throw-up', which was commonly created with the bubble letter font as it 'usually consists of a two- or three-letter name that is formed, usually rounded, into a single unit that can be sprayed quickly and with a minimum of paint on the sides of a train'.[15] This new format therefore also relocated graffiti art's mobile spatiality from inside a subway car to its outside surface. The spatial relocation further enabled graffiti art to become visible to a wider urban public, namely to 'outsiders' in Goffman's terms, while the trains rolled 'through diverse neighbourhoods, allowing communication between various black and Hispanic communities throughout the five boroughs and larger New York population and disseminating graffiti writers' public performance'.[16]

While Rose links graffiti art's new spatial practices and new 'fronts' to an African-American and Latino context, Castleman is more cautious with his observations on graffiti artists' ethnic backgrounds, explaining that 'possibly most writers[...] are poor blacks, Hispanics, and whites',[17] yet overall graffiti artists belonged to 'every race, nationality, and economic group in New York City'.[18] This statement is further affirmed by an officer from the New York Transit Police Department's graffiti squad, who notes that graffiti art was being produced by 'kids that live in New York City. They range from the ultra-

12 Castleman, *Getting Up*, p. 28.
13 Rose, *Black Noise*, p. 42.
14 Castleman, *Getting Up*, p. 25.
15 Castleman, *Getting Up*, p. 29.
16 Rose, *Black Noise*, p. 43.
17 Castleman, *Getting Up*, p. 67.
18 Castleman, *Getting Up*, p. 67.

rich to the ultra-poor. There is no general classification of the kids'.[19] Thus, from the onset of its emergence in New York City, graffiti art addressed a wider range of social and cultural sensibilities beyond the 'thirdspace' of one particular neighbourhood. While the artists' ethnic and social backgrounds were thus irrelevant to an authentic engagement in graffiti art, its placement on the outside of subway trains became the most important factor in assessing a painter's social identity as an artist. New graffiti formats were specifically tailored to the 'firstspace' surface of the subway car façade.

These subway-specific formats included the 'top-to-bottom', which reached from the ground to the top of the subway car, while the 'end-to-end' referred to a piece reaching from one side of the car to the other.[20] The extension of these pieces became the 'whole car', which, as the name reveals, refers to graffiti art that covers an entire side of a subway car. With the first whole car sprayed in 1973, by the 'mid-1970s the best writers in the city were specializing in the painting of enormous whole-car murals that often contained caricatures, cartoon characters, outdoor scenes, holiday settings, and even the writers' own interpretations of life in the city'.[21] Soon, the creation of such whole cars was considered to be 'the epitome of style and skill, and those writers who achieve them are much admired'.[22] Thus, graffiti art's social discourse in terms of gaining respect became deeply tied to the 'fronts' of its mobile urban 'firstspaces'.

However, the new spatial emphasis in graffiti art also influenced another social aspect of the art form beyond its gaining of a respected social status and individual admiration. It changed the dynamics of writing in solitude to producing graffiti art within a group.[23] As Castleman explains, the immense work required for spraying whole cars led to graffiti art being 'frequently painted by groups who share paint and skills and generally work from a plan drawn in advance that outlines the design and colors to be used'.[24] While graffiti groups had already existed as an outcome of the 'thirdspace' experience of New York City, they previously formed as a direct security measure against violent local street gangs. These early graffiti groups were therefore 'similar to fighting gangs in that they sometimes purposefully engaged in rumbles with other gangs, limited membership to writers from their home turf and [...] were into territory'.[25] It was not until 1973 – the same year as the first whole car

19 Kevin Hickey, quoted in Castleman, *Getting Up*, p. 67.
20 Rose, *Black Noise*, p. 42.
21 Castleman, *Getting Up*, p. 60.
22 Castleman, *Getting Up*, p. 36.
23 Castleman, *Getting Up*, p. 84.
24 Castleman, *Getting Up*, p. 35.
25 Castleman, *Getting Up*, p. 96.

creation – that graffiti art crews were formed for the purpose of practising art aside from the mere territorial appropriation of urban 'firstspaces'. These crews have since become 'informal in structure, have no hierarchy of officers, do not require members to wear identifying colors, and were not formed for the sake of defence against fighting gangs but only for companionship and occasional joint writing ventures'.[26]

Thus, graffiti art's trialectics of being were deeply influenced and affected by the overall urban dynamics of New York City at the time. Its historicality even begins in this urban realm, namely as a spatial response to the lifestyles of the multifaceted post-industrial American metropolis. It is this modern urban environment which, according to historian Joe Austin, 'appears within, shapes and partially constitutes the artwork itself. The city and its myriad writings are fundamental contextual references without which graffiti art is poorly understood'.[27] The only initial commonality between hip-hop's main artistic elements was, therefore, the shared cityspace of New York and its all-encompassing urban 'thirdspace' experience, which nurtured personal hunger to gain social respect while providing a distraction from everyday life through engagement in art.

Graffiti art's maturity and vibrant movement eventually mobilized it into being integrated as a hip-hop element. According to DJ Kool Herc, 'I was the guy with the art. I liked graffiti flyers. My graffiti friend used to do my flyers'.[28] With Kool Herc being the initiator, local DJs began turning to graffiti art as a marketing tool for the promotion of their neighbourhood block parties. Graffiti writers began to paint 'murals for DJs' stage platforms and design posters and flyers to advertise hip hop events'.[29] However, as DJ Afrika Bambaataa explains, it was not until the early 1980s when New York City's urban art movements became commercialized and marketed outside of their home territory that 'everything started coming into place, we started doing shows and traveling into different boroughs. Then we started traveling to different states and that's when we threw it all together'.[30]

Framed as part of a united hip-hop movement, graffiti art finally became globally disseminated as its visual element and has since been able to create 'a culturally rich visual history'[31] of various urban spatialities. Consequentially,

26 Castleman, *Getting Up*, p. 107. 'Colors' refer to the colour marked on one's jacket or vest that signified membership of a specific gang. B-boy crews initially mimicked this colour identification code as well (Banes, *Writing Dancing*, p. 128).

27 Austin, 'More to see than a Canvas in a White Cube', 38.

28 George, 'Hip-Hop's Founding Fathers speak the Truth', p. 45.

29 Rose, *Black Noise*, p. 35.

30 DJ Afrika Bambaataa in George, 'Hip-Hop's Founding Fathers speak the Truth', p. 45.

31 Austin, 'More to see than a Canvas in a White Cube', 35.

according to Austin, graffiti art's 'collectively sustained duration, its historically complex social and institutional development, and its aesthetic sophistication place it among the longest-running, global visual culture movements originating within the 20th century, and perhaps **the most** important of the last decades'.[32] In the following section, this visual cultural movement will be explored in its German manifestation. Close readings of graffiti art will focus on typographical aspects in an attempt to facilitate a better understanding of the various social, spatial and historical perspectives of graffiti art's urban expression in a contemporary German cultural context.

Reading the Typographic Style of Graffiti Art

The idea that style, in connection to specific materiality, is able to signify and communicate a social identity has not only been subject to graffiti art's norms and practices. Linguist Hartmut Stöckl links this ability to typography in general and explains that typography is both 'Stilmittel und soziales Signal' [stylistic device and social signal].[33] Taking Stöckl's views on typography as a blueprint with which to analyse graffiti art's trialectics of being, this study will apply Stöckl's four main typographic categories to close readings of graffiti art works in Germany. These consist of *micro-, meso-, macro- and paratypography.*

Microtypography describes the most basic type of typographic features, which Stöckl refers to as the formal structures of letters and symbols, such as font, style, colour or size.[34] In graffiti art, this category of typography applies to the stylistic choice of the personalized font in the 'way you write your name, the letters you use, their shape, flow and form, the colours you choose'.[35] *Mesotypography*, on the other hand, captures the composition of a text on a surface, such as the spacing of letters.[36] In graffiti art, the composition of a text is often defined by the format, such as the creation of tags, throw-ups or more elaborate pieces. German graffiti scholar Stefan Meier further notes that focussing on the *mesotypography* of a piece of graffiti art may reveal the graffiti writer's technical ability and experience. If, for instance, letters leave drips and traces of running paint on the remaining surface which interfere with the *mesotypographic* layout of the piece, it can be deduced that this piece

32 Austin, 'More to see than a Canvas in a White Cube', 35.

33 Hartmut Stöckl, 'Typographie: Gewand und Körper des Textes – Linguistische Überlegungen zu typographischer Gestaltung', *Zeitschrift für angewandte Linguistik*, 41 (2004), 5–48 (p. 7).

34 Stöckl, 'Typographie', 22.

35 MacDonald, *The Graffiti Subculture*, p. 71.

36 Stöckl, 'Typographie', 22.

was created by a beginner who did not have much spray-can control.[37] The third category, *macrotypography*, relates to the creative organization of textual units. Creativity is often expressed through the addition of images, figures and caricatures.[38] In graffiti art, *macrotypographical* elements usually serve to enhance the visual impact of a written name or message by adding 'decorations that are frequently worked into the letters of a name, ranging from simple lines, swirls, arrows, and stars to highly complex caricatures and other drawings'.[39]

In order for these three typographic aspects to be identifiable as belonging to the graffiti art movement, the last category, *paratypography*, becomes the most relevant, as it links graffiti art to its urban context. Stöckl divides *paratypography* into 'die beiden Kategorien Material und Praktik des Signierens. Das Material bezeichnet dabei die stoffliche Qualität des Zeichenträgers, die Praktik des Signierens bezieht sich auf verfügbare Herstellungsverfahren, d.h. auf Techniken und benötigte Werkzeuge zum "Zeichenmachen"' [the two categories of the material and the practice of signing. *Material* denotes the material quality of the sign carrier, the *practice of signing* refers to the available manufacturing process, meaning the techniques and the tools required to 'create signs'].[40] *Paratypography* therefore pertains to both the materiality of a text in terms of the tools employed to create it and to the 'firstspace' surface on which graffiti art is placed, with Castleman stating that the 'style that one displays on the trains means the most'.[41] Stöckl's latter *paratypographic* category refers to the aerosol spray-paint which, according to Hilary Greenbaum and Dana Rubinstein, 'came in small, easy-to-conceal, easy-to-steal cans. It was paint and brush in one. It dried quickly. It worked well on building materials and subway cars'.[42]

With these four typographic categories at hand Meier, for instance, distinguishes between the different social aspirations of individual graffiti artists, noting:

> Während es gilt, auf mikro- und mesotypografischer Ebene einen möglichst markanten, unverwechselbaren Schriftzug zu entwickeln, markiert man auf paratypografischer Ebene bestimmte Stadtbezirke als 'Reviere', hinterlässt

37 Meier, 'Stylelife', p. 202.
38 Stöckl, 'Typographie', 22.
39 Castleman, *Getting Up*, p. 25.
40 Stöckl, 'Typographie', 37.
41 Castleman, *Getting Up*, 21.
42 Hilary Greenbaum and Dana Rubinstein, 'The Origin of Spray Paint', *New York Times Magazine*, 4 November 2011, http://www.nytimes.com/2011/11/06/magazine/who-made-spraypaint.html [accessed 9 October 2013].

> Spuren auf den Streifzügen und macht so innerhalb und außerhalb der Szene auf sich aufmerksam.[43]
>
> [While it is important to develop the most distinctive, unmistakable font possible on the micro- and mesotypographical level, you mark certain city districts as your 'territory' on a paratypographical level, leaving behind traces on your wanderings and thus attracting attention to yourself within and outwith the scene.]

This analysis will take the use of typography in understanding graffiti art one step further, namely by applying it to close readings of graffiti art's social, spatial and historical relevance within German cultural contexts. After a brief introduction of graffiti art's adaptation in West Germany, a comparative analysis will examine how this element of hip-hop has been appropriated in Hamburg and Oldenburg and how it has influenced the visual experience of these contemporary German cityspaces.

The Visibility of Graffiti Art in West Germany

> Das ist unsere Kunst gerade zurzeit. Das ist unser Stil. Das ist unsere Generation einfach.[44]
>
> [This is our art form at this precise time. This is our style. This is simply our generation.]

This statement by Hamburg graffiti artist Tasek not only reveals graffiti art's presence in Germany but highlights its importance to contemporary German artists ever since it reached West Germany as part of the mediated hip-hop movement in the 1980s. With the practice of spraying letters on urban surfaces being influenced by New York City graffiti art's socio-spatial norms, different West German graffiti communities quickly adapted distinct fonts in order to become identifiable within West Germany's urban landscape. West Berlin's graffiti community, for example, was known for adhering to the 'wild style' font,[45] while Hamburg and German cities from the Ruhr area became known for their creation of a distinct German 'simple style'.[46] This style was

43 Meier, 'Stylelife', pp. 204–05.

44 Tasek, interviewed by author, 20 August 2012.

45 Jürgen Deppe and Odem, *Odem – On the Run: Eine Jugend in der Graffiti-Szene* (Berlin: Schwarzkopf & Schwarzkopf, 1997), pp. i–ix and p. 161; cf. Moe, interviewed by author, 11 March 2012; Asek, interviewed by author, 21 March 2012.

46 Tasek, interviewed by author, 20 August 2012.

also referred to as the 'Dortmund style' since Dortmund's graffiti community employed it in the most unscrupulous and unrelenting ways.[47] According to Tasek, this simple style was:

> ein typischer Bombingsstyle, den man halt nachts viel gemacht hat. Das waren halt ganz geradlinige Letters mit ganz dicken Outlines. Alles ganz perfekt und sauber exekutiert. Ganz simple Farben reingefüllt. Nicht großartig irgendwelche Fadings und Ge-*shizzl*, und gar nicht viel Characters und so was, sondern einfach nur straighte Blockletters sozusagen. Mit einem bisschen Swing drinne. Aber halt sehr geradlinig letztendlich so. Also fast Deutschland-typisch sozusagen.[48]
>
> [a typical bombing style that you did a lot at night. Letters with very straight lines and very fat outlines. Everything perfectly and cleanly executed. Filled with very simple colours. Not many fadings and shit and not many characters and things like that but just straight block letters. With a bit of swing. But very straight in the end. Almost typically German, so to speak.]

By linking the *micro*- and *macrotypographical* features of the Dortmund style to an overall German stereotype, Tasek engages in a cultural discourse that can be understood as a 'form of splitting and multiple belief, [which] requires, for its successful signification, a continual and repetitive chain of other stereotypes' (*LOC*, p. 110). This is established through the repetitive sequence of straight and perfectly executed spray-painted lines. Its successful signification is further enhanced through the iterative pattern of the 'bombing' tradition, which ensures high visibility to 'outsiders'. Thus, the German simple style became known for the:

> Qualität der technischen Umsetzung und die Quantität durch die nächtlichen Umsetzungen. Dadurch war das auf jeden Fall echt eine massive Sache. Und die auch plötzlich dafür gesorgt hat, dass da echt alle plötzlich auch hingeguckt haben so: 'Was machen denn die deutschen Verrückten da so? Da geht ja mächtig was!'.[49]
>
> [quality of the technical realization and the quantity due to the realization at night. That definitely led to it becoming a massive thing. And which also all of a sudden made sure that everyone, all of a sudden, watched it, like: 'What are the crazy Germans doing there? Something is really going on!']

With Hamburg graffiti writer Delles concluding that 'was typisch deutsch ist,

47 Deppe and Odem, *Odem*, p. 263 and p. 291.

48 Tasek, interviewed by author, 20 August 2012. 'Bombing' refers to the practice of producing large quantities of illegal graffiti.

49 Tasek, interviewed by author, 20 August 2012.

ist so dieser Dortmund Style' [what is typically German is this Dortmund style],[50] the stereotypically German attributes characterizing this style compellingly parallel the initial German adaptation of b-boying as 'straight German power'. The characteristics of the Dortmund-style typography and the kinaesthetics of the straight-German-power tradition exhibit the same qualities in terms of the clean execution and creation of straight lines which provided the art forms with a German national identity. However, while in b-boying these characteristics could have been a logical cultural consequence of an existing tradition of gymnastics, no prior national artistic tradition can be identified as having been influential on Germany's simple graffiti style. Rather, Moe states that 'manche von meinen Jungs aus der Crew, die sind eben an Kunst nur über Graffiti rangekommen' [some of my guys in the crew only got to art through graffiti].[51] Indeed, the aesthetic appearance of the simple style's 'throw-up' formats was secondary to its efficient function of visibility. Nevertheless, Delles stresses that German artists invented a national style that was 'innovativ. Sind wohl nicht die schönsten Buchstaben, aber es ist was Eigenes' [innovative. Maybe not the prettiest letters but it is something individual].[52] Thus, while 'straight German power' was criticized by Jango as lacking *das gewisse Eigene*,[53] the independently created German graffiti style was understood as being just that: unique.

However, this uniqueness did not prove strong enough to withstand other aesthetic impulses. By the late 1990s, and hence after German unification, West German graffiti art departed from its previous nationally representative style and ended as an aesthetic of pluralism. One reason for this transformation was the changing forces of its forms of spatial communication, for the advent of the Internet opened up wider possibilities for exchanging and experiencing graffiti art beyond the 'firstspaces' of its production sites. Through the creation of online graffiti-art platforms such as 'streetfiles' and its successor 'streetpins', which is described as 'a photo sharing community for streetart & graffiti artists and all other interested people',[54] photographic images of graffiti-art murals, canvases and trains could instantly be globally disseminated. The artists' aims have moved beyond creating and maintaining 'lokale Stile, wo die Leute sich beeinflussen. [Graffiti] folgt zwar immer noch denselben Regeln, aber der Spielplatz ist verändert worden, weil durch das Internet ist das eine völlig dezentralisierte Geschichte geworden' [local styles in which people influenced

50 Beatboy Delles, interviewed by author, 21 May 2012.

51 Moe, interviewed by author, 11 March 2012; this statement refers to his crew in West Berlin.

52 Beatboy Delles, interviewed by author, 21 May 2012.

53 Jango, interviewed by author, 8 June 2012.

54 Anonymous, 'Graffiti & Streetart Photo Community', *Streetpins.com | Graffiti & Streetart Photo Community*, http://www.streetpins.com/ [accessed 2 October 2013].

each other. [Graffiti] still follow the same rules but the playground has changed because through the Internet it has become such a decentralized thing].[55]

This spatial decentralization has had an impact not only on the creation of distinct local fonts and styles but also on the consumption of graffiti art. Moe explains:

> Streetfiles hat Graffiti nach Hause auf deinen Bildschirm gebracht und ist eine sehr bequeme Sache und für jemand wie ich, der so gut wie keine Freizeit mehr besitzt wegen Familie und Vollzeitjob und noch ehrenamtliche Arbeit ist es unmöglich, dass ich alle [Graffiti] *Places* aufsuche.[56]
>
> [Streetfiles has brought graffiti to your screen at home and is a very convenient thing for someone like me who has almost no free time any more due to a family and a full-time job and volunteering, it's impossible for me to seek out all [graffiti] *places*.]

While these changing dynamics influence contemporary practices of graffiti art, Tasek emphasizes that the task of a graffiti artist is to engage in these changes and to produce graffiti art in ways that are meaningful in a contemporary cultural context. He explains:

> Je mehr *true to the old school* die Leute auch über Jahre geblieben sind, desto cooler ist das zwar irgendwie, aber dann ist das halt immer noch nicht authentisch, weil wenn du etwas stilecht kopierst macht dich das noch nicht zum authentischen Künstler.[57]
>
> [The *truer to the old school* people stay over the years, the cooler it is somehow, but it is still not authentic yet because when you copy the style of something precisely, then that does not make you an authentic artist].

As graffiti art has become 'eine Identifikation' for contemporary German artists, Tasek concludes that this identification only happens if it is 'aus dir selbst entstanden im Abgleich mit deinem Umfeld und deiner Umgebung und deinen Fragen' [created out of yourself in alignment with your environment and your questions].[58] The strategies with which graffiti art has become relevant for contemporary German artists and their urban environment will therefore be explored in the following comparative analysis.

55 Tasek, interviewed by author, 20 August 2012.
56 Moe, interviewed by author, 11 March 2012.
57 Tasek, interviewed by author, 20 August 2012.
58 Tasek, interviewed by author, 20 August 2012.

Hamburg and the Metropolitan Messages of Graffiti Art

The beginnings of graffiti art in Hamburg remain captured on Hamburg's 'firstspaces' up to this very day. Delles explains: '[D]er erste wirklich bekannte Sprüher aus Hamburg, der wirklich Buchstaben gemalt hat, das war Eric. Es gibt auch immer noch Bilder, wie am Berliner Tor [...] von 1984 oder so' [[T]he first really well-known sprayer from Hamburg, who really painted letters, was Eric. There are still pictures like the one at the Berliner Tor [...] from 1984 or so].[59] These images thus coincide with the year in which hip-hop was being introduced through American films. However, early graffiti art in Hamburg was also influenced by the circulation of hard-copy graffiti sketches created by Shoe, a writer from Amsterdam, and Bando from Paris.[60] This Eurocentric influence is comparable to Britcore's relevance for Hamburg's early hip-hop sound. More drawings by Shoe, and hence from the closer Dutch border, reached and circulated in Hamburg. This European intervention led to the fact that 'von denselben Sachen basierend etwas Eigenes entwickelt wurde, oder eigene Swings und Flows entwickelt [wurden]' [something individual was developed based on the same things, or individual swings and flows were developed].[61] This new style went beyond solely mimicking American graffiti art fonts. Nonetheless, the virtual visibility of stylistic approaches has led to the outcome that 'diesen klassischen Hamburg Stil, den gibt es so nicht mehr' [this classical Hamburg style does not exist anymore].[62] While it was once known for its unique, individual, simple-block-letter graffiti fonts, Hamburg's cityspace is now described by local graffiti artist Davis as home to a 'multikulti' style.[63]

While *multikulti* in Germany has been declared dead by Germany's leading conservative politicians, it remains very much alive in the cityspace of Hamburg. Here, *multikulti*, in the sense of graffiti art, on the one hand refers to the pluralism of styles that have converged from different cultures and different cityspaces. On the other hand, it is also the case that Hamburg's sprayer community comprises many cultural backgrounds. Davis specifically names Turkish, Polish, Russian and ethnic German as the main ethnic groups.[64] In a humorous account, he asserts that local hip-hop artists of African descent remain relatively absent in this element and instead engage in hip-hop dance

59 Beatboy Delles, interviewed by author, 21 May 2012.

60 Tasek, interviewed by author, 20 August 2012; cf. Davis, interviewed by author, 20 August 2012.

61 Tasek, interviewed by author, 20 August 2012.

62 Tasek, interviewed by author, 20 August 2012.

63 Davis, interviewed by author, 20 August 2012.

64 Davis, interviewed by author, 20 August 2012.

as this art form supposedly resonates more meaningfully with their natural physique and cultural background.[65] While such ironic statements hint at an alleged division of cultures, the general consensus nevertheless reveals that, as with graffiti art's social discourse in New York City, it is irrelevant whether one is 'schwarz, weiß, reich, arm, krank, gesund, groß, klein, dick, dünn, Mann oder Frau [...]. Das spielt einfach alles keine Rolle' [black, white, rich, poor, sick, healthy, big, small, fat, thin, man or woman [...]. That is all just completely irrelevant].[66] The important aspect for gaining a respected social identity as a graffiti artist in Hamburg is, therefore, based on the creation of an individual typographic style presented on selected 'fronts' in urban 'firstspaces'.

These urban 'firstspaces' also include mobile train canvases since the size of Hamburg's cityspace requires a railway transit system for inner-urban transportation. Indeed, Eric's historical graffiti piece already shows that Hamburg's early writers immediately imitated the original metropolitan discourse of graffiti art by writing on rail-traffic terrain.[67] However, unlike New York City's traditional subway canvases, Hamburg's train-graffiti pieces have been placed on urban railway cars rather than on its subway line. This substitution of mobile urban 'firstspaces' is due to the urban train system's low number of circulating cars, as these provide a greater chance for a top-to-bottom or a whole car to run. This is mainly because the subway line has enough cars for a spray-painted one to be exchanged immediately after its detection by authorities.[68] In other words, the same symbolic value of visibility that was previously attached to New York City's subway spatiality has been inscribed on Hamburg's urban railway cars, which disseminate graffiti art throughout the Northern German metropolis. An example is provided by the whole car created by graffiti group BK, who not only adapt graffiti art's socio-spatial practices to their local German cityspace, but also fuse them with a cultural-historical discourse pertaining to a German cultural context (see Figure 8). A close reading of this piece will highlight the typographic strategies chosen for the creation of this culturally hybrid, yet nevertheless German, graffiti-art piece.

The black outline around the train car serves to define the canvas's elongated rectangular shape, which at the same time imitates the conventional format of a German vehicle registration plate. The silver filling within the outline further offers a contrast to the four black letters and four black numbers situated in

65 Davis, interviewed by author, 20 August 2012. While over half the active, independent hip-hop dancers training in Hamburg in 2012 were of African descent, it remains problematic to locate their interest in dance solely in their ethnic heritage.

66 Tasek, interviewed by author, 20 August 2012.

67 'Berliner Tor' is the name of a subway and an urban railway station in Hamburg.

68 Udu, interviewed by author, 13 May 2012.

Figure 8: A 'whole car' by BK on Hamburg's urban railway line

(Source: https://streetpins.com/photos/snaqq/snaqq_1373733544-639x477.jpg)

Figure 9: Smiley Face and Tag by OZ

(Copyright: author)

the frame. The letters and digits specifically adhere to the *microtypographic* '*FE-Schrift*' (*fälschungserschwerende Schrift*) [writing that is difficult to counterfeit] which has been employed on German licence plates since 2000. The piece's *mesotypography* also follows the established arrangement of the vehicle registration codes: the letters 'HH' on the left are the abbreviation for 'Hansestadt Hamburg'. The remaining letter combinations serve to present the graffiti crew's identity, while the numbers capture the piece's year of creation.

The inclusion of *macrotypographical* symbols further adds to the faithful replication of the vehicle registration plate. Germany's countrycode 'D', sprayed in white paint, is located on a blue strip to the far left side of the canvas above which a ring of twelve yellow stars symbolizes the flag of Europe. Other *mesotypographic* accents include two circles placed above each other between Hamburg's prefix and BK's name. The top orange circle replicates the safety inspection seal, whereby the orange colour signifies its fictional expiration date in 2007 and adds a realistic touch to the fact that this imitation of the licence plate was done in 2006.[69] Below, Hamburg's white and red coat-of-arms represents Hamburg's status as a city-state.

This highly detailed and sophisticated whole car thus infuses graffiti art's norms and practices with German cultural signification. While from a spatial perspective the choice of the 'firstspace' of the Hamburg urban train façade and the piece's format become a meaningful social sign for the local graffiti community, the creativity of the whole car becomes evident when reading it as a 'secondspatial' representation of contemporary Germany, signified through the symbolic codes of German registration plates. Therefore, BK's metropolitan message rests on knowledge of the contemporary German cultural context. From a historical perspective, moreover, the piece's message only makes sense in the modern era, enabled by the invention of motorized vehicles as a consequence of the urban industrialization of society. More specifically, the historicality of this piece dates back to 2000, when the *microtypography* of the licence plates became established.

At the same time, the codes can also be read anew from a social perspective as they come to signify the successful act of illegally creating a whole car. BK ridicule officialdom by re-functioning the usefulness of the codes pertaining to official registration laws to represent their deviant social behaviour as local German citizens. By blending these two forms of cultural knowledge into one graffiti-art form, BK ultimately create a 'third space' which 'challenges

69 Anonymous, 'Anlage IX (zu § 29 Absatz 2, 3, 5 bis 8) – Prüfplakette für die Untersuchung von Kraftfahrzeugen und Anhängern', *StVZO* (Bundesministerium der Justiz und für Verbraucherschutz, 2012), http://www.gesetze-im-internet.de/stvzo_2012/anlage_ix_139.html [accessed 10 September 2013].

the binary that separated the containment of meaning within an artwork and the establishment of a framework for making meaning within culture, by suggesting that both art and culture are in a reflexive process that is co-constitutive'.[70]

This co-constitutiveness of German culture and graffiti art is also traceable beyond BK's whole car and its circulation through Hamburg. Sprayer OZ, for example, engaged in the same appropriation of mobile 'firstspaces' in order to re-negotiate the binary of art and culture.[71] Delles highlights the fact that 'du siehst überall OZ' [you see OZ *everywhere*],[72] explaining that 'im Endeffekt [...] er alle Lines [hat], alle S-Bahnen, alle Yards hat der abgedeckt. Und das hat kein weiterer Sprüher bis jetzt hinbekommen' [ultimately, he has covered all the lines, all the tram lines, all the yards. And no other sprayer has managed that yet].[73] However, in contrast to the communal works by BK, OZ had been spraying in solitude in Hamburg since the mid-1980s.[74] Since then he has visually dominated Hamburg's cityspace through his vast number of spray-painted traces, which appear most commonly as black smiley faces or as his tag OZ, created by two connecting letters spray-painted in black ink with a dot acting as a *macrotypographic* marker placed in the lower elbow of the Z (see Figure 9).

The dissemination of these social symbols has provided OZ with the local status of 'Weltmeister von Hamburg sozusagen. Also was Quantität angeht' [world champion of Hamburg, so to speak. Quantity-wise].[75] However, the main difference between OZ's approach to German graffiti art and that of BK is not only his individual engagement but that OZ gained his reputation without adhering to graffiti art's typographic norms, aside from its *paratypography*. As Tasek explains, OZ's presentation of self has not been 'über Stil, nicht über Szene-Affinität oder *Realness* oder *Coolness* irgendwie [...], sondern einfach nur [über] harte Fakten und zwar in Masse' [about style, about affinity to the scene or about *realness* or *coolness* [...], but just about hard facts, masses of them].[76] Rather than writing stylized letters in order to communicate a social identity within the local graffiti community, OZ's tags, smiley faces and abstract designs,[77] which do 'not depict recognizable scenes or objects,

70 Papastergiadis, 'Hybridity and Ambivalence', 47.

71 OZ died on 25 September 2014.

72 Beatboy Delles, interviewed by author, 21 May 2012.

73 Beatboy Delles, interviewed by author, 21 May 2012.

74 Insa Gall and Martin Kopp, 'Der Sprayer Von OZ', *DIE WELT*, 16 December 1999, http://www.welt.de/print-welt/article593031/Der-Sprayer-von-OZ.html [accessed 2 October 2013].

75 Tasek, interviewed by author, 20 August 2012.

76 Tasek, interviewed by author, 20 August 2012.

77 OZ's artistic output other than smiley faces and his tag includes painted surfaces made up of circles and dots placed on colourful backgrounds.

but instead [are] made up of forms and colours that exist for their own expressive sake',[78] have served to bring colour into 'das braune Deutschland' [brown Germany].[79] With Hamburg's contemporary architecture and human geography supposedly tainted by the country's politically 'brown' Nazi history, OZ's performative claim to this urban 'firstspace' becomes a material discourse grounded in a historical context.

OZ's politically-charged *paratypographical* demonstration also reveals itself as his voiceless form of communication. On the one hand, his graffiti art was able to mask his 'abomination of the body', namely the 'attribute' of his cleft palate, which inhibits proper pronunciation of the German language.[80] On the other hand, the colouring of Hamburg's 'firstspace' further became a strategy with which to manage OZ's 'tribal stigma' of Jewish heritage. As a newspaper article in *Die Welt* reports:

> Der Sprayer und sein Hass auf die Nazis: Elternlos aufgewachsen in Heimen, beharrt er seit Jahren darauf, Jude zu sein – vielleicht gerade, weil sich der Mann ohne Herkunft eine solche verschaffen möchte. 'Im Heim hat man mir erzählt, meine Mutter wäre Jüdin', behauptet er.[81]
>
> [The sprayer and his hatred of Nazis: having grown up in homes without his parents, he has been insisting for years that he is Jewish – maybe because that is how the man without an origin wants to create one for himself. 'In the home they told me that my mother was Jewish', he claims.]

Thus, OZ's choice of style served to react visibly against (neo-)Nazism, with abstract art having been banned in Nazi Germany for not conforming to a supposed German artistic aesthetic. By visually challenging the German historical present, OZ's urban oeuvre and spatial narrative open up a 'third space' which 'refers to the visible manifestation of difference within identity as a consequence of the incorporation of foreign elements'.[82] While successfully re-functioning graffiti art's foreign *paratypographic* norms and practices into a socio-historical discourse pertaining to Germany, OZ's identity as a

78 Ian Chilvers, 'Abstract Art', in *The Oxford Dictionary of Art*, 3rd edn (Oxford: Oxford University Press, 2004), p. 2.

79 Udu, interviewed by author, 13 May 2012; brown was the colour of the former German NSDAP party.

80 Udu, interviewed by author, 13 May 2012. Insa Gall and Martin Kopp write that OZ was 'wegen seiner Gaumenspalte als "Teufelsbrut" gebrandmarkt' [was branded as 'the spawn of the devil' because of his cleft palate] (Insa Gall and Martin Kopp, 'Der Sprayer von OZ', http://www.welt.de/print-welt/article593031/Der-Sprayer-von-OZ.html [accessed 2 October 2013].

81 Gall and Kopp, 'Der Sprayer Von OZ'.

82 Papastergiadis, 'Hybridity and Ambivalence', 40.

graffiti artist has nevertheless remained ambivalent within the local hip-hop community. His choice of *paratypography*, the visibility of traces and the creation of an innovative style[83] have become 'für viele aus der Graffitiszene ein Qualitätsmerkmal sozusagen, was ihm Heroenstatus eingebracht hat' [a sort of hallmark of quality for many members of the graffiti scene which brought him the status of a hero].[84] However, at the same time OZ was 'trotzdem nie so wirklich ein Teil einer Szene' [never really part of the scene][85] due to his 'Stilistik und durch seine Ausnahmestellung' [style and exceptional position].[86]

Nevertheless, in the end OZ's expressive power has become 'einfach ein Metakonstrukt [...] dadurch, dass es so politisch für die Stadt Relevanz bekommen hat' [quite simply a meta-construct because it has become so politically relevant for the city].[87] In other words, OZ's personal approach to graffiti art has created a local identity for the German cityspace of Hamburg beyond a hip-hop-related context. Its relevance as an urban identity marker is summarized in the slogan 'Hamburg ohne OZ ... ist München!' [Hamburg without OZ ... is Munich!],[88] which circulated on a placard in front of Hamburg's court room during OZ's hearing in 2011.[89]

While some members of Hamburg's graffiti community have honoured OZ's quantitative engagement by providing him with the status of world champion, local artist DAIM has gained the same status for his qualitative approach to graffiti art, namely for becoming 'weltweit bekannt für 3-Ds' [known world-wide for 3-Ds].[90] DAIM became initially involved in graffiti art through an interest in hip-hop culture and a previous fascination for the art works of Spanish Surrealist artist Salvador Dalí and Dutch Post-Impressionist painter Vincent van Gogh. Through this latter interest, DAIM acquired an understanding for different techniques of paint application and of visual effects beyond the defining aesthetics of graffiti art. With these insights, DAIM began to ask himself: 'Warum muss eigentlich immer die klassische schwarze Outline um die ganzen Buchstaben rumgesprüht werden?' [Why does

83 Beatboy Delles, interviewed by author, 21 May 2012.

84 Tasek, interviewed by author, 20 August 2012.

85 Tasek, interviewed by author, 20 August 2012.

86 Tasek, interviewed by author, 20 August 2012.

87 Tasek, interviewed by author, 20 August 2012.

88 Anonymous, Picture #5, 'Streetart-Mythos OZ: Die Stadt als Galerie', *SPIEGEL ONLINE Fotostrecke*, 29 July 2011, http://www.spiegel.de/fotostrecke/streetart-mythos-oz-die-stadt-als-galerie-fotostrecke-71007-5.html [accessed 10 September 2013].

89 OZ was in court and in prison on multiple occasions due to his graffiti art; many people demonstrated against his conviction. The issue was whether OZ should be understood as an artist or as a vandal, which is how the local authorities of Hamburg viewed him.

90 Beatboy Delles, interviewed by author, 21 May 2012.

the classic black outline always have to be sprayed around all the letters?].[91] Through investigating this aesthetic custom DAIM omitted the classic black outline when spraying letters, a feature which had previously been an identity marker of the Dortmund style. Rather, DAIM chose to construct his letters through variations of shade and light and different hues of colour.[92]

Thus, while OZ challenged the socio-historical discourse of graffiti art through his quantitative approach, DAIM ruptures graffiti art's previously established aesthetic boundaries, posing:

> powerful questions about the effects of difference within cultural objects, the process of incorporating foreign symbols or utilizing different media and the articulation of a critique against domination. Much of the debate around these kinds of artistic practices has tended to take an absolute position, with critics either celebrating the mobility of culture or mourning the loss of authenticity.[93]

In line with Papastergiadis's observations, DAIM's three-dimensional approach was initially dismissed by other German graffiti writers who mourned the loss of the supposedly authentic practice of graffiti art, deeming his typographic style not to be graffiti art at all.[94] However, DAIM was able to mitigate this apprehensive reaction by adhering to the spatiality of graffiti art as well as to the social discourse of presenting himself through the continual repetition of his style, with which he could repeatedly 'show new sides of graffiti art'.[95] In this way DAIM's technique has provided him with a style, 'den man sofort, ob man von tausend Meter oder von fünf Meter entfernt, sofort lesen kann' [which you can immediately read, whether you are standing a thousand metres or five metres away],[96] fulfilling the ultimate objective of a skilled graffiti writer.[97]

By having 'gotten up' meaning, having gained 'recognition and acceptance of [his] work by other writers (and possibly the public in general)',[98] DAIM, together with Tasek and colleague Heiko Zahlmann, have further transcended graffiti art's illegality by making it their legal profession. In line with this development, the three artists have founded the graffiti artist association 'Getting Up'. The institution provides 'back' regions where the artists are able

91 DAIM, 'Opel Corsa – DAIM & Loomit Interview', *DAIM*, 24 January 2011, http://www.youtube.com/watch?v=LZJfbiUDgY8 [accessed 20 September 2013].

92 DAIM, 'Opel Corsa'.

93 Papastergiadis, 'Hybridity and Ambivalence', 45–46.

94 DAIM, 'ARTotale "Die Kunst der Kontrolle" PART 1 – Leuphana Urban-Art Project Lüneburg', *Reinkingprojekte*, 16 March 2010, http://www.youtube.com/watch?v=-v_ak4GZVkg [accessed 20 September 2013].

95 DAIM, *DAIM: Daring to Push the Boundaries* (Hamburg: Reisser, 2004), p. 6.

96 Beatboy Delles, interviewed by author, 21 May 2012.

97 MacDonald, *The Graffiti Subculture*, p. 71.

98 Castleman, *Getting Up*, p. 19.

to plan, practise and perfect their technical skills as professionals; this also includes preparing art works for art-gallery exhibitions. This, in turn, serves to elevate their social status as artists beyond the hip-hop community. Indeed, the 'secondspatial' hip-hop identity of the artist association 'Getting Up' becomes especially relevant to determining Tasek's art works, since his pieces have become 'inzwischen von der Form her ziemlich weit weg [...] von Graffiti, aber sich halt immer eben noch auf dieselben Gesetzmäßigkeiten [beziehen]' [considerably distanced from graffiti in terms of form, but they still refer to the same rules].[99]

Moreover, Tasek adheres to graffiti art's trialectics, such as the spatiality in which 'Dinge draußen entstehen und dass Dinge auch schnell wieder vergehen' [things are created outside and quickly vanish again][100] and the need 'die Stadt als multiplen Platz wahrzunehmen' [to perceive the city as a multiple space].[101] By moving 'wie ein Wanderer zwischen den Welten, wie ein Nomade' [like a wanderer between the worlds, like a nomad][102] Tasek has re-negotiated graffiti art's normative typographic guidelines. Having discovered this grey area between graffiti art's cultural relevance and its spatial and stylistic boundaries, Tasek explains: '[A]b da [hat] [...] Hip-Hop für mich Sinn gemacht als Szene und als Identifikation für mich. Und das versuche ich halt heutzutage als urbanen Künstler in meinen Arbeiten auch weiterzutragen' [[F]rom then on hip-hop made sense to me, as a scene and identification for myself. And that is what I, as an urban artist, still try to carry onwards in my work].[103] An example of this grey zone is found in the legal communal graffiti piece 'Repeat', which Tasek created in Hamburg together with DAIM, Heiko Zahlmann and the Berlin graffiti artist Stohead in 2010 (see Figure 10). A close reading of this piece will further elaborate on the typographic strategies employed by Tasek and with which he aims to address stylistically his 'soziale Fragen, politische Fragen, natürlich auch existenzielle Fragen' [social questions, political questions, of course existential questions].[104]

The piece spans multiple walls leading into the entry of an underground car park in the Hamburg district of Altona. While it comprises the artists' individual graffiti styles, such as DAIM's recognizable 3D design, their unity is *microtypographically* expressed through the use of the same colour combinations. The individual styles are mainly presented in shades of white and grey, as well as in orange and yellow.

99 Tasek, interviewed by author, 20 August 2012.
100 Tasek, interviewed by author, 20 August 2012.
101 Tasek, interviewed by author, 20 August 2012.
102 Tasek, interviewed by author, 20 August 2012.
103 Tasek, interviewed by author, 20 August 2012.
104 Tasek, interviewed by author, 20 August 2012.

Figure 10: 'Repeat'

(Copyright: ©2010 courtesy getting-up/STAMP/altonale)

Tasek's contribution to this mural consists of white letters that create the word 'REPEAT'. It appears in different *microtypographic* sizes, yet always in the same straight, angular shapes. The gaps within the capitalized letters R, P and A are, moreover, filled with white paint. The piece's *mesotypography* is characterized by the word's random and repeated appearance all over the cemented *paratypogaphic* surface. This includes partial overlapping of the individual words as well as of *mesotypographic* interruptions through white lines of paint dripping from one letter onto the one placed below. From a typographic perspective then, Tasek's letters are not a reflection of graffiti art's emphasis on creating a personal identity through a distinct flow and swing of letters. Rather, his letters are rigid and fixed with dripping paint further challenging the supposed skill of a graffiti artist. This aspect becomes especially interesting when regarding Tasek's performance as a graffiti artist who has 'gotten up' precisely because of his talent and skill, yet who now even replaces the spray can by a paint roller with which to write his letters.

By re-articulating graffiti art's stylestic norms while remaining within the familiar spatial framework, Tasek's grey zone and the newness and meaningfulness that emerge from it are further enhanced by the piece's contemporary social discourse. Inspired by the 'thirdspace' experience of the 'repetitive aspects of urban life',[105] the graffiti artist explains that the:

> mantric repetition of the term 'repeat' reflects complex, constantly changing social structures, and simultaneously reduces these to one self-denominating formula: Repeat. A motif that is completely separated from place, content

105 Anonymous, 'Repeat – Tiefgarageneinfahrt', *Getting-up*, 18 October 2010, http://getting-up.org/en/2010/10/repeat_tiefgarageneinfahrt/ [accessed 20 September 2013].

> and function, but that nevertheless consistently follows its own rules; a motif trapped in itself.[106]

The aesthetic expression of the trapped motif further mimics the iterative graffiti art practice of tagging, with the difference being the dissemination of a verb rather than a personal pseudonym. Moreover, while the mural becomes a 'firstspace' that at the same time influences the 'thirdspace' experience within Hamburg, the fact that the motif is supposed to present a separation from a distinct cityspace highlights the:

> difficulties in defining the sense of place in the context of art [through] the strategic use of boundaries in new kinds of artistic practice. The juxtaposition of different signs and the contrast of alternative perspectives are not only recurring features in the composition of artworks but also strategies that artists utilize in order to provoke new forms of cross-cultural communication.[107]

In the spatial narrative of 'Repeat', such forms of cross-cultural communication are evident in the strategic employment of English as a global linguistic sign with which Tasek is able to disseminate his metropolitan message beyond urban and even national boundaries. However, in this way the message simultaneously detaches the graffiti-art piece from a German urban 'firstspace'. In other words, from a spatial perspective the mural can only become a German cultural sign if it is encountered as a 'thirdspace' experience in its territorial location. Here its social meaning relates to a historicality pertaining to any contemporary urban lifestyle in which the repetitiveness and anonymity of metropolitan life are socially expressed through Tasek's iterative, yet at the same time impersonal, style. This hybrid measure does, therefore, 'not point to an ideal stage of accomplishment, but rather to the process of critical interaction that occurs within and against the structure of a binary'.[108] In critically interacting with the norms and practices of graffiti art, Tasek's ambivalent positioning within the traditional graffiti-art movement has estranged the art form through its contact with other cultural presences, while making it relevant for spatial, social and historical discourses pertaining to contemporary global, urban 'thirdspace' experiences.

Hence, as an interim summary of the first analysis of graffiti art's appropriation in Hamburg, it can be stated that close readings of hip-hop's visual art form have illustrated the variety of social, spatial and historical discourses expressed through graffiti art. However, these close readings have

106 Gerrit Peters (Tasek), *The Artists* (Gettingup.de, n.d.), http://getting-up.org/en/artists/gerrit-peters-tasek/ [accessed 20 September 2013].
107 Papastergiadis, 'Hybridity and Ambivalence', 46.
108 Papastergiadis, 'Hybridity and Ambivalence', 62.

also revealed a slight divergence in the relationship of graffiti art and artists to hip-hop culture. Since graffiti art has always existed before and then parallel to hip-hop, it remains a relative of hip-hop, although not every expression of graffiti art fits into the framework of hip-hop culture's intentions and motivations. Nevertheless, spatiality has remained the most important feature through which to determine a writer's engagement in this art form. Its spatial functions have been adapted to Hamburg's cityspace while the metropolitan messages have been grounded in multicultural social, spatial and historical discourses pertaining to Hamburg and Germany, as well as to Europe and beyond. Four examples of local graffiti art, ranging from communal to individual, from legal to illegal pieces, have served to highlight the aesthetic and typographic strategies employed in order to make graffiti art meaningful as a contemporary art movement. They have shown that Hamburg's graffiti-art style has become pluralistic and cosmopolitan, a style previously defined by Davis as *multikulti*. Indeed, Tasek characterizes his local writing community as 'weltoffen [...], zwar reserviert, aber doch offen, und tolerant' [open-minded [...], a bit reserved, but open and tolerant].[109] Nonetheless, at the same time this cultural and artistic open-mindedness has also blurred the art form's identifiable Germanness when compared to its previous 'simple style'. Whether this only relates to Hamburg will be explored in the following analysis, which examines graffiti art's manifestation in the contrasting cityspace of Oldenburg.

Oldenburg and the Provincial Messages of Graffiti Art

Graffiti art in Oldenburg started to appear between 1989 and 1990,[110] thus dating to six years later than graffiti art's first visible traces in Hamburg. Nevertheless, despite the delay Moe stresses that graffiti art 'an[fing] und das ist für so eine große Stadt doch relativ früh' [started and that was relatively early for the size of such a city].[111] With the hype of the first hip-hop films having already passed, the rise of Oldenburg's graffiti art was, rather, indebted to 'zwei, drei wirklich gute Maler, [die] zu der Zeit aktiv waren' [two, three really good painters who were active at that time].[112] With only three artists needed to transform the 'firstspaces' of Oldenburg into a colourful 'thirdspace' experience, local graffiti artist Sbek remembers that:

109 Tasek, interviewed by author, 20 August 2012.
110 Moe, interviewed by author, 11 March 2012.
111 Moe, interviewed by author, 11 March 2012.
112 Moe, interviewed by author, 11 March 2012.

> [ich] [...] durch meine Stadt gefahren [bin]. Habe Wände gesehen. Vereinzelnd. Und das hat mich total gepackt. Hab' mich immer schon für Schrift interessiert und dann gesehen, wie Menschen mit der Spraydose Schrift an die Wand sprühen. War total cool!.
>
> [I drove through my city. Saw walls. Here and there. And that fascinated me. I was always interested in writing and then I saw how people were writing on the walls with spray cans. That was totally awesome!].[113]

In his encountering of graffiti art in Oldenburg, Sbek's understanding of it, therefore, 'does not presuppose an original which the process can refer back to, nor does it impose fixed terms of meaning'.[114] Rather, Sbek experienced graffiti art as an inherent part of urban life in Oldenburg.

However, despite the size of the cityspace and the low number of graffiti artists, local writer Asek explains: '[S]o einen richtigen Oldenburg Style gibt es halt eigentlich kaum so' [a real Oldenburg style really barely exists].[115] With Oldenburg's graffiti-art community having established itself later than communities in other German cities, it can be argued that the short time span between its establishment as a local art movement and the rise of graffiti art circulating on the Internet has caused Oldenburg's graffiti community to remain largely identity-less in terms of creating a typical local font. Indeed, Asek adds that 'gerade durch das Internet und dadurch, dass die Leute ja auch alle reisen, [...] sich das einfach total [vermischt]' [especially through the Internet and because people travel, everything just blends together completely].[116] In this sense, Oldenburg's contemporary stylistic diversity is comparable to Hamburg's *multikulti* style, with the main difference being that Oldenburg's graffiti-art community is mainly comprised of ethnic German writers, like its local rap community.

Just as the practice and performance of rap established themselves in accordance with Oldenburg's spatiality, graffiti art has been subject to a comparable urban adaptation. Since Oldenburg lacks an inner-urban rail transportation system, mobile visibility and communication have been pursued on the metal canvases of regional train lines, where the same formats of top-to-bottoms and whole cars remain valid criteria with which to interpret artistic skills. However, within this regional locomotive realm, graffiti art's train-writing norms have also been re-defined and have become more sophisticated as artists have re-interpreted different train models as status symbols. Asek explains:

113 Sbek, interviewed by author, 7 March 2012.
114 Papastergiadis, *The Turbulence of Migration*, p. 136.
115 Asek, interviewed by author, 21 March 2012.
116 Asek, interviewed by author, 21 March 2012.

> [E]ntscheidend ist wie lange der Zug fährt und wie das Bild auf dem Zug ist. Das ist eigentlich sogar noch entscheidender. Aber ein Güterzug wird nicht so hoch angesehen, wie jetzt eine NordWestBahn. Also diese Ränge gibt es natürlich schon.[117]

> [[I]t is decisive how long a train runs and how long the piece stays on the train. That is even more decisive. But a freight train is not so highly valued as a NordWestBahn. These ranks do exist.]

Moreover, while train pieces in New York City and in Hamburg served communication between crews in different neighbourhoods and boroughs within the cityspace, Oldenburg's main railway station is located on the regional network line. By stating: 'Ich hab' *gestern* erst einen [Zug in Oldenburg] gesehen. [...] War eine Osnabrücker Crew' [Just *yesterday* I saw one [a train in Oldenburg]. [...] It was a crew from Osnabruck],[118] Sbek reveals that graffiti art placed on regional train lines allows for messages and the social status of local writers to transcend urban boundaries, enabling much wider geographical communication via train.

However, in order for artists to communicate within the cityspace of Oldenburg different 'firstspaces' need to be re-appropriated, since '[n]atürlich [...] Züge geil [sind], aber nur dann, wenn du auch ein System hast, das dir die Möglichkeit bietet. [...] Graffiti braucht seinen Gegenwert in Form von Sichtbarkeit' [of course trains are awesome, but only if you have a system that provides you with the opportunity. [...] [G]raffiti needs its equivalent value in form of visibility].[119] In Oldenburg, this equivalent value is already realized due to its small-scale cityspace, with local graffiti artist Tosh explaining: '[D]u kannst ja in Oldenburg super schnell *Fame* kriegen. Wenn du einmal los gehst und dir wirklich mal Mühe gibst, dann bist du sofort bekannt. Es fällt sofort auf' [[Y]ou can get *fame* really fast in Oldenburg. If you just go out and really make an effort then you will get famous immediately. It stands out immediately].[120] Writer Delles from Hamburg perceives the written presentation of self through graffiti art as a far greater achievement in Oldenburg than in a metropolis, for in:

> einer Großstadt wie Hamburg ist es im Endeffekt viel einfacher [illegales Graffiti zu malen] als in Oldenburg, ne? Wenn du in Oldenburg einen Train

117 Asek, interviewed by author, 21 March 2012. The NordWestBahn is a private railway company whose trains connect to Bremen, Wilhelmshaven and Osnabrück when passing through Oldenburg.

118 Sbek, interviewed by author, 7 March 2012.

119 Shark, quoted in Loh and Verlan, 'ist doch alles so schön bunt hier – Zehn Vorurteile zum Thema Graffiti', in Loh and Verlan, *25 Jahre Hip-Hop in Deutschland*, pp. 315–19 (p. 317).

120 Moe, interviewed by author, 11 March 2012.

> malst, ist es da so, als würde einer zehn Banken überfallen. Malt hier einer einen Train fällt das gar nicht großartig auf. Deswegen. Die Leute in den kleinen Städten riskieren im Endeffekt viel mehr, weil im Sumpf der Großstadt hier geht das unter. Wenn du in Oldenburg in der Innenstadt ein Tag machst, dann kriegst du gleich sofort 2000 Euro Strafe. Wenn du hier ein Tag machst, fällt das gar keinem auf.[121]
>
> [ultimately it's much easier to paint illegal graffiti in a large city like Hamburg than in Oldenburg, right? If you paint a train in Oldenburg it's as if somebody were robbing ten banks. If someone paints a train here it doesn't really attract much attention. That's why. Ultimately, people from the smaller cities risk much more because here it gets submerged in the swamp of the metropolis. If you tag in the city centre of Oldenburg then you are immediately fined 2000 Euros. If you tag here, nobody notices.]

Delles's perspective thus re-negotiates the urban conditions that originally framed graffiti art's social statements as being exclusively tied to metropolitan cityspaces and lifestyles.

By taking advantage of Oldenburg's spatial privilege and by risking prosecution, graffiti artist Indiz has attained the highest social status as 'King. Auch wenn wir das immer mit einem Lächeln sagen, "King Indiz". Aber er kriegt Respekt. Er kriegt Anerkennung von uns allen für seine Art' [King. Even if we always say it with a smile, 'King Indiz'. But he gets respect. He is acknowledged by all of us for his manner].[122] According to Moe, 'kaum einer ist so publik in der Stadt, wie er, was illegale Bilder angeht' [hardly anyone in the city has such a high public profile as he does for his illegal pieces].[123] One of Indiz's strategies for gaining public visibility through graffiti art has been to adapt graffiti art's practice of 'bombing' to local noise-barrier walls. As Oldenburg's automobile routes pass directly through its city centre, the roads' noise-barrier walls offer similar symbolic features of spatial centrality and hence visibility to subway or urban railway cars in metropolitan cities. Thus, by re-appropriating these material 'firstspaces' as personal graffiti-art canvases, Indiz is 'der, wenn du auch an der Autobahn lang fährst, alle paar Meter ein Bild irgendwo von sich hat' [the one, when you also drive down the

121 Beatboy Delles, interviewed by author, 21 May 2012. In 2014, an annual statistic released by the German police revealed that Oldenburg registered nearly three times more graffiti-related damage than Hamburg. The statistic does not, however, clarify what type of 'graffiti' is included and whether the spray-painting was part of a hip-hop discourse or merely due to acts of random vandalism (Matthias Stolz, 'Deutschlandkarte: Graffiti', *Zeitmagazin*, 26 (2014), p. 10).

122 Moe, interviewed by author, 11 March 2012.

123 Moe, interviewed by author, 11 March 2012.

Figure 11: 'Indiz'

(Copyright: author)

motorway, who has painted a piece every couple of metres].[124] Moreover, Moe acknowledges 'mit was für einer Genauigkeit der seine Sachen macht' [the real precision with which he does his things],[125] a feature which has provided Indiz with 'eine[m] sehr wiedererkennbaren Stil' [a very recognizable style] (see Figure 11).[126]

Indiz's throw-up reaches over three PVC panels that make up a noise-barrier wall and its *microtypography* is characterized by fat, simple capital letters painted in silver. Their outline consists of a pale blue-and-black border. The *mesotypography* is defined by a tight composition of the letters that creates the name as a single unit. Any gaps are filled with a black background. With no *macrotypographic* features enhancing the piece at first sight, it can be argued that the angular pointed shapes placed above the two 'i's serve as a *macrotypographical* addition, while simultaneously signifying the orthographic dot of the lower case 'i'.

Indiz's typographic style fits Tasek's description of the German simple style: straight block letters defined through thick outlines, simple colour fillings as well as a slight swing, all executed with a clean spraying technique.[127] However, the similarities are actually rooted in the same aim of being fast and efficient.

124 Moe, interviewed by author, 11 March 2012.
125 Moe, interviewed by author, 11 March 2012.
126 Moe, interviewed by author, 11 March 2012.
127 Tasek, interviewed by author, 20 August 2012.

Beyond the efficiency and perfection of his individual style, Indiz's large, public presentations of self become especially revealing when we know that 'wenn du den irgendwo treffen würdest, der ist unsichtbar' [if you were to meet him somewhere, he is invisible].[128] Thus, from a social perspective, Indiz's presentation of self through graffiti art has become 'seine Kommunikation. Komplett!' [his communication. Completely!].[129] Indiz also engages in a discourse with the local German authorities, since his pseudonym is at the same time a German legal term which refers to a piece of circumstantial evidence. Indiz's visual discursive strategy creates a political 'catch-me-if-you-can' game with Oldenburg's officials in which Indiz's evidence of illegal activity, literally speaking, 'provides a narrative structure characteristic of modern political rationality: the marginal integration of individuals in a repetitious movement between the antinomies of law and order' (*LOC*, p. 222). Indiz demonstrates the way in which graffiti art's repetitive practice of 'bombing' can be culturally translated as a systematic visual disruption of law and order in a modern German cultural context, something which reveals itself through the German linguistic code of 'Indiz' and its spatial location in Oldenburg's 'firstspatial' territory.

While Indiz is thus 'King of Oldenburg' due to his quantitative output, which parallels OZ's achievement and social status in Hamburg, Sbek can be compared to DAIM for being considered 'der beste Sprüher in Oldenburg' [the best sprayer in Oldenburg][130] when it comes to quality. As we have seen in Jordan MC's rap track 'One Love', the connection between rap and graffiti art as part of an overall hip-hop culture is captured not only in 'shout outs' to Sbek in the form of rap lyrics but also in the employment of graffiti art as a marketing tool during, for example, the annual public 'One Love' rap concert in Oldenburg. A spray-painted stage sign with the writing 'One Love' and local hip-hop caricature 'Cody' holding two speakers creates the stage decoration for the local rap show, highlighting the interconnectedness of local rap and graffiti-art practices in a manner similar to graffiti art's initial involvement in the hip-hop movement in the Bronx (see Figure 12).

While this piece of graffiti art appears only once a year in Oldenburg's city centre, in 2010 Sbek and his crew BRS legally re-appropriated a wall in the local pedestrian precinct to ensure longevity for their mural 'Bohlens Richtige Söhne' [Bohlen's Real Sons] (see Figure 13). In it they engage in a dialectical play on contemporary German cultural knowledge and graffiti art's practices in order to represent Oldenburg. The following close reading of the piece's

128 Moe, interviewed by author, 11 March 2012.
129 Moe, interviewed by author, 11 March 2012.
130 Moe, interviewed by author, 11 March 2012.

Figure 12: 'One Love'

(Copyright: Andre Elten)

Figure 13: 'Bohlens Richtige Söhne'

(Copyright: author)

typographic characteristics will explain how this dialectic play is achieved.

The black and purple background of the cement canvas carries the title, which is *mesotypographically* located above the six individual names that make up BRS. The left half of the canvas shows the names Mast, Topar and Ponshoe written underneath one another, while Sbek, Tosh and Flome appear on the right half. As the individual style of each name represents the writers' social selves, the unity of the crew and communal creation of this piece are *microtypographically* expressed through the shared use of the colours yellow, orange and red in three-dimensional fonts. The *macrotypography* of the mural further includes seven male faces. One of the faces is placed mid-centre in the canvas with the remaining six characters forming a circle around it. The targeted visualization of individual facial expressions, as well as of different hair colours and fashion accessories, further serves to distinguish them.

Smaller and more detailed *macrotypographic* elements include white stars sprayed on the *microtypographic* borders of the letters and characters, while the remaining space at the bottom of the frame is filled with light blue writing dedicating the mural 'Für Vatti' [to Daddy] and displaying the graffiti artists' signatures (unfortunately covered by a parked car). The mural's typographic characteristics therefore locate the piece in the realm of graffiti art. Yet, beyond its showing off of styles and skills, another message is revealed when looking at the title and spray-painted characters. In order to extract this meaning the viewer has to be aquainted with the German language, with German popular culture and especially with the local hip-hop community in Oldenburg.

The identities of 'Bohlen's real sons' refer to the members of the local graffiti crew, a reference which become evident in two ways. On the one hand, the pop artist and entertainment figure Dieter Bohlen used to be an Oldenburg local prior to his commercial success. This shared urban connection is emphasized through the targeted *mesotypography* of the six 'sons' surrounding their *Vatti*, assuming Bohlen's face is recognized by the viewer. BRS's written dedication follows a traditional graffiti norm as 'writers frequently dedicate their pieces to fellow writers or other friends or relatives or to popular public figures.'[131] On the other hand, the wider meaning reveals itself if we know that each word of the mural title begins with the letters that make up the crew's name BRS. However, this identification is not fixed, for in the past the same combination of letters has also signified an abbreviation for 'BullRiderS'. Hence, BRS's vacillating identity 'makes the structure of meaning and reference an ambivalent process [and] destroys this mirror of representation in which cultural knowledge is customarily revealed as an integrated, open, expanding code' (*LOC*, p. 54).

131 Castleman, *Getting Up*, p. 43; Castleman's observations were conducted in New York City during the early 1980s.

This ambivalence of cultural knowledge relates to a hip-hop discourse as well.

In communicating a local affiliation with a figure representing German show business, BRS's parodic presentation of self contradicts the norms and values of hip-hop culture. Dieter Bohlen is a living symbol of the pop music industry's supposed artificiality and exploitative commodification of art. Thus, his persona and social identity stand in stark contrast to hip-hop culture's norm of 'keeping it real'.[132] As graffiti artists in particular are known to be motivated by a desire to create art for non-commercial purposes due to the re-appropriation of public, urban 'firstspaces' as canvases, Moe explains: 'Wir waren schon immer Leute, die kommerziell eigentlich gar nicht greifbar waren' [We were always people who weren't really tangible commercially].[133] This statement especially resonates with Oldenburg's appropriation of graffiti art, in contrast to Hamburg where the professionalization of hip-hop art forms has led it to its commodification as well. Moe asserts that graffiti art as a non-commercial practice captures the:

> Spirit der ganzen Geschichte. Also zu sagen: 'Das kann man nicht kaufen'. Niemand kann sich einen Zug zuhause hinstellen. Das würde sich einfach nicht lohnen. [...] Weil für mich findet das draußen statt. Ich finde, das sollte Menschen zugänglich sein und deshalb habe ich auch Probleme mit [kommerziellem] Rap und überhaupt mit der Verwertbarkeit dieser Popkultur.[134]
>
> [spirit of the whole thing. To say: 'I can't buy that'. Nobody can put a train in their house. It just wouldn't be worth it. [...] Because for me it has to happen outside. I think it should be accessible to people and that is why I also have problems with [commercial] rap and in general with the commercial exploitation of this pop culture.]

Since the spirit of graffiti art is kept intact by BRS's non-commercial intentions and *paratypographic* tools and materiality, the tension between pop and hip-hop culture's juxtaposed values is instead created through their fictional spatial narrative: this presents the graffiti artists as the show businessman's next generation and hence as the carriers of commercialized and hence artificial values of artistic performance. However, BRS create this ironic paradox by locating their contradictory social identity in the liminal space of the German linguistic sign. Being Bohlen's 'real' sons, BRS disrupt the sense of 'realness' through their targeted introduction of the adjective *richtige* in their descriptive relationship to Bohlen. The choice of word not only fits the letter *R* but in so doing implements the term 'richtig' as an ambivalent linguistic sign. If we

132 Menrath, *Represent what...*, p. 102

133 Moe, interviewed by author, 11 March 2012.

134 Moe, interviewed by author, 11 March 2012.

lack insight into hip-hop culture's concept of 'realness', the use of the German term is merely understood as 'true' or 'proper'. If the term were to address the 'realness' discourse of hip-hop directly, the linguistic sign would have had to be written in English, since that is the language in which the concept has established itself in German hip-hop culture. Thus, the German translation 'richtige' opens up its signification to other interpretations beyond hip-hop culture's norms and practices.

However, the hybrid outcome of the cultural translations and playful, juxtaposing enunciations through which German contemporary culture is fused with a graffiti-art discourse still becomes symbolic of a German local identity. From a spatial perspective, the mural's central placement promotes a visibility that influences the 'thirdspace' experience of Oldenburg, for both 'outsiders' and fellow writers. Moreover, from a social perspective, BRS's contemporary identification as Bohlen's sons also enables Polish-born writer Tosh to be read as a local German, in a manner comparable to Das Bo's participation in the rap track 'Nordish by Nature'. Having re-located from Poland to Oldenburg as a child, Tosh states that he is:

> Deutscher, weil ich lebe hier seit etlichen Jahren. Ich kann besser deutsch als polnisch. Und ich bin halt Deutscher so. Aber ich habe meine Wurzeln nicht vergessen. Und ich bin auch ein Künstler. Und welcher Nationalität ich jetzt angehöre, das ist natürlich die Frage so. Ich würd schon sagen: 'Ich bin ein deutscher Künstler'.[135]
>
> [German because I've been living here for many years. I can speak better German than Polish. And I am simply German. But I haven't forgotten my roots. And I am also an artist. And which nationality I have, that is of course the question. I would say: 'I am a German artist'.]

Requiring neither language skills nor his physical body in order to express himself artistically, the graffiti artist reveals his local German cultural affiliation by claiming Oldenburg's territory, namely its 'firstspaces', through graffiti art. The management of this 'stigma' of foreignness can be contrasted to MicFire and Roulette, who share an Eastern European background yet rely on the spoken language, with which they create real-and-imagined rap narratives located between Russia and Germany.

While an engagement in graffiti art enables Tosh to integrate his German identity through local 'firstspatial' narratives, a similar affirmation by Moe is visible in his communal graffiti-art piece 'Nordlichter' [Northern Lights], created with BRS member Sbek (see Figure 14). In contrast to 'Bohlens Richtige Söhne', this piece was painted outside Oldenburg's 'firstspaces', namely in the

135 Tosh, interviewed by author, 23 March 2012.

Figure 14: 'Nordlichter'

(Copyright: Sbek & Moe)

Bavarian city of Coburg, where the 'writer's social connections – including city and neighborhood (often codes for ethnic identity in the USA) – are acknowledged, visually maintained and conventionally expected'.[136]

The *microtypography* of 'Nordlichter' consists of Sbek's name written in a slick, entangled 3-D style, produced in shades of white and black and surrounded by a red and blue outline. The only exception to this pattern is provided by the letter *E*, which is painted in shades of orange and red. Moreover, this letter wraps itself around the *macrotypographical* inclusion of an anchor placed between the *E* and the *K*. Besides this anchor, Sbek's piece is further framed by other *macrotypograhical* attributes, which have been created by Moe. These include a white seagull placed on the left and a grey seal on the right side of 'Sbek'; they look in each other's direction. While both animals are portrayed with blue hats on their heads, the seal also has a pipe resting in its mouth and wears a red cloth with white dots around its neck as well as an inflatable red float around its body which bears the inscription 'ABS'. It is these detailed, targeted inclusions of *macrotypographical* features that visually maintain the graffiti artists' social connections.

The inclusion of 'ABS' performs the conventionally expected identification with one's locality as these letters represent the graffiti crew of which Sbek and Moe are members. Moreover, Moe's characters and Sbek's anchor symbolically allude to a more general maritime theme. Especially Moe's addition of traditional nautical elements that define his characters serves to exaggerate the animals' geographical affiliation with the North Sea and hence with a Northern German region. This particular 'secondspace' metaphor is also evident in the piece's title, 'Nordlichter' [Northern Lights], colloquially labelling people from

136 Austin, 'More to see than a Canvas in a White Cube', 36.

the Northern (German) region. However, while Oldenburg is located in the North of Germany it does not border the North Sea, nor does it have any large sea port. The arbitrary title of the piece and its theme could therefore also refer to Hamburg graffiti artists, as that city's rappers, music producers and hip-hop dancers have identified with this maritime space as well. In this case, the maritime theme alludes to a Northern German 'secondspace' which is culturally appropriated (rather than geographically shared) by Oldenburg's artists as a regional identity set in contrast to its Bavarian 'firstspace' locality.

In terms of graffiti art, the expression of this regional identity places Sbek, the Oldenburg native, in a hip-hop-related context represented by his *microtypographic* style and name. Moe, however, engages in a more abstract identity-discourse by disguising his original local background, since his reputation in Oldenburg is 'der coole Moe aus Berlin' [cool Moe from Berlin].[137] In identifying with Northern Germany, Moe, however, admits that '[i]ch [...] jetzt ein Landei geworden [bin]. Ich gehöre jetzt zur Provinz irgendwo dazu' [I've become a country bumpkin. Now I somehow belong to the provinces].[138] It is this provincial message which he communicates through his *macrotypographic* identification as a 'Nordlicht', highlighting the way a graffiti artist can indeed 'have authentic attachments to a place and develop a form of cultural identity that is influenced by movement'.[139] This movement does not, however, refer only to Moe's spatial relocation. It also refers to the social and historical perspective of his stylistic presentation of self. He explains that he has 'einen Namen, den ich auch ab und zu mal schreibe: MOE' [a name that I even write now and then: MOE].[140] At the same time, Moe also emphasizes: '[I]ch liebe einfach die Herausforderung Figuren zu zeichnen' [I just love the challenge of drawing characters].[141] Without writing his name as a presentation of his social identity, Moe presents his self instead through characters. In the case of 'Nordlichter' the graffiti artist especially identifies with the seagull 'Moe die Möwe' [Moe the seagull], which figuratively 'auf Styles [scheißt]' [shits on styles], namely on Sbek's letter *S*. This symbolic dismissal of typographic style iterates Moe's approach to graffiti art's norms and practices.

While adhering to graffiti art's *paratypography*, Moe expresses his interest in 'Comic und Cartoonisten. Also Comiczeichner, französisch, belgisch. Ja? Also so ganz klar europäische Schule und politische Cartoons' [comic and cartoonists. Comic illustrators, French, Belgian. Yeah? So, really very clearly

137 Moe, interviewed by author, 11 March 2012.
138 Moe, interviewed by author, 11 March 2012.
139 Papastergiadis, 'Hybridity and Ambivalence', 49.
140 Moe, interviewed by author, 11 March 2012.
141 Moe, interviewed by author, 11 March 2012.

the European school and political cartoons].[142] Thus, Moe's adaptation of graffiti art has become 'eher europäisch angehaucht vom Stil' [rather a bit European in terms of style].[143] Since West Berlin's graffiti community initially represented itself through an adherance to a 'wild style' font, this disruption 'hat natürlich auf dem ersten Blick erst mal nicht in dieses amerikanische Graffiti reingepasst' [did not really fit into these American graffiti at first glance][144] and 'hat natürlich auch in meiner Crew zu Stress geführt, weil die gesagt haben: "Kannst du nicht amerikanischer malen? Kannst du nicht mehr malen, wie die in New York?"' [led to aggravation in my crew because they said: 'Can't you paint in a more American style? Can't you paint more like them in New York?'].[145] This drastic cultural and hence stylistic re-articulation compares to DAIM's similar rupture of graffiti art's previously established aesthetic boundaries through his interest in other European art forms.

Exemplifying the idea that by 'taking matter out of one place and putting it in another, there is both the disruption and reordering of the conventional codes and structures',[146] Moe further defies the common understanding of graffiti art as exclusively defined by stylized letters while at the same time contesting traditional European art movements by spray-painting on urban walls. It is here that Moe's presentation of self fully performs its disruption and re-ordering since he engaged in this *macrotypographical* approach to graffiti art as a personal act of demonstration. It was an art form:

> wo dein Vater dir nicht reinreden kann. Wo er dich nicht ständig kritisieren kann. Also Comic und Graffiti waren die einzigen Kunstdisziplinen, wo ich mich frei bewegen konnte. Ohne, dass er da groß qualitativ mir was zu sagen konnte. [...] Wo ich sogar so ein bisschen in Opposition zu ihm gehen konnte.[147]
>
> [where your father couldn't butt in. Where he couldn't constantly criticize you. So comic and graffiti were the only artistic disciplines where I could move freely. Without having him be able to tell me something about quality. [...] Where I could even declare opposition to him a bit.]

Motivated by artistic rebellion against his own father, a former art teacher in West Berlin, Moe's approach to graffiti art has thus ultimately created a new niche 'weil ich mich nicht messbar mache, durch die Schrift, die die meisten malen' [because I can't be measured by the letters most people paint].[148] He

142 Moe, interviewed by author, 11 March 2012.
143 Moe, interviewed by author, 11 March 2012.
144 Moe, interviewed by author, 11 March 2012.
145 Moe, interviewed by author, 11 March 2012.
146 Nikos Papastergiadis, *Cosmopolitanism and Culture* (Cambridge, UK: Polity, 2012), p. 131.
147 Moe, interviewed by author, 11 March 2012.
148 Moe, interviewed by author, 11 March 2012.

further explains: '[I]ch kann dadurch natürlich ohne in Konkurrenz zu treten deren Bilder ergänzen, aufwerten' [in this way I can support and upgrade their pictures, of course without being in competition].[149] This 'third space' of Europeanized cartoon graffiti art becomes visible in the example of 'Nordlichter', where Moe's intervention of stylistic difference fuses with Sbek's traditional appropriation of graffiti art.

Summary

This comparative analysis of graffiti art has presented insights into the ways in which graffiti art has distanced itself from the 'narrow range of identity-community sensibilities present within New York City during the 1970s'.[150] By partially splitting from or transforming the original spatial, social and historical circumstances that have shaped graffiti art, spray-painters in Hamburg and in Oldenburg nevertheless continue to base it on 'style, space, identity, and reimagining the city'.[151] However, not every expression of graffiti art ties in with hip-hop culture, as it is the only art form that exists clearly within and outside it. Graffiti art thus proposes the largest deviation from and ambiguity within hip-hop's overall norms and practices – an ambiguity which is, furthermore, created by graffiti artists themselves. This chapter captures primarily graffiti artists whose motivation is linked to hip-hop, or who have been adopted by the local hip-hop community, and whose spatialized meanings and messages have been specifically re-adjusted to the spatial conditions of their respective German cityspace. This addresses Papastergiadis's question of 'whether authenticity is bound to the "roots" of traditional forms of attachment, intimacy and proximity, or whether the multiple "routes" of modernity are the only pathways to freedom, criticality and innovation'.[152] It seems as though Papastergiadis's latter option is the case, for while graffiti artists in Germany initially appropriated the 'lore, language, and techniques of graffiti writing',[153] Moe states: 'Es war schon so, dass dieses enge amerikanische Graffiti zwar wichtig war, um was zu starten, um eine Bewegung loszutreten, aber ich habe schon den Eindruck, dass Deutschland zu einer eigenen Sprache gefunden hat' [It was the case that these tight American graffiti were important to start

149 Moe, interviewed by author, 11 March 2012.

150 Austin, 'More to see than a Canvas in a White Cube', 36.

151 Alastair Pennycook, 'Spatial Narrations: Graffscapes and City Souls', in *Semiotic Landscapes – Language, Image, Space*, ed. by Adam Jaworski and Crispin Thurlow (New York: Continuum, 2010), pp. 137–50 (p. 141).

152 Papastergiadis, 'Hybridity and Ambivalence', 47–48.

153 Castleman, *Getting Up*, p. 69.

something, to start a movement, but I am under the impression that Germany has found its own language].[154]

Writers in Hamburg and Oldenburg have re-positioned themselves in a liminal space between the aesthetic norms that recognize the art form as hip-hop's visual element and cultural codes. These relate the art form's meaning to their own social, spatial and historical contexts, which are linked to 'locale, resistance, innovation, affirmation, and cultural identity within a complex web of spatialised meanings and practices'.[155] In Hamburg, this meant that the priority of graffiti art's visibility was inscribed into the local urban railway system while in Oldenburg other fixed urban 'firstspaces' had to suffice as visible canvases within the city. However, train art still existed on regional train lines, allowing for a sophistication of guidelines concerning mobile communication in terms of geographical outreach and the symbolic value attached to the train model on which graffiti art was placed.

Close readings of BK's and BRS's piece moreover showed that graffiti art remains a communal art practice in which the local messages of the pieces become primarily meaningful through their cultural content and placement on Hamburg's urban railway car and on a wall in Oldenburg's city centre. Such successful re-signification of New York City's metropolitan spatial discourse further proves that the size of a cityspace has become irrelevant in authentic engagement in graffiti art, with graffiti art in smaller urban environments even being treated as more remarkable achievements than in large cityspaces. An engagement in graffiti art has further allowed Tosh and Moe to affirm themselves as Oldenburg locals through their creation of, and participation in, communally spray-painted urban narratives with which they represent, albeit at times in a geographically arbitrary fashion, their city of Oldenburg. In Hamburg, an arbitrariness concerning the messages of graffiti art was shown by OZ, who employed his individually-created spatialized narrative to demonstrate against his 'stigmata'. In this way OZ's artistic expression was contextualized in a historical German cultural and political discourse in which his visual resistance towards his national environment challenged graffiti art's aesthetic norms. Despite him having been a rather controversial graffiti artist, OZ's output and works have shown that graffiti art has become a relevant marker for the city's identity and a powerful form of communication for the artist, one similar to Indiz's playful spray-painted traces throughout Oldenburg.

Other case studies in this comparative analysis also presented various

154 Moe, interviewed by author, 11 March 2012.

155 Murray Forman, '"Ain't no Love in the Heart of the City" – Hip-Hop, Space and Place', in *That's the Joint!*, ed. by Forman and Neal, pp. 225–27 (p. 225).

motivations for engaging in graffiti art that were linked to a more general interest in art. By justifying why he does graffiti art, Sbek from Oldenburg, for example, explains:

> [E]s gibt verschiedene Kunstformen. Es gibt Leute, die Realismus malen. Die malen dann halt nur Realismus. Es gibt Leute, die interessieren sich für Kubismus. Es gibt Leute, die interessieren sich dafür und dafür und ich interessiere mich für Schrift und das ist so meine persönliche Kunstform, die ich mache und die mache ich mit Leidenschaft.[156]
>
> [[D]ifferent art forms exist. There are people who paint Realism. They just paint Realism then. There are people who are interested in Cubism. There are people interested in this and in that and I am interested in writing and that is my personal art form that I pursue with passion.]

By equating graffiti art with established European art movements, Sbek at the same time elevates the social status of hip-hop's painted art form. This approach to graffiti art was also shared by Hamburg writer DAIM, who even combined his knowledge and interest in European art styles with graffiti-art practices. This resulted in his *microtypraphic* 3-D style. Similarly, Moe has fused his fascination for European cartoons with the practice of graffiti art by expressing himself solely through *macrotypographic* aspects rather than through letters. Thus, DAIM and Moe have created hybrid graffiti-art styles in which two cultural temporalities and stylistic priorities – the American graffiti art of the 1970s and even older European aesthetic expressions – are implemented as a personal artistic statement. Aside from the aesthetically motivated hybridization of graffiti art, Tasek has even taken a step towards opening the artistic and cultural boundaries of graffiti art in order to engage with profounder questions about practices of modern urban life beyond the German national realm. This new approach is captured in his choice to name himself an urban artist rather than a graffiti artist.

Therefore, while graffiti art has become *unsere Kunst*, *unser Stil* and *unsere Generation*, as claimed by Tasek, it does not project a homogeneous, holistic contemporary German cultural entity. It reveals itself as a multicultural statement and therefore as contrary to Germany's early appropriation of graffiti art, whose label of the German 'simple style' even relied on a self-stereotype. The sum of the examples in this comparative analysis has shown that in both cityspaces the development of graffiti art into a relevant language for its artists has resulted in the hybridization and diversification of styles and presentation of self without proposing a post-hybrid identity. The colourful images represent a heterogeneity which, perhaps deceptively, does not even

156 Sbek, interviewed by author, 7 March 2012.

reflect the multicultural composition of the local graffiti-art communities. Oldenburg's predominantly ethnic German writers represent themselves with the same diversity as Hamburg's sprayers. This normalized state of aesthetic and cultural diversity has, rather, been mobilized through access to the Internet and cheaper international travel beyond local and even national realms.

However, the colourful artistic hybridity of graffiti art nevertheless influences the experience of the German city and provides Germany's provincial and metropolitan 'firstspaces' with a local identity. Thus, Tosh concludes:

> [I]ch merke immer, wenn ich außerhalb mit dem Auto unterwegs war und dann fahre ich nach Oldenburg rein und erkenne immer an den Graffitis: 'Eeeyyy! Geil!'. Das ist so, als ob du in eine alte Gegend kommst und du siehst die alten Häuser. Das sind Zeichen! Also das sind ja wirkliche Zeichen, dass man in der Heimat ist![157]

> [I always notice after I have been travelling by car outside the city and then I drive back into Oldenburg and I recognize it due to the graffiti: 'Eyyy! Awesome!'. It's like coming back to an old district and you see the old houses. These are signs. They are really signs that you are home!]

157 Tosh, interviewed by author, 23 March 2012.

CONCLUSION

This study provides insights into the ways in which hip-hop's four main elements have become culturally relevant and meaningful for its practitioners in Hamburg and in Oldenburg. In so doing, it both adds to the scant body of literature on the totality of hip-hop culture and fosters an awareness of hip-hop's aesthetic forces beyond the commercial focus on rap and its sub-genre of gangsta rap. While graffiti art presents a slight exception in terms of its relationship to hip-hop culture, since it has always been practised outside the hip-hop movement, the theoretical framework and methods of analysis applied in this study show how hip-hop's art forms are shaped and re-reshaped through processes of cultural hybridization and that these influence the expression of identity and belonging by artists in Germany.

The consideration of spatiality, historicality and sociality reveals that hip-hop practised in Hamburg and Oldenburg exists in a hybrid state, with artists mixing hip-hop norms with cultural codes peculiar to their city, to Germany or even to Europe. In some cases, this cultural hybridization has also transcended into an expression of post-hybridity. In this state, artists have engaged in cultural mixture to represent their German identity, showing that cultural diversity is not necessarily a factor separating them from German society. Rather, they understand it as being an inherent part of contemporary Germany, as rapper Harris mentions in the introductory statement to this work. Despite his African-American and German heritage, he feels:

> deutsch, und er will sich dieses Gefühl genauso wenig wegnehmen lassen wie seinen Fußball. Nicht von denen, die ihn wegen seiner Hautfarbe in die Schublade 'nicht von hier' stecken. Und nicht von denen, die seinen Ruf versauen, weil sie kein Deutsch sprechen. Es gibt nämlich die 'neuen Deutschen', das sind Leute wie er, und die 'alten Deutschen', die noch nicht richtig kapiert haben, wer die neuen Deutschen sind.[1]
>
> [German and he does not want this feeling, or his football, to be taken away from him. Not by those who, due to his skin colour, put him in the drawer marked 'not from here'. And not by those who destroy his reputation because they cannot speak German. There are the 'new Germans' now, those are are people like him, and the 'old Germans' who do not yet really understand who the new Germans are.]

1 Pham, 'Deutscher Patriot', p. 17.

Such observations on the 'new Germans', with their claims to recognition and belonging to German society despite their perceived 'otherness',[2] also form part of the case studies in this volume. These contemporary examples were initially contrasted to the early stages of hip-hop's manifestation in West Germany, when hip-hop practices mimicked those presented in American hip-hop films or imitated other European countries' appropriation of hip-hop. However, eventually hip-hop artists presented the new art forms as self-stereotypical German performances which emphasized cleanliness, exactness, rigidness and straightness. The interviews conducted for this study revealed that DJs in Germany focused on honing precise scratching techniques, while b-boys created the 'straight German power' style defined by clean, well-executed movements. Rappers, on the other hand, articulated themselves in clear and proper German; while German graffiti artists became known for their straight and precisely sprayed 'simple style'. However, through close readings of contemporary hip-hop material, this analysis also presents examples that show how hip-hop has dissolved into the cultural diversification of its previous German identity.

This diversification is examined in two urban realms which until now have not been analysed in any full-length ethnographic hip-hop study. By looking at hip-hop practised in Hamburg and Oldenburg, this research project engages with Soja's observation that:

> studying cityspace presents a potentially endless variety of exemplifications and interpretations. Faced with such complexity, we explore and explain as much as we can, choosing those specific examples and instances which most closely reflect our particular objectives and projects for obtaining useful, practical knowledge, knowledge that we can use not just to understand the world but to change it for the better.[3]

Thus, this monograph is the first to consider the ways in which hip-hop artists occupy, comprehend and experience their urban space, deeming it relevant towards understanding the expression of their identity as German hip-hop artists and producers of contemporary German art and culture. The choice of the two Northern German cities presents hip-hop as an artistic cultural movement that is equally practised by ethnic minorities and the ethnic majority, distancing itself from the common notion that hip-hop is solely an expression of the minority.

Furthermore, the selection of these two particular cities made it possible to view hip-hop from a metropolitan and professional as well as a provincial and

2 Cf. Saied, *Rap in Deutschland*; Stehle, *Ghetto Voices*; and Templeton, 'What's so German about It?'.

3 Soja, *Postmetropolis*, p. 12.

leisure-pursuit perspective. This has shown that hip-hop in a smaller German city resembles the way hip-hop was originally lived in the Bronx, with artists supporting each others' art forms and working together to engage in hip-hop as a non-commercial pastime. Hip-hop in the larger metropolitan city of Hamburg was originally practised in the same way, yet eventually moved towards professionalization and commodification, made possible by the city's commercial structures. This, in turn, has also disrupted the interconnectedness of hip-hop's different elements and artists, who nowadays work nearly exclusively together to stage professional events or to realize commercial projects. Fieldwork observations at a local rap festival in Hamburg in the summer of 2012, for instance, revealed that the backstage regions of dancers and rappers were separated. Dancers were not allowed to enter the rappers' domains despite performing on the same stage at the same hip-hop event.

By examining these differences through a theoretical framework which took spatiality, historicality and sociality into consideration, this study also demonstrates that these three components have become useful perspectives when determining hip-hop's cultural adaptation, aesthetics and practices in the respective German cityspaces. Having looked at hip-hop from a spatial perspective, this study contributes to existing knowledge of the relationship between spatial logics and hip-hop which was previously introduced in Forman's research on rap, space and place. However, this study provides further insights into the spatial implications of graffiti art, hip-hop music and dance with regard to the formation and expression of identity, whereby the theoretical distinction between 'first-', 'second-' and 'thirdspaces' has deepened the understanding of these spatial influences.

The spatial analysis of rap shows that this art form enables the dissemination of messages from multiple spatial perspectives, such as the street, the living room or even Germany or Russia. This is because rappers' notion of spatial authenticity can be solely rooted in 'secondspaces'. These are created through words and hence the imagination rather than through the physical appropriation of spaces. This lyrical creation of space therefore allows for a wider flexibility in terms of spatial narratives, enabling rappers to express more complex and controversial identity discourses when situated between physical-*and*-imagined spaces. Since rappers only require their voice to present themselves, their art form can be consumed aurally and can therefore be produced and disseminated faster than, for example, video or film. Moreover, like music productions, the power of words and sound is able to reach a large audience in a comparatively short period of time.

Performances of hip-hop dance and graffiti art, on the other hand, unfold in 'firstspace' realms and hence as live 'thirdspace' experiences. In other words, their art form is deemed 'unreal' if it is not performed in public urban areas. Indeed, the connection through which material or metaphorical space determines the expression of identity and presentation of self through art has been underexplored in Hip-hop Studies as well as in other research areas concerned with art and socio-cultural movements. While videos and photographs of dance and graffiti art also circulate on the Internet as mediated versions of the art forms, they still require a previous performance in a particular 'firstspace' and need to be consumed visually. It is, therefore, the body of the dancer that creates the experience in hip-hop dance while graffiti art presents itself as colourful traces without the presence of the artist's physical self. This also leads to a further differentiation, where, in the case of rap and music productions, the cityspace influences the artists' messages and identities, while conversely dancers and graffiti artists influence the experience of the city. Thus, the relationship between space and art is different according to the spatial appropriations and perspectives in which the art forms engage.

By presenting their art form at live public 'firstspaces' hip-hop dancers in Hamburg can, furthermore, contribute physically to the multicultural 'secondspace' notion of Hamburg which influences the hip-hop sound of its music producers. However, while the music producers have employed the image of Hamburg as culturally open-minded in progressing towards their development of a local sound, Hamburg does not seem to offer the same multicultural conditions for its dancers. Hamburg's metropolitan cityspace provides all the 'firstspaces' required for pursuing hip-hop dance, including its own competitions. Therefore, Hamburg can also inhibit cultural exchange, as dancers do not have to travel to other places in order to compete, practise and perform their art form. Hamburg can thus be understood as an arbitrary space when it comes to cultural open-mindedness.

Apart from providing new approaches to studying cultural identity through a consideration of 'spatiality', this study also contributes to critical theory by proposing a new perspective on, and concept of, cultural hybridity through its consideration of 'historicality'. Since hybridity captures the mixture of two cultural elements which may produce a new, 'third', space, this monograph shows that hybridity can also alter something old or, in other words, something 'first'. In this case, this 'first' space has been Germanness or a local German identity. Examples indicate that DJs and music producers aim to mix cultural sounds in order to represent their city or nation and even understand the art of mixing cultural sounds as the only way – beyond the use of German lyrics – to create a German hip-hop music genre. While the social situation has, in reality, not been able to achieve this cultural mixture in German hip-hop music, thus revealing a discrepancy between the imagined ability of hip-hop as compared to its actual realization, music producers in Hamburg nevertheless attempt to create a unique sound. With the city's image of a culturally open-minded 'secondspace' that forms a 'gateway to the world', an image grounded in its local Hanseatic history of seafarers and pirates, Hamburg even suits the idea of cultural and musical mixing as a representation of its locality within the wider German nation. By engaging in this maritime-infused image of Hamburg, local music producers from culturally mixed backgrounds can represent their cultural hybridity through hip-hop music as a normal state of German identity since it stems from the open-minded and multicultural cityspace of Hamburg.

This approach has also become visible in the local adaptation of hip-hop dance. As socio-cultural or ethnic dances which would reflect a German cultural identity, such as the Bavarian 'Schuhplattler',[4] remain extremely scarce in northern Germany, early hip-hop dancers were not able to use any pre-established dance tradition which could have been re-cycled into a German approach to hip-hop. Rather, dancers in Hamburg have relied on their cultural knowledge of dance from foreign traditions in order to engage faithfully in hip-hop dance. Through their incorporation of this knowledge and experience into their expression of dance, the hybridized approach and performance have become a representation of Hamburg as well as of their German identity when competing nationally or internationally.

While rappers have also been able to express themselves as German, despite having different cultural and ethnic roots, their specific cultural messages are primarily supported by their choice of language. These linguistic options are also dependent on the 'secondspaces' that rappers seek to represent or the 'firstspaces' in which they practise. However, their use of language can also become arbitrary signs, allowing for the disguise and distortion of national identities. The proper pronunciation of German enables culturally hybrid artists to present themselves as the national majority of Germany, while the use of street slang, German which borrows vocabulary from other languages and even Russian contests traditional notions of German culture, even if the rapper who expresses himself in this manner is ethnically German. Thus, language may not suffice as an inclusive statement of Germanness if the listener does not identify with its register, dialect or multilingual expressions.

Finally, German graffiti art's expression has become a culturally hybrid art form, most notably through the global influence of the Internet. It therefore has no German identity of its own anymore; yet when displayed on urban walls and hence on German geographical terrain it can influence the local

4 In 2014, the Bavarian b-boy crew "DDC" performed a successful Schuhplattler-b-boy routine on German television. Cf: 'DDC – "Breakdance in Lederhosen – 20 Jahre Feste – ARD – Okt 2014 | DDC Breakdance"', *DDC Breakdance* YouTube, 26 October 2014, https://www.youtube.com/watch?v=0GKUyjBrNFI [accessed 30 June 2016].

experience of a German city. While this study therefore shows that the practice and outcome of cultural hybridity are not only a necessity for creating new art, it also shows that newness in German hip-hop does not aim at threatening existing national norms, values and traditions. Rather, through culturally-induced alteration, culturally hybrid hip-hop artists affirm an identity linked to a German city, region and nation. In other words, while the concept of the 'third space' implies a disruption of the homogeneous national whole, post-hybridity emphasizes the national whole by showing that it can also exist as a heterogeneous cultural entity, with multiculturalism tied to the same shared emotional affiliation, geographical locality and language. Indeed, the immediate identification of each element of hip-hop as a regional, urban or national representation of Germany is enabled through a particular use of language. This has been manifested in German lyrical samples, by dancing to German music, rapping in the German language or having a tag or a title of a piece sprayed in German or filling it with German cultural codes and symbols in German cityspaces.

By considering 'sociality' as a final cultural component, hip-hop can also be seen as facilitating acceptance of this state of cultural diversity since, according to DJ Kool Herc, hip-hop has 'bridged the culture gap. It brings white kids together with Black [*sic*] kids, brown kids with yellow kids. [...] It gets past the stereotypes and people hating each other because of those stereotypes'.[5] Hip-hop therefore has the ability to open up a liminal space of cultural recognition and to deconstruct the common stereotyping captured in Jango's summarizing statement: 'Die Deutschen sagen: Du bist Ausländer. Die Ausländer sagen: Du bist Deutsch!' [Germans say: 'You are a foreigner'. Foreigners say: 'You are German!'].[6] By allowing artists to fuse their foreign backgrounds into an art form with which to represent their city or nation, hip-hop can provide the tools to overcome a supposed 'stigma' of foreignness and to show how 'the stigmatized individual can come to feel that he should be above passing, that if he accepts himself and respects himself he will feel no need to conceal his failing' (*STGM*, p. 101).

However, the successful or realistic outcome of hip-hop's supposed ability to overcome the culture gap remains problematic. One of the issues is convincing the audience of the artist's 'passing' through an engagement in hip-hop. While public performances by local hip-hop dancers, for instance, contribute to the multicultural image of Hamburg, these artists might not be understood as actually being from the city as they engage in a globally adapted art form. The same can hold true for rap lyrics and the articulation of German that

5 Kool Herc in Chang, *Can't Stop, Won't Stop*, p. xi.

6 Jango, interviewed by author, 8 June 2012.

can be misinterpreted by the common listener as messages from the minority. Dance, on the other hand, only relies on body and movement as a presentation of self. Hence, black or brown skin tones and other 'attributes' become the predominant signs of the hip-hop dancer's socio-cultural performance, which can also be interpreted as signs of 'otherness'. Furthermore, without any German dance tradition re-appearing in hip-hop dance, nor any other directly enunciated identifier of Germanness, such as the spoken language, hip-hop dance remains in a state of hybridity rather than post-hybridity from an 'outside' perspective.

While culturally hybrid artists attempt to overcome their 'otherness' by destroying 'the constant principles of the national culture that attempt to hark back to a "true" national past, which is often represented in the reified forms of realism and stereotype' (*LOC*, p. 218), the art of hip-hop also remains in a socio-cultural struggle to be identified as a German cultural movement. This affects its ethnic German practitioners as well. By trying to re-frame hip-hop's supposed foreignness as familiar Germanness, hip-hop artists choose to present their art form as a high-class artistic expression. This strategy has been mostly rooted in paralleling as well as fusing hip-hop with a classical artistic context and has attempted by these means to elevate hip-hop's social status to *deutsche Hochkultur*. An examination of the ways in which hip-hop is practised and perfected in specific 'back' regions and consequently performed in designated 'front' regions thus reveals how Das DJ Orchester blended classical performance norms into their DJ show in order to make a statement about their status as musicians. Hip-hop dancers have danced on theatre stages and to classical German music in order to improve their reputation as professional performers. Rappers, on the other hand, have compared their art form to canonical German poetry and Germany's linguistic and literary traditions. Finally, some graffiti artists equate their art form to past European art movements. Others even fuse these European approaches in their spray-painted aesthetic in order to achieve fame and respect through artistic innovation. Their images are even displayed in art galleries.

While hip-hop practised in Hamburg and in Oldenburg still struggles at times to be understood and respected as a German art form, it is also used as a mobilizer for successful integration and intercultural communication. Hip-hop dancers in Hamburg thus aim to teach social and personal values through their art form, while b-boying has also been named 'ein Beispiel für gelungene Integration' [an example of successful integration][7] by Deutsche Welle host

7 Hajo Schumacher, 'Talk mit Breakdancer Vartan Bassil | Typisch Deutsch', Interview by Hajo Schumacher, *Deutsche Welle*, 1 October 2012, http://www.youtube.com/watch?v=SMwniRnibZ4 [accessed 12 June 2013].

Hajo Schumacher after talking to Berlin b-boy Vartan Bassil about his positive experience as a Lebanese-Armenian growing up in Germany. At the end of the interview, the German television host concludes:

> [A]lle [in Deutschland] stehen vor der großen Herausforderung, die sich Integration nennt. Was genau ist das eigentlich? Da gehen die Meinungen ziemlich auseinander. Einigkeit herrscht aber darüber, dass Kunst und Kultur, wir sehen es hier mit dem Breakdance, dabei helfen.[8]
>
> [[E]veryone [in Germany] is confronted by the great challenge called integration. But what is it actually? Opinions differ greatly in this matter. But unity does exist about the fact that art and culture can help. We see it here with break dance.]

Indeed, this observation is not new to Hip-hop Studies, with Cheesman already having observed that the 'elective affinity between hip hop and ethnic minority youth encouraged educationalists and social workers to develop inner-city projects harnessing hip hop to goals of multiculturalist integration'.[9] This is because hip-hop's art forms and cultural norms and practices allow the inclusion of different histories and cultural understandings. Most importantly, hip-hop permits the expression of personal artistic freedom. While hip-hop dance has already been associated with this liberty, it is no coincidence that the creative and improvised practice of rapping, as well as dancing and turntabling, is called '*free*styling'. Similarly, Moe points out that graffiti art in Germany 'eben auch *befreit* worden [ist]. Durch Street Art und durch Konzepte, die jetzt weit über dieses Streetbombing oder Trainbombing hinausgehen' [has been *freed*. Through street art and through concepts that now reach farther than street bombing or train bombing].[10] In this statement he touches upon the hybridization of graffiti art which has transcended its aesthetic and cultural boundaries towards a more democratic engagement.

However, it does not seem as if the integration of cultural pluralism in hip-hop has been or can be adapted to a wider society when we consider the ongoing debates and problematics of multiculturalism and parallel societies in Germany. With hip-hop struggling to be accepted as a German cultural movement, it remains difficult to disseminate a message of cultural belonging through an art form that is often understood as being the opposite, namely as a movement of resistance and of the minority. Moreover, intercultural communication and co-operation are also lacking in hip-hop itself, for example, in German hip-hop music productions whose supposed absence of cultural exchange has been

8 Schumacher, 'Talk mit Breakdancer Vartan Bassil | Typisch Deutsch'.

9 Cheesman, 'Polyglot Pop Politics', 198.

10 Moe, interviewed by author, 11 March 2012.

mentioned by interviewees. In line with these statements, this research project also establishes that different ethnicities remain more represented than others within hip-hop's individual elements. In other words, there is a separation of ethnicities and cultures among hip-hop's art forms.

In Hamburg, DJing and the production of music tend to be practised mainly by ethnic Germans, with some artists being half-German. Only a few Turkish DJs have proved exceptions to this observation. In hip-hop dance, however, ethnic German male dancers remain very scarce. Rather, dancers with Asian, African and Middle Eastern heritages dominate this element in Hamburg. Rap, on the other hand, does not feature any Asian cultural backgrounds at all but mainly represents ethnic German, African and Eastern European heritages. MicFire and Roulette from Oldenburg have proved exceptional cases. They neglect their ethnic Germanness in order to affirm their Eastern European identity, which is positively influenced by their German cultural environment. Finally, graffiti art is mainly pursued by ethnic Germans and Eastern Europeans as well as by artists of Middle Eastern descent.

Thus, ethnic Germans engage in all hip-hop art forms but, remarkably, least of all in dance. Turkish ancestries, on the other hand, have hardly appeared in rap compared to the other elements. This is especially interesting if we consider that early German Hip-hop Studies focused heavily on the Turkish minority's engagement in rap. The reason for this roughly outlined cultural separation within the different elements remains unclear. Only graffiti writer Davis has proposed that it is due to the supposedly different ethnic conditions of the artists, thus hinting at a problematic of cultural integration and exchange in Hamburg's graffiti art community, despite hip-hop's supposed ability to integrate and assimilate. While this observation opens further areas of investigation, it also highlights the fact that the generalization of the results and perceptions within this study is, of course, subject to limitations.

Since the time frame for the investigation lasted from January until September 2012, this monograph invites further comparative studies in order to define the longevity of the results. Over time, the debate on German *Leitkultur* may have changed or the aims and artistic expressions of hip-hop may have shifted, since hip-hop 'has never been a static form; it has always been subject to change and hybridity owing to ongoing influences that are generated through multiple connections and contacts'.[11] This also includes the growing influence of the Internet and other mediatization processes, which have already altered the practice of graffiti art and of rap, with online photo communities and YouTube videos re-arranging the spatial, social and historical dynamics of the artists' presentations of self.

11 Forman, *The 'hood Comes First*, p. 199.

Furthermore, the models of identity processes presented in this study may not be transferable to every hip-hop artist in Hamburg and in Oldenburg. Conversely, not every local inhabitant from a foreign cultural background may feel the same way towards Germany as the hip-hop artists who feature in this analysis. It would, therefore, be interesting to compare the experiences of individuals with the same cultural predisposition in order to identify the extent to which the norms and practices of hip-hop culture have shaped the aforementioned identity discourses. While religion and religious affiliations are omitted as a marker of cultural identity in this study, their inclusion in further analyses could add another perspective to the contemporary dynamics of identity formations in hip-hop culture. Similarly, the issue of gender in hip-hop should be addressed, since nearly all interviewees who participated in this study were male. While this ratio faithfully represents the gender dynamics of the two hip-hop communities, this aspect requires further research into female artists' engagement in hip-hop's art forms and whether their aims and objectives also re-negotiate the representation of their identity and national affiliation.

Moreover, since this study looks at two cityspaces within Germany, more comparative urban analyses need to be conducted in order to transfer the insights and results onto the wider German nation. These could include other hip-hop strongholds, such as Munich in Southern Germany, or Dessau and Leipzig in former East Germany. This would serve to highlight differences and similarities in the historical development of hip-hop and the regional and urban variation and strategies with which artists make hip-hop a meaningful form of German artistic expression. Extending this idea, it would then be compelling to see whether other art movements and cultural lifestyles have had the same power to bridge and blend cultures into representing one national identity in the way hip-hop has been able to do within the German cultural landscape.

Finally, the focus of this analysis can be broadened beyond hip-hop as well. While this study has shed light on the different nuances of identity, ranging from hybrid constructions to the emergence of post-hybrid identity formations expressed through the hip-hop culture practised in Hamburg and in Oldenburg, these different layers of identity have been detected through a targeted focus on spatiality, historicality and sociality. This study therefore suggests that this three-dimensional theoretical framework is applicable to other studies of cultural identity which also aim at detecting the changing dynamics of culture, identity and belonging in Germany, since as b-boy Vartan claims:

> mittlerweile [...] Deutschland immer bunter [wird]. Das sieht man auch bei der Nationalmannschaft. Und ich finde das einfach wunderschön, weil Deutschland *hat* Farbe. Und warum soll man nicht dazu stehen und das ist auch eine tolle Sache, so offen und bunt zu sein.[12]
>
> [Germany is becoming more colourful. You can see it in the national [football] team. And I find it beautiful because Germany *has* colour. And why should you not stand behind that and it is also a great thing, to be so open and colourful.]

Indeed, two years after research for this study had been conducted, an article in *Spiegel International* addressed the question of what it meant to be German in 2014 by stating that 'Germany in 2014 is a very different country than [*sic*] it was in 1984, not to mention 1994 or 2004. [. . .] There's a new feeling of what it means to be German'.[13] This 'new feeling' is summarized in the sentence that 'Germany has become one society, but also a diverse one'.[14] However, at the same time the article also states that '[i]mmigration and integration nevertheless remain difficult issues. Chancellor Angela Merkel's conservative Christian Democrats still don't like thinking of Germany as a country of immigration'.[15] In this sense, this research project sees itself as a contribution to the complex discourse of identity formation in a multicultural German society.

12 Vartin Schumacher, 'Talk mit Breakdancer Vartan Bassil | Typisch Deutsch'.

13 Sven Böll and others, 'The Bearable Lightness of Being: How Germans are Learning to Like Themselves', *SPIEGEL ONLINE*, 17 July 2014, http://www.spiegel.de/international/germany/football-championships-help-boost-german-image-at-home-and-abroad-a-981591.html [accessed 18 July 2014].

14 Böll and others, 'The Bearable Lightness of Being'.

15 Böll and others, 'The Bearable Lightness of Being'.

APPENDIX

List of Interviewees (in alphabetical order)

Asek (m)	Graffiti artist	21 March 2012 in Oldenburg
Azad (m)	Popping dancer	25 May 2012 in Hamburg
Backenfutter (m)	Rapper	24 August 2012 in Hamburg
Beatboy Delles (m)	B-boy/graffiti artist	21 May 2012 in Hamburg
Blacky White (m)	Music producer	10 July 2012 in Hamburg
Boran (m)	Freestyle rapper	5 April 2012 in Oldenburg
Can (m)	Hip-hop dancer	21 May 2012 in Hamburg
CB (m)	Rapper	24 August 2012 in Hamburg
Davis (m)	Graffiti artist	20 August 2012 in Hamburg
D-Flame (m)	Rapper/DJ	26 July 2012 in Hamburg
DJ Ben Kenobi (m)	DJ	3 July 2012 in Hamburg
DJ Dope (m)	DJ	20 January 2012 in Oldenburg
DJ Mirko Machine (m)	DJ/music producer	10 May 2012 in Hamburg
DJ Mixwell (m)	DJ/music producer	19 June 2012 in Hamburg
DJ Placeebo (m)	DJ	26 July 2012 in Hamburg
DJ Stylewarz (m)	DJ/music producer	12 June 2012 in Hamburg
DJ Vito (m)	DJ/music producer	21 June 2012 in Hamburg
Gizmo (m)	B-boy	17 July 2012 in Hamburg
Henry the First (m)	Rapper/singer	25 January 2012 in Oldenburg
Jango (m)	B-boy/DJ	8 June 2012 in Hamburg

JayHuttz (m)	Rapper	24 August 2012 in Hamburg
Jill (f)	Graffiti artist	14 March 2012 in Oldenburg
Jordan MC (m)	Freestyle rapper	21 February 2012 in Oldenburg
J-Smart (m)	Rapper/music producer	25 January 2012 in Oldenburg
Juiz (m)	Rapper	21 February 2012 in Oldenburg
K-Four (m)	Rapper	9 February 2012 in Oldenburg
Luc von Mensing (m)	Rapper	31 March 2012 in Oldenburg
Macentosh (m)	Freestyle rapper	21 February 2012 in Oldenburg
Maxi (m)	Rapper	31 March 2012 in Oldenburg
Metin (m)	Former b-boy	4 May 2012 in Hamburg
MicFire (m)	Rapper	14 February 2012 in Oldenburg
Moe (m)	Graffiti artist	11 March 2012 in Oldenburg
Nan-D (m)	Freestyle rapper	4 July 2012, e-mail
Nate57 (m)	Rapper	21 August 2012 in Hamburg
Newman o.t.B. (m)	Rapper	11 February 2012 in Oldenburg
Philipp Kabbe (m)	Graffiti artist	20 August 2012 in Hamburg
Raphael (m)	Beatboxer	20 January 2012 in Oldenburg
Ronin (m)	Rapper	25 February 2012 in Oldenburg

Roulette (m)	Rapper	14 February 2012 in Oldenburg
Samy Deluxe (m)	Rapper/music producer	29 July 2012 in Hamburg
Sbek (m)	Graffiti artist	7 March 2012 in Oldenburg
Sleepwalker (m)	Music producer	5 June 2012 in Hamburg
SonnyTee (m)	B-boy/graffiti artist	29 August 2012 in Hamburg
Stee (m)	Freestyle rapper	26 July 2012 in Hamburg
Stephen Long (m)	Rapper	24 August 2012 in Hamburg
Stylez-Tyson (m)	Rapper/music producer	14 March 2012 in Oldenburg
Tasek (m)	Graffiti/urban artist	20 August 2012 in Hamburg
Telly Tellz (m)	Rapper	22 August 2012 in Hamburg
Tim Beam (m)	Artist and event manager	8 August 2012 in Hamburg
Torch (m)	Rapper/DJ	29 August 2012 in Hamburg
Tosh (m)	Graffiti artist	28 March 2012 in Oldenburg
Udu (f)	Graffiti activist	13 May 2012 in Hamburg

Semi-Structured Interview Questions

Aim	Question
Introduction to conversation	Wer bist du?
Introduction to interview topic	Wann und wie bist du mit Hip-Hop involviert geworden?
Gaining an awareness of the interviewee's practical involvement in hip-hop	Wieviele Hip-Hop-Künste beherrschst du?
Gaining an awareness of the personal importance of hip-hop for interviewee	Warum Hip-Hop und nicht eine andere Musik-, Tanz-, Kunstrichtung?
Understanding the communal aspect of hip-hop	Wie sieht es mit Hip-Hop Crews in Deutschland aus?
Gaining an awareness of the priority of hip-hop in the interviewee's life	Wie viel Zeit investierst du im Durchschnitt in der Woche für Hip-Hop?
Understanding the level of importance regarding hip-hop from the United States	Warum ist die Hip-Hop-Szene der USA ein Vorbild?
Gaining an insight into the development of hip-hop in order to understand better its current state	Wie hat sich die Hip-Hop-Szene, in der du dich bewegst, über die Jahre verändert?
Aiming at revealing a Germanness in hip-hop that is perhaps not known to the common consumer	Was ist "deutsch" am Hip-Hop der aus Deutschland stammt?
Aiming at discerning differences and similarities between the two cities and their hip-hop communities	Wie würdest du die Hip-Hop-Szene in Hamburg/Oldenburg beschreiben oder charakterisieren?
Gaining an awareness of the interviewee's investment in keeping hip-hop alive in Germany and passing on knowledge	Warum gibst du Unterricht in deinem Hip-Hop Element?
Gaining an awareness of hip-hop's potential future dynamics and current state in Hamburg and Oldenburg	Wie sieht es mit dem Nachwuchs aus?
Revealing complexities and issues within hip-hop that artists may want to tackle	Was sind deine Ziele als Hip-Hop-Künstler?
Giving the interviewee the opportunity to share final additional information	Gibt es etwas, was dir unbedingt noch wichtig ist, mir auf den Weg zu geben?

BIBLIOGRAPHY

Anonymous, Picture #5, 'Streetart-Mythos OZ: Die Stadt als Galerie', *SPIEGEL ONLINE Fotostrecke*, 29 July 2011, http://www.spiegel.de/fotostrecke/streetart-mythos-oz-die-stadt-als-galerie-fotostrecke-71007-5.html [accessed 10 September 2013]

— '2012 Top 40 Official Singles Chart UK Archive,' The Official Charts Company, 7 April 2012, http://www.officialcharts.com/archive-chart/_/1/2012-04-07/ [accessed 21 February 2013]

— 'Anlage IX (zu § 29 Absatz 2, 3, 5 bis 8) – Prüfplakette für die Untersuchung von Kraftfahrzeugen und Anhängern', *StVZO* (Bundesministerium der Justiz und für Verbraucherschutz, 2012), http://www.gesetze-im-internet.de/stvzo_2012/anlage_ix_139.html [accessed 10 September 2013]

— 'Ausländische Bevölkerung in Deutschland 2011', *Statistisches Jahrbuch Deutschland und Internationales* (Wiesbaden: Statistisches Bundesamt, 2012), https://www.destatis.de/DE/Publikationen/StatistischesJahrbuch/StatistischesJahrbuch2012.pdf?__blob=publicationFile, 20.2.2012. [accessed 21 April 2014]

— 'Census Reveals German Population Lower than Thought', *BBC News Europe*, 31 May 2013, http://www.bbc.co.uk/news/world-europe-22727898 [accessed 31 May 2013]

— 'Germany. Statistisches Amt für Hamburg und Schleswig-Holstein', *Hamburger Stadtteilprofile 2013*, 15th edn (Hamburg: Anstalt des Öffentlichen Rechts, 2013), http://www.statistik-nord.de/uploads/tx_standocuments/NR15_Statistik-Profile2013.pdf [accessed 1 April 2014]

— 'Graffiti & Streetart Photo Community', *Streetpins.com | Graffiti & Streetart Photo Community* (Streetpins, 2013), http://www.streetpins.com/ [accessed 2 October 2013]

— 'Repeat – Tiefgarageneinfahrt', *Getting-up*, 18 October 2010, http://getting-up.org/en/2010/10/repeat_tiefgarageneinfahrt [accessed 20 September 2013]

— 'Who goes to German Pegida "anti-Islamisation" rallies?', *BBC News Europe*, 13 January 2015, http://www.bbc.com/news/world-europe-30776182 [accessed 13 January 2015]

Adaso, Henry, 'What is Conscious Rap?', in *Rap/Hip-Hop* (About.com, n.d.), http://rap.about.com/od/genresstyles/p/ConsciousRap.htm [accessed 30 October 2013]

Alim, Samy H., *Roc the MIC Right: The Language of Hip Hop Culture* (New York: Routledge, 2006)

Amenda, Lars, '"Welthafen" Hamburg – Kultur- und Technikgeschichtliche Perspektiven', in *Hamburgs Geschichte Einmal Anders: Entwicklung der Naturwissenschaften, Medizin und Technik*, ed. by Gudrun Wolfschmidt, Nuncius Hamburgensis – Beiträge zur Geschichte der Naturwissenschaften, 7 (Norderstedt: on Demand, 2009), pp. 238–49

Amrine, Douglas, *Hamburg* (London: Dorling Kindersley, 2012)

Androutsopoulos, Jannis, 'Einleitung', in *HipHop – Globale Kultur, Lokale Praktiken*, ed. by Jannis Androutsopoulos (Bielefeld: transcript, 2003), pp. 9–23

— 'HipHop und Sprache: Vertikale Intertextualität und die drei Sphären der Popkultur', in *HipHop – Globale Kultur, Lokale Praktiken*, ed. by Jannis Androutsopoulos (Bielefeld: transcript, 2003), pp. 111–36

Angrosino, Michael, *Doing Ethnographic and Observational Research* (London: SAGE, 2007)

Auer, Peter, 'A Post-Script: Code-switch and Social Identity', *Journal of Pragmatics*, 37 (2005), 403–10

Austin, Joe A., 'More to see than a Canvas in a White Cube: For an Art in the Street', *City*, 14 (2010), 33–47

Ayto, John, 'Pretzel', in *The Diner's Dictionary: Word Origins of Food and Drink*, 2nd edn (Oxford: Oxford University Press, 2012), http://www.oxfordreference.com [accessed 2 September 2013]

Bade, Klaus J., '"Leitkultur"-Debatte: "Zuwanderung wird als Bedrohung empfunden"', *SPIEGEL ONLINE*, 24 November 2004, http://www.spiegel.de/kultur/gesellschaft/leitkultur-debatte-zuwanderung-wird-als-bedrohung-empfunden-a-329285.html [accessed 10 January 2015]

Bakker, Hans, and Theo Bakker, 'The Club DJ: A Semiotic and Interactionalist Analysis', *Symbolic Interaction*, 29 (2006), 71–82

Banes, Sally, *Writing Dancing in the Age of Postmodernism* (Hanover, NH: University Press of New England, 1994)

Baumann, Gerd, *The Multicultural Riddle – Rethinking National, Ethnic, and Religious Identities* (New York and London: Routledge, 1999)

Beauftragte für Migration, Flüchtlinge und Integration, 'Staatsangehörigkeit: Das Geburtstortprinzip', *Die Bundesregierung* (Presse- und Informationsamt der Bundesregierung, 2015), http://bundesregierung.de/Webs/Breg/DE/Bundes regierung/BeauftragtefuerIntegration/Staatsangehoerigkeit/geburtsortprinzip/_node.html [accessed 20 January 2015]

Bennett, Andy, 'Hip-Hop am Main: Die Lokalisierung von Rap-Musik und HipHop-Kultur', in *HipHop – Globale Kultur, Lokale Praktiken*, ed. by Jannis Androutsopoulos (Bielefeld: transcript, 2003), pp. 26–42

Berns, Jan, and Peter Schlobinski, 'Constructions of Identity in German Hip-hop Culture', in *Discourse Constructions of Youth Identities*, ed. by Jannis Androutsopoulos and Alexandra Georgakopoulou (Amsterdam: Benjamins, 2003), pp. 197–219

Bhabha, Homi K., 'Culture's in Between', *Artforum International*, 32 (1993), 167–70

— *The Location of Culture* (London: Routledge, 1994)

Birken-Silverman, Gabriele, '"Isch bin New School und West Coast ... du bisch doch ebe bei de Southside Rockern": Identität und Sprechstil in einer Breakdance-Gruppe von Mannheimer Italienern', in *HipHop – Globale Kultur, Lokale Praktiken*, ed. by Jannis Androutsopoulos (Bielefeld: transcript, 2003), pp. 273–96

Böll, Sven, and others 'The Bearable Lightness of Being: How Germans are Learning to Like Themselves', *SPIEGEL ONLINE*, 17 July 2014), http://spiegel.de/international/germany/football-championships-help-boost-german-image-at-home-and-abroad-a-981591.html [accessed 18 July 2014]

Bonnett, Alastair, 'Constructions of Whiteness in European and American Anti-Racism', in *Debating Cultural Hybridity – Multi-Cultural Identities and the Politics of Anti-Racism*, ed. by Pnina Werbner and Tariq Modood (London and New Jersey: Zed Books, 1997), pp. 173–92

Brown, Timothy S., '(African-)Americanization and Hip Hop in Germany', in *The Vinyl ain't Final – Hip Hop and the Globalization of Black Culture*, ed. by Dipannita Basu and Sidney J. Lemelle (London and Ann Arbor: Pluto, 2006), pp. 137–50

Burkard, Stefan, *HipHop am Pranger – Wie die Medien eine Kultur verteufeln* (Hamburg: Diplomica, 2013)

Butterwege, Carolin, 'Von der "Gastarbeiter"-Anwerbung zum Zuwanderungsgesetz: Migrationsgeschehen und Zuwanderungspolitik in der Bundesrepublik', *Grundlagendossier Migration* (Bundeszentrale für politische Bildung, 15 March 2005), http://www.bpb.de/gesellschaft/migration/dossiermigration/56377/migrationspolitik-in-der-brd?p=all [accessed 20 January 2015]

Castleman, Craig, *Getting Up: Subway Graffiti in New York* (Cambridge, MA: The MIT Press, 1982)

— 'The Politics of Graffiti', in *That's the Joint! The Hip-Hop Studies Reader*, ed. by Murray Forman and Marc Anthony Neal, 2nd edn (New York: Routledge, 2012), pp. 14–34

Castree, Noel, Rob Kitchin, and Alisdair Rogers, 'Identity', in *A Dictionary of Human Geography* (Oxford University Press, 2013), pp. 231–32

Chang, Jeff, *Can't Stop, Won't Stop: A History of the Hip-hop Generation* (New York: Picador, 2005)

Cheesman, Tom, 'Polyglot Pop Politics – Hip Hop in Germany', *Debatte*, 6 (1998), 191–214

— 'Talking "Kanak": Zaimoglu contra Leitkultur', in *Multicultural Germany: Arts, Media, and Performance*, ed. by Deniz Göktürk and Barbara Wolbert (= *New German Critique*, 92 (2004)), pp. 82–99

Chilvers, Ian, 'Abstract Art', in *The Oxford Dictionary of Art*, 3rd edn (Oxford: Oxford University Press, 2004), p. 2

Colvin, Sarah, *Ulrike Meinhof and West German Terrorism: Language, Violence, and Identity* (Rochester, NY: Camden House, 2009)

DAIM, *DAIM: Daring to Push the Boundaries* (Hamburg: Reisser, 2004)

DeFrantz, Thomas F., 'The Black Beat Made Visible: Body Power in Hip Hop Dance', in *Of the Presence of the Body: Essays on Dance and Performance Theory*, ed. by Andre Lepecki (Middletown, CT: Wesleyan University Press, 2004), pp. 64–81

Deppe, Jürgen and Odem, *Odem – On the Run: Eine Jugend in der Graffiti-Szene* (Berlin: Schwarzkopf & Schwarzkopf, 1997)

Desmond, Jane C., 'Embodying Difference: Issues in Dance and Cultural Studies', in *Meaning in Motion: New Cultural Studies of Dance*, ed. by Jane C. Desmond (Durham, NC: Duke University Press, 1997), pp. 29–54

Dimitriadis, Greg, 'Hip-Hop: From Live Performance to Mediated Narrative', *Popular Music*, 15 (1996), 179–94

DuBois, Andrew, 'Close Reading: An Introduction', in *Close Reading: The Reader*, ed. by Frank Lentricchia and Andrew DuBois (Durham: Duke UP, 2003), pp. 1–40

Elflein, Dietmar, 'From Krauts with Attitudes to Turks with Attitudes: Some Aspects of Hip-Hop History in Germany', *Popular Music*, 17 (1998), 255–65

Evans, Tonya M., 'Sampling, Looping and Mashing …Oh My!: How HipHop Music is Scratching more than the Surface of Copyright Law', *Fordham Intellectual Property, Media & Entertainment Law Journal*, 21 (2011), 843–904

Fernando, S. H., Jr, *The New Beats: Exploring the Music, Culture, and Attitudes of Hip-Hop* (New York: Anchor/Doubleday, 1994)

Forman, Murray, '"Represent": Race, Space and Place in Rap Music', *Popular Music*, 19 (2000), 65–90

— *The 'hood Comes First: Race, Space, and Place in Rap and Hip-Hop* (Middletown, CT: Wesleyan University Press, 2002)

— '"Ain't no Love in the Heart of the City" – Hip-Hop, Space and Place', in *That's the Joint! The Hip-Hop Studies Reader*, ed. by Murray Forman and Marc Anthony Neal, 2nd edn (New York: Routledge, 2012), pp. 225–27

Foster, Susan Leigh, *Reading Dancing: Bodies and Subjects in Contemporary American Dance* (Berkeley, CA: University of California Press, 1986)

— 'Choreographies of Gender', *Signs: Journal of Women in Culture and Society*, 24 (1998), 1–21

Fouroutan, Naika, in '"Junge Muslime möchten das Land mit gestalten" – Naika Foroutan im Gespräch', *Goethe Institut: Migration und Integration*, June 2012, http://www.goethe.de/lhr/prj/daz/mag/igd/de9494836.htm [accessed 22 January 2015]

Friedrich, Malte, *Urbane Klänge. Popmusik und Imagination der Stadt* (Bielefeld: transcript, 2010)

Fuchs, Oliver, and Hannes Ross, 'Udo Lindenberg und Jan Delay: "Wir haben den Nasensound"', *Stern*, 28 March 2008, http://www.stern.de/kultur/musik/udo-lindenberg-und-jan-delay-wir-haben-den-nasensound-615113.html [accessed 12 April 2013]

Gall, Insa, and Martin Kopp, 'Der Sprayer Von OZ', *DIE WELT*, 16 December 1999, http://www.welt.de/print-welt/article593031/Der-Spra yer-von-OZ.html [accessed 2 October 2013]

Gems, Gerald R., and Gertrud Pfister, *Understanding American Sports* (London: Routledge, 2009)

Genette, Gerard, *Palimpsestes: la littérature au second degré* (Paris, Ed. du Seuil, 1982)

— *Palimpsests: Literature in the Second Degree*, trans. by Channa Newman and Claude Doubinsky (Lincoln and London: University of Nebraska Press, 1997)

George, Nelson, *Hip-Hop America* (New York: Penguin Books, 1998)

— 'Hip-Hop's Founding Fathers Speak the Truth', in *That's the Joint! The Hip-Hop Studies Reader*, ed. by Murray Forman and Marc Anthony Neal, 2nd edn (New York: Routledge, 2012), pp. 43–55

Goffman, Erving, *The Presentation of Self in Everyday Life* (New York: Anchor, 1959)

— *Stigma: Notes on the Management of Spoiled Identity* (New York: Simon & Schuster, 1963)

Goodman, Nelson, *Languages of Art: An Approach to a Theory of Symbols* (New York: Bobbs-Merrill, 1968)

Greenbaum, Hilary, and Dana Rubinstein, 'The Origin of Spray Paint', *New York Times Magazine*, 4 November 2011, http://www.nyti mes.com/2011/11/06/magazine/who-made-spray-paint.html [accessed 9 October 2013]

Güngör, Murat, and Hannes Loh, *Fear of a Kanak Planet: HipHop zwischen Weltkultur und Nazi-Rap* (Höfen: Hannibal, 2002)

Gurney, Joan Neff, 'Female Researchers in Male Settings', in *Experiencing Fieldwork: An Inside View of Qualitative Research*, ed. by William B. Shaffir and Robert A. Stebbins (Los Angeles, CA: SAGE, 1991), pp. 53–61

Hadley, Michael L., *Count Not the Dead: The Popular Image of the German Submarine* (Annapolis, MD: Naval Institute, 1995)

Hartmann, Andreas, 'Hip-Hop in Deutschland', *Musik*, September 2007, http://www.goethe.de/kue/mus/pop/de2621937.htm [accessed 15 January 2014]

Herzog, Todd, 'Hybrids and Mischlinge: Translating Anglo-American Cultural Theory into German', *The German Quarterly*, 70 (1997), 1–17

Johnson, Simon, 'Rap Music Originated in Medieval Scottish Pubs, Claims American Professor', *The Telegraph*, 28 December 2008, http://www.telegraph.co.uk/culture/music/3998862/Rap-music-originated-in-medieval-Scottish-pubs-claims-American-professor.html [accessed 22 April 2012]

Katz, Mark, *Capturing Sound: How Technology has Changed Music* (Berkeley, CA: University of California, 2010)

— *Groove Music – The Art and Culture of the Hip-Hop DJ* (New York: Oxford University Press, 2012)

Kaya, Ayhan, *Constructing Diasporas: Turkish Hip-Hop Youth in Berlin* (Warwick: University of Warwick, 1997)

— '"Scribo Ergo Sum": Islamic Force und Berlin-Türken', in *HipHop: Globale Kultur – Lokale Praktiken*, ed. by Jannis Androutsopoulos (Bielefeld: transcript, 2003), pp. 246–72

— 'German-Turkish Transnational Space: A Separate Space of Their Own', *German Studies Review*, 30 (2007), 483–502

Kimminich, Eva, 'Tanzstile der Hip Hop Kultur. Bewegungskult und Körperkommunikation', in *KiF – Kulturen im Fokus* (Potsdamer Kulturanalysen, 2013), http://www.kulturenfokus.de/content/tanzstile-der-hip-hop-kultur [accessed 23 June 2014]

Klein, Gabriele, and Malte Friedrich, *Is this real? Die Kultur des HipHop* (Frankfurt am Main: Suhrkamp, 2003)

— 'Populäre Stadtansichten. Bildinszenierungen des Urbanen im HipHop', in *HipHop – Globale Kultur, Lokale Praktiken*, ed. by Jannis Androutsopoulos (Bielefeld: transcript, 2003), pp. 85–101

Krims, Adam, *Rap Music and the Poetics of Identity* (Cambridge: Cambridge University Press, 2000)

Kugelberg, Johann (ed.), *Born in the Bronx – A Visual Record of the Early Days of Hip Hop* (New York: Rizzoli, 2007)

Lacasse, Serge, 'Intertextuality and Hypertextuality in Recorded Music', in *The Musical Work: Reality or Invention?*, ed. by Michael Talbot (Liverpool: Liverpool University Press, 2000), pp. 35–58

Langer, Nils, 'Low German', in *Standardizations of German – From Past to Present*, ed. by Ana Deumert and Wim Vandenbussche (Amsterdam: John Benjamins, 2003), pp. 282–302

Lepa, Steffen, and Malte Pelleter, '"Sampling" als kulturelle Praxis des HipHop', in *HipHop Meets Academia: Globale Spuren eines lokalen Kulturphänomens*, ed. by Karin Bock, Stefan Meier and Gunter Süss (Bielefeld: transcript, 2007), pp. 199-213

Ley, David, and Roman Cybriwsky, 'Urban Graffiti as Territorial Markers', *Annals of the Association of American Geographers*, 64 (1974), 491–505

Loh, Hannes and Sascha Verlan, *25 Jahre Hip-Hop in Deutschland* (Höfen: Hannibal, 2006)

Lossau, Julia, 'Spatial Turn', in *Handbuch Stadtsoziologie*, ed. by Frank Eckhard (Wiesbaden: VS Verlag für Sozialwissenschaften, 2012), pp. 185–98

MacDonald, Nancy, *The Graffiti Subculture: Youth, Masculinity, and Identity* (London and New York: Palgrave Macmillan, 2001)

McLeoud, Kembrew, 'Authenticity within Hip-Hop and Other Cultures Threatened with Assimilation', in *That's the Joint! The Hip-Hop Studies Reader*, ed. by Murray Forman and Marc Anthony Neal, 2nd edn (New York: Routledge, 2012), pp. 165–78

Manuel, Peter, 'Music as Symbol, Music as Simulacrum: Postmodern, Pre-modern, and Modern Aesthetics in Subcultural Popular Musics', *Popular Music*, 14 (1995), 227–39

Marcus, George E., 'Ethnography in/of the World System: The Emergence of Multi-Sited Ethnography', *Annual Review Anthropology*, 24 (1995), 95–117

Martinez-Morrison, Amanda, 'Black and Tan Realities: Chicanos in the Borderlands of the Hip-Hop Nation', in *The Voices of Latin/o American Hip-Hop*, ed. by Christopher Dennis (= *alter/nativas: Latin American Cultural Studies Journal*, 2 (Spring 2014)), http://alternativas.osu.edu/en/issues/spring-2014/essays1/martinez-morrison.html [accessed 17 August 2014]

Meier, Stefan, 'Stylelife: Graffiti als "typographisches" Ausdrucksmittel sozialen Stils', in *Express yourself! Europas kulturelle Kreativität zwischen Markt und Underground*, ed. by Eva Kimminich and others (Bielefeld: transcript, 2007), pp. 193–208

Menrath, Stefanie, *Represent what... Performativität und Identitäten im HipHop* (Hamburg: Argument, 2001)

Merkel, Angela, in 'Integration: Merkel erklärt Multikulti für Gescheitert', *SPIEGEL ONLINE*, 16 October 2010, http://www.spiegel.de/politik/deutsch

land/integration-merkel-erklaert-multikulti-fuer-gescheitert-a-723532.html [accessed 25 February 2014]

Merz, Friedrich, 'Einwanderung und Identität', *Die Welt*, 25 October 2000, http://www.welt.de/print-welt/article540438/Einwanderung-und-Identitaet.html [accessed 10 January 2015]

Mikos, Lothar, 'Interpolation and Sampling: kulturelles Gedächtnis und Intertextualität im HipHop', in *HipHop: Globale Kultur – Lokale Praktiken*, ed. by Jannis Androutsopoulos (Bielefeld: transcript, 2003), pp. 64–84

Mitchell, Tony, ed., *Global Noise: Rap and Hip-hop outside the USA* (Middletown, CT: Wesleyan University Press, 2001)

— Introduction: Another Root – Hip-Hop Outside the USA', in *Global Noise: Rap and Hip-hop outside the USA*, ed. by Tony Mitchell (Middletown, CT: Wesleyan University Press, 2001), pp. 1–29

Mraz, Steve, 'European Spotlight: Verna Mae Bentley-Krause', *Stars and Stripes*, 14 July 2008, http://www.stripes.com/news/european-spotlight-verna-mae-bentley-krause-1.80960 [accessed 3 September 2014]

Munderloh, Marissa K., '*Heb die Fahne hoch, Santa Pauli Patriot!*: A Case Study of Urban Place-Making in Rap Music', in *Place-Making in urbanen Diskursen – Interdisziplinäre Beiträge zur Stadtforschung*, ed. by Beatrix Busse and Ingo H. Warnke, Diskursmuster – Discourse Patterns, 7 (Boston/Berlin: de Gruyter 2014), pp. 421–42

Musante DeWalt, Kathleen, and Billie R. DeWalt, *Participant Observation: A Guide for Fieldworkers* (Lanham, MD: Rowman & Littlefield, 2011)

Neal, Mark Anthony, 'Post-industrial Soul: Black Popular Music at the Crossroads', in *That's the Joint! The Hip-Hop Studies Reader*, ed. by Murray Forman and Marc Anthony Neal, 2nd edn (New York: Routledge, 2012), pp. 476–502

Nohl, Arnd-Michael, 'Interkulturelle Bildungsprozesse im Breakdance', in *HipHop – Globale Kultur, Lokale Praktiken*, ed. by Jannis Androutsopoulos (Bielefeld: transcript, 2003), pp. 297–320

O'Connor, Alan, 'Local Scenes and Dangerous Crossroads: Punk and Theories of Cultural Hybridity', *Popular Music*, 21 (2002), 225–36

Ogbar, Jeffrey O. G., *Hip-Hop Revolution – The Culture and Politics of Rap* (Lawrence, KA: University Press of Kansas, 2007)

Pabon, Jorge, 'Physical Graffiti', in *That's the Joint! The Hip-Hop Studies Reader*, ed. by Murray Forman and Marc Anthony Neal, 2nd edn (New York: Routledge, 2012), pp. 57–62

Papastergiadis, Nikos, *The Turbulence of Migration: Globalization, Deterritorialization and Hybridity* (Cambridge: Polity, 2000)

— 'Hybridity and Ambivalence: Places and Flows in Contemporary Art and Culture', *Theory, Culture and Society*, 22 (2005), 39–64

— *Cosmopolitanism and Culture* (Cambridge: Polity, 2012)

Pautz, Hartwig, 'The Politics of Identity in Germany: the Leitkultur Debate', *Race & Class*, 46 (2005), 39–52

Pennay, Mark, 'Rap in Germany: The Birth of a Genre', in *Global Noise: Rap and Hip-hop outside the USA*, ed. by Tony Mitchell (Middletown, CT: Wesleyan UP, 2001), pp. 111–33

Pennycook, Alaistair, 'Spatial Narrations: Graffscapes and City Souls', in *Semiotic Landscapes - Language, Image, Space*, ed. by Adam Jaworskiand Crispin Thurlow (New York: Continuum, 2010), pp. 137–50

Peschke, Andre, *Hip-Hop in Deutschland - Analyse einer Jugendkultur aus pädagogischer Perspektive* (Hamburg: Diplomica, 2010)

Peters, Gerrit, 'The Artists' [n.d.], http://getting-up.org/en/artists/gerrit-peters-tasek/ [accessed 20 September 2013]

Pham, Khuê, 'Deutscher Patriot: Der Rap-Musiker Harris ist dunkelhäutig – und stolz auf sein Land. In seinen Texten beschimpft er Integrationsverweigerer', *Die Zeit - Politik*, 47 (18 November 2010), p. 17

Poschardt, Ulf, *DJ Culture* (Hamburg: Rogner und Bernhard, 1995)

Potter, Russell A., *Spectacular Vernaculars: Hip-Hop and the Politics of Postmodernism* (Albany, NY: State University of New York, 1995)

Rappe, Michael, 'Rhythmus-Sound-Symbol: Struktur und Vermittlungsformen einer Oral Culture am Beispiel des Hip-Hop', in *Expressyourself! Europas kulturelle Kreativität zwischen Markt und Underground*, ed. by Eva Kimminich and others (Bielefeld: transcript, 2007), pp. 137–56

Rivera, Raquel Z., *New York Ricans from the Hip Hop Zone* (New York: Palgrave Macmillan, 2003)

Robitzky, Niels, *Von Swipe Zu Storm: Breakdance in Deutschland* (Hamburg: Backspin, 2000)

Rode, Dorit, *Breaking. Popping. Locking. Tanzformen der HipHop-Kultur* (Marburg, Tectum, 2006)

Rose, Tricia, *Black Noise - Rap Music and Black Culture in Contemporary America* (Middletown, CT: Wesleyan University Press, 1994)

— *The Hip Hop Wars: What We Talk about When We Talk about Hip Hop - and Why It Matters* (New York: BasicCivitas, 2008)

Roskind, Robert, *Rasta Heart: A Journey into One Love* (Blowing Rock, NC: One Love, 2001)

Rühle, Alex, and Dirk Peitz, 'Interview mit Bushido, Loh, Güngör - Harte Texte und die Härte der Nazis', *Süddeutsche Zeitung - Kultur*, 11 May 2010, http://www.sueddeutsche.de/kultur/interview-mit-bushido-loh-guengoer-harte-texte-und-die-haerte-der-nazis-1.425538-2 [accessed 30 May 2012]

Saied, Ayla Güler, *Rap in Deutschland – Musik als Interaktionsmedium zwischen Partykultur und urbanen Anerkennungskämpfen* (Bielefeld: transcript, 2012)

Salaverría, Heidi, 'Tanz um Anerkennung. Ästhetik und Alterität – von Breaking bis Krumping', in *Expressyourself! Europas kulturelle Kreativität zwischen Markt und Underground*, ed. by Eva Kimminich and others (Bielefeld: transcript, 2007), pp. 209–38

Sarrazin, Thilo, in 'Sarrazin droht Ausschluss aus der SPD', *taz.de*, 5 October 2009, http://www.taz.de/1/archiv/digitaz/artikel/?ressort=ba&dig=2009/10/05/a0116&cHash=500e526491 [accessed 10 January 2015]

— *Deutschland schafft sich ab: Wie wir unser Land aufs Spiel setzen* (Stuttgart: Deutsche Verlags-Anstalt, 2010)

— in 'Merkels Aussage vernebelt das Problem', *Die Welt*, 20 January 2015, http://www.welt.de/politik/deutschland/article136566652/Merkels-Aussage-zum-Islam-vernebelt-das-Problem.html [accessed 21 January 2015].

Schensul, Stephen L., Jean J. Schensul, and Margaret Diane LeCompte, *Essential Ethno-graphic Methods: Observations, Interviews, and Questionnaires* (Walnut Creek, CA: AltaMira, 1999)

Schloss, Joseph, *Making Beats – The Art of Sample-based Hip-hop* (Middletown, CT: Wesleyan UP, 2004)

— *Foundation: B-boys, B-girls, and Hip-hop Culture in New York* (Oxford: Oxford University Press, 2009)

Schmelz, Andrea, 'Immigration and Integration Policies and Practices in Germany', in *Immigration Worldwide: Policies, Practices, and Trends*, ed. by Uma A. Segal, Doreen Elliot, and Nazneen S. Mayada (New York: Oxford University Press, 2010), pp. 63–78

Schröer, Sebastian, 'Raum und Inszenierung', in *HipHop Meets Academia: Globale Spuren eines lokalen Kulturphänomens*, ed. by Karin Bock, Stefan Meier and Gunter Süss (Bielefeld: transcript, 2007), pp. 247–62

Shusterman, Richard, *Performing Live – Aesthetic Alternatives for the Ends of Art* (New York: Cornell University Press, 2000)

Skey, Michael, 'Why do Nations Matter? The Struggle for Belonging and Security in an Uncertain World', *British Journal of Sociology*, 64 (2013), 81–98

Small, Christopher, *Music of the Common Tongue: Survival and Celebration in African American Music* (Hanover, NH: University Press of New England, 1987)

Soja, Edward W., *Thirdspace: Journeys to Los Angeles and Other Real-and-imagined Places* (Cambridge, MA: Blackwell, 1996)

— *Postmetropolis: Critical Studies of Cities and Regions* (Malden, MA: Blackwell Pub., 2000)

— 'Vom "Zeitgeist" zum "Raumgeist". New Twists on the Spatial Turn', in *Spatial Turn: Das Raumparadigma in den Kultur- und Sozialwissenschaften*, ed. by Jörg Döring and Tristan Thielmann (Bielefeld: transcript, 2008), pp. 241–62

Sorge, Samy, *Dis wo ich herkomm* (Reinbeck: Rohwolt, 2009)

Soysal, Levent, 'Rap, Hiphop, Kreuzberg: Scripts of/for Migrant Youth Culture in the WorldCity Berlin', in *Multicultural Germany: Arts, Media, and Performance*, ed. by Deniz Göktürk and Barbara Wolbert (= *New German Critique*, 92 (2004)), pp. 62–81

Stadt Oldenburg, 'Statistik', *Entwicklung der Einwohnerzahl 1978–2012* (Fachdienst Stadtinformation und Geodaten, 2012), http://www.oldenburg.de/fileadmin/oldenburg/Benutzer/PDF/40/402/0202-2012-Z-Internetx.pdf [accessed 20 March 2012]

Stalling Huntington, Carla, *Hip Hop Dance: Meanings and Messages* (Jefferson, NC: McFarland, 2007)

Stehle, Maria, *Ghetto Voices in Contemporary German Culture* (New York: Camden House, 2012)

Stöckl, Hartmut, 'Typographie: Gewand und Körper des Textes – Linguistische Überlegungen zu typographischer Gestaltung', *Zeitschrift für angewandte Linguistik*, 41 (2004), 5–48

Stolz, Matthias, 'Deutschlandkarte: Graffiti', *Zeitmagazin*, 26 (2014), 10

Stross, Brian, 'The Hybrid Metaphor: From Biology to Culture', *The Journal of American Folklore*, 112 (1999), 254–67

Templeton, Inez H., 'What's so German about It? Cultural Identity in the Berlin Hip Hop Scene' (unpublished doctoral thesis, University of Stirling, 2005) https://dspace.stir.ac.uk/bitstream/1893/75/1/Inez%20Templeton%20-%20Thesis%20PDF%20Version.pdf [accessed 31 May 2013]

Thum, Frida, 'Und woher kommst du wirklich?', *Zeit Online*, 16 September 2014, http://www.zeit.de/gesellschaft/zeitgeschehen/2014-08/deutsch-identitaet-migranten-sarrazin [accessed 10 January 2015]

Tickner, Arlene B., 'Aquí en el Ghetto: Hip-hop in Colombia, Cuba and Mexico', *Latin American Politics and Society*, 50 (2008), 121–46

Turpin, Tilman, 'Die Leitkultur-Debatte: Fragen nach Identität und Integration in Deutschland', in *Die Zukunft der Demokratie: L'avenir de la démocratie*, ed. by Thomas Bedorf, Felix Heidenreich and Marcus Obrecht (Berlin: LIT, 2009)

Van Treeck, Bernhard, 'Styles – Typographie als Mittel zur Identitätsbildung', in *HipHop: Globale Kultur – Lokale Praktiken*, ed. by Jannis Androutsopoulos (Bielefeld: transcript, 2003), pp. 102–10

Verlan, Sascha, 'HipHop als schöne Kunst betrachtet', in *HipHop: Globale Kultur – Lokale Praktiken*, ed. by Jannis Androutsopoulos (Bielefeld: transcript, 2003), pp. 138–46

Von Dirke, Sabine, 'Hip-Hop Made in Germany: From Old School to the Kanaksta Movement', in *German Popular Culture – How "American" is It?*, ed. by Agnes C. Mueller (Ann Arbor: The University of Michigan Press, 2004), pp. 96–112

Wallis, Emma, 'Make Me a German' (Deutsche Welle, 8 August 2013), http://www.dw.de/make-me-a-german/a-17007958 [accessed 9 June 2014]

Wicker, Hans-Rudolph, 'From Complex Culture to Cultural Complexity', in *Debating Cultural Hybridity – Multi-Cultural Identities and the Politics of Anti-Racism*, ed. by Pnina Werbner and Tariq Modood (London and New Jersey: Zed Books, 1997), pp. 29–45

Williams, Justin A., 'Musical Borrowing in Hip-Hop Music: Theoretical Frameworks and Case Studies' (unpublished doctoral thesis, University of Nottingham, 2009), http://eprints.nottingham.ac.uk/11081/1/JustinWilliams_PhDfinal.pdf

Young, Jennifer R., 'Brooklyn Beats: Hip Hop's Home to Everyone from Everywhere', in *Hip Hop in America: A Regional Guide*, ed. by Mickey Hess (Santa Barbara, CA: Greenwood Press, 2010), pp. 75–106

Yuval-Davis, Nira, 'Ethnicity, Gender Relations and Multiculturalism', in *Debating Cultural Hybridity – Multi-Cultural Identities and the Politics of Anti-Racism*, ed. by Pnina Werbner and Tariq Modood (London and New Jersey: Zed Books, 1997), pp. 193–208

Videography

'24. März 2012: Sonne', *Kanal von lizzarteos*, YouTube, 31 March 2012, http://www.youtube.com/watch?v=KdH895tVPHk [accessed 11 April 2012]

'Talk mit Breakdancer Vartan Bassil | Typisch Deutsch', Interview by Hajo Schumacher, *Deutsche Welle*, YouTube, 1 October 2012, http://www.youtube. com/watch?v= SMwniRnibZ4 [accessed 12 June 2013]

'Opel Corsa – DAIM & Loomit Interview (German)', *DAIM*, YouTube, 24 January 2011, http://www.youtube.com/watch?v=LZJfbiUDgY8 [accessed 20 September 2013]

'ARTotale "Die Kunst Der Kontrolle" PART 1 – Leuphana Urban-Art Project Lüneburg', *Reinkingprojekte*, YouTube, 16 March 2010, http://www.youtube.com/watch?v =v_ak4GZVkg [accessed 20 September 2013]

'DJ Orchester – Mirko Machine, DJ Mixwell, DJ Stylewarz', *Guesi2007*, YouTube, 18 November 2011, http://www.youtube.com/watch?v=Bxv2y5Izll4 [accessed 1 January 2012]

'DDC – "Breakdance in Lederhosen – 20 Jahre Feste – ARD – Okt 2014 | DDC Breakdance"', *DDC Breakdance* YouTube, 26 October 2014, https://www.youtube.com/watch?v=0GKUyjBrNFI [accessed 30 June 2016]

'Juiz feat. Starchild, Jordan MC und Macentosh – "4x4"', *JuizySupport*, YouTube, 6 November 2013, http://www.youtube.com/watch?v=XxdfdcjR3n0 [accessed 12 February 2014]

'Samy Deluxe – Weck Mich Auf', *SamyDeluxeVEVO*, YouTube, 20 January 2012, http://www.youtube.com/watch?v=yiWd14IoN2Y [accessed 12 May 2014]

Scratch, dir. by Doug Pray and performed by Afrika Bambaataa, Mos Def and Fab 5 Freddy (Palm Pictures, 2001) [DVD]

Seehofer, Horst, in 'Integrationsdebatte: Von Der Leyen versus Seehofer: "Eintrittsschwellen Senken"', *Frankfurt Allgemeine Zeitung für Deutschland – Inland* 16 October 2010, http://www.faz.net/aktuell/po litik/inland/integrationsdebatte-von-der-leyen-versus-seehofer-eintrittsschwellen-senken-11056459.html [accessed 27 February 2014]

Discography

Absolute Beginner, *Bambule* (Buback/Universal Music, 1998) [CD]

Advanced Chemistry, *Fremd im eigenen Land* (MZEE Records, 1992), maxi-single [CD]

— *Blast Action Heroes* (Buback/Motor, 2003) [LP/CD]

Bentley-Krause, Verna Mae, *Ich liebe deutsche Land (Da Det De Det De Dä)* (Rare, 2001), maxi-single [CD]

Black Sabbath, 'Paranoid', *Paranoid* (Vertigo, 1970) [CD]

Delay, Jan, *Irgendwie, irgendwo, irgendwann* (EMI, 1999), single [CD]

Delay, Jan, 'Feuer', *Mercedes Dance* (Buback/Universal Music Group, 2007) [CD]

Deluxe, Samy, 'Dis Wo ich Herkomm', *Dis Wo ich Herkomm* (EMI, 2009) [CD]

— 'Feuer, Verbrannt, Asche' (2012), https://www.youtube.com/watch?v=Fe6IVrkGO1M [accessed 9 June 2016]

— 'Hände Hoch', *Schwarz Weiß* (EMI, 2011) [CD]

— 'Poesialbum', *Schwarz Weiß* (EMI, 2011) [CD]

— 'Reimemonsta 2011', *Schwarz Weiß* (EMI, 2011) [CD]

— 'Schwarz Weiß', *Schwarz Weiß* (EMI, 2011) [CD]

Fettes Brot, *Nordish by Nature* (Alternation (2), 1995), maxi-single [CD]

Fresh Familee, 'Ahmet Gündüz', *Coming from Ratinga* (Ratingan, 1992) [LP]

Grandmaster Flash and the Furious Five, *The Message* (Sugar Hill Records, 1982) [CD]

Jordan MC, 'One Love' (2007), single, https://www.youtube.com/watch?v=rBp6gWIqiQs [accessed 9 June 2016]

Juiz feat. None aka Starchild, Jordan & Macentosh, '4x4', *Eigenregie* (Cubetribe Studio, 2014) [CD]

K-Four, 'The Beginner', *The Beginner* (Str8 Team Ent., 2012), mixtape, http://www.datpiff.com/K-Four-The-Beginner-mixtape.371741.html [accessed 9 June 2016]

Lindenberg, Udo und das Panikorchester, 'Ich bin beim Bund', *Odyssee* (Polydor, 1983) [CD]

MicFire, 'Made in Germany', *Made in Germany* (Mafyo & Star Trip Loopers, 2013), EP, https://www.youtube.com/watch?v=VCv7mgNLhRI [accessed 9 June 2016]

Mobb Deep, *Survival of the Fittest* (Loud Records, 1995), single [CD]

Nate57 & Telly Tellz, 'Nur die Starken überleben', *Verrückte Ratten* (Rattos Locos Records, 2009), mixtape, http://deutscher-hip-hop.com/?path=download&contentid=2282 [accessed 9 June 2016]

NewMan on the Block, 'Ich bin Deutschland', *Kategorie Gangsta* (2011), mixtape [CD]

Stylez-Tyson, 'OneLove' (2012), single, https://www.youtube.com/watch?v=i8jCkOfYy_Q [accessed 30 June 2016]

Telly Tellz, *Mischlingskind* (Rattos Locos Records, 2010), mixtape, https://www.youtube.com/watch?v=piaLY6m5k-I [accessed 25 November 2016]

INDEX

CPSIA information can be obtained
at www.ICGtesting.com
Printed in the USA
LVHW010354021219
638755LV00001B/2/P

9 780854 57255